Design for Personalisation

The principle of personalisation appears in a range of current debates among design professionals, healthcare providers and educationalists about the implications of new technologies and approaches to consumer sovereignty for 'mass' provision. The potential of new technologies implies systems of provision that offer bespoke support to their users, tailoring services and experiences to suit individual needs. The assumption that individual choice automatically increases wellbeing has underlain the re-design of public services. Ubiquitous personalisation in screen-based environments gives individuals the sense that their personality is reflected back at them. Advances in Artificial Intelligence mean our personal intelligent agents have begun to acquire personality. Given its prevalence, it is appropriate to identify the scope of this phenomenon that is altering our relationship to the 'non-human' world.

This book presents taxonomy of personalisation, and its potential consequences for the design profession as well as its ethical and political dimensions through a collection of essays from a range of academic perspectives. The thought-provoking introduction, conclusion and nine chapters present a well-balanced mixture of in-depth literature review and practical examples to deepen our understanding of the consequences of personalisation for our professional and personal lives. Collectively, this book points towards the implications of personalisation for design-led social innovation.

This will be valuable reading for professionals in the design industry and health provision, as well as students of product design, fashion and sociology.

Iryna Kuksa is a Senior Research Fellow in Art and Design at Nottingham Trent University, UK. In her research, Iryna investigates the challenges, and opportunities, encountered by scholars, practitioners and educators in using immersive virtual environments and in applying 3D visualisation as research methodology. Her broad research interests enable her to make creative and inventive connections between various areas of knowledge, identifying exciting research questions and methodologies.

Tom Fisher is a Professor of Art and Design Research in the School of Art and Design at Nottingham Trent University, UK. His academic background combines Art History, Design and Sociology and he has led research funded by the AHRC on industrial heritage, innovation in relation to new textile technologies and for Defra on sustainable clothing. He is a member of the Design Research Society Council and leads the Special Interest Group OPEN (Objects, Practices, Experiences, Networks). His current research seeks to deepen connections between design and research in the human sciences by focusing on skills in material practices.

Design for Social Responsibility
Series Editor: Rachel Cooper

Social responsibility, in various disguises, has been a recurring theme in design for many years. Since the 1960s several more or less commercial approaches have evolved. In the 1970s designers were encouraged to abandon 'design for profit' in favour of a more compassionate approach inspired by Papanek. In the 1980s and 1990s profit and ethical issues were no longer considered mutually exclusive and more market-oriented concepts emerged, such as the 'green consumer' and ethical investment. The purchase of socially responsible, 'ethical' products and services has been stimulated by the dissemination of research into sustainability issues in consumer publications. Accessibility and inclusivity have also attracted a great deal of design interest and recently designers have turned to solving social and crime-related problems. Organisations supporting and funding such projects have recently included the NHS (research into design for patient safety); the Home Office has (design against crime); Engineering and Physical Sciences Research Council (design decision-making for urban sustainability).

Businesses are encouraged (and increasingly forced by legislation) to set their own socially responsible agendas that depend on design to be realised. Design decisions all have environmental, social and ethical impacts, so there is a pressing need to provide guidelines for designers and design students within an overarching framework that takes a holistic approach to socially responsible design. This edited series of guides is aimed at students of design, product development, architecture and marketing, and design and management professionals working in the sectors covered by each title. Each volume includes: The background and history of the topic, its significance in social and commercial contexts and trends in the field. Exemplar design case studies. Guidelines for the designer and advice on tools, techniques and resources available.

Design for Micro-Utopias
Making the Unthinkable Possible
John Wood

Design for Inclusivity
A Practical Guide to Accessible, Innovative and User-Centred Design
Roger Coleman, John Clarkson, Julia Cassim

Design for Sustainability
A Practical Approach
John Wood

Design for Sport
Anxo Cereijo Roibás, Emmanuel Stamatakis

Design for Services
Anna Meroni, Daniela Sangiorgi

Design for Transport
A User-Centred Approach to Vehicle Design and Travel
Edited by Mike Tovey

Design for Policy
Christian Bason

Design Against Crime
Caroline L Davey, Andrew B Wootton

Design for Healthcare
Edited by Emmanuel Tsekleves and Rachel Cooper

Design for Personalisation
Edited by Iryna Kuksa and Tom Fisher

Design for Personalisation

Edited by Iryna Kuksa and
Tom Fisher

LONDON AND NEW YORK

First published 2017
by Routledge
2 Park Square, Milton Park, Abingdon, Oxon OX14 4RN

and by Routledge
711 Third Avenue, New York, NY 10017

Routledge is an imprint of the Taylor & Francis Group, an informa business

© 2017 selection and editorial matter, Iryna Kuksa and Tom Fisher; individual chapters, the contributors

The right of Iryna Kuksa and Tom Fisher to be identified as the authors of the editorial material, and of the authors for their individual chapters, has been asserted in accordance with sections 77 and 78 of the Copyright, Designs and Patents Act 1988.

All rights reserved. No part of this book may be reprinted or reproduced or utilised in any form or by any electronic, mechanical, or other means, now known or hereafter invented, including photocopying and recording, or in any information storage or retrieval system, without permission in writing from the publishers.

Trademark notice: Product or corporate names may be trademarks or registered trademarks, and are used only for identification and explanation without intent to infringe.

British Library Cataloguing-in-Publication Data
A catalogue record for this book is available from the British Library

Library of Congress Cataloging-in-Publication Data
A catalog record for this book has been requested

ISBN: 978-1-4724-5739-4 (hbk)
ISBN: 978-1-315-57663-3 (ebk)

Typeset in Bembo
by Swales & Willis Ltd, Exeter, Devon, UK

Contents

List of figures ix
Notes on contributors xi
Foreword xv

Introduction: design and personalisation – by a person or for a person? 1
IRYNA KUKSA AND TOM FISHER

PART I
Personalising consumption, retail and digital spaces 15

1 Personalisation and fashion design 17
TONY KENT

2 Making it mine: personalising clothes at home 34
AMY TWIGGER HOLROYD

3 Wearable technology as personalised fashion: empowering or oppressive? 51
CONOR FARRINGTON

PART II
Personalising communication, marketing and manufacture 71

4 Who is really in control? Pitfalls on the path to personalisation and personality 73
JON OBERLANDER

5 What will designers do when everyone can be a designer? 91
MATT SINCLAIR

6 The history and application of additive manufacturing for design personalisation 113
GUY BINGHAM

PART III
Personalising health   131

7 The 4 Ps: problems in personalising a public service
   (a personal view of personalisation in the NHS)   133
   KATH CHECKLAND

8 Designing for personalisation in predictive and preventive
   medicine   150
   OLGA GOLUBNITSCHAJA, HEINZ LEMKE, MARKO KAPALLA
   AND TONY KENT

9 Towards a Person-Centred Approach to design for
   personalisation   170
   SARAH KETTLEY, RICHARD KETTLEY AND RACHEL LUCAS

   Conclusion: what happens next? Themes and principles
   for a personalised future   192
   TOM FISHER AND IRYNA KUKSA

   Index   206

Figures

2.1	Design variations offered by sewing patterns	40
2.2	Hand-knitted cardigan in the early stages of transformation, with samples	43
2.3	The same cardigan after re-knitting, with samples and calculations	43
3.1	Cute Circuit Pink & Black Dress	66
3.2	dbCHRONICLE™ bag	67
4.1	Extract from a personalised web page generated by ILEX, the Intelligent Labelling Explorer	76
4.2	The Five Factor Model of personality	79
4.3	Some possible ways of saying 'The music was good'	81
5.1	Industrial design process model	94
5.2	A classification of consumer involvement in New Product Development	98
5.3	Bone Cuff in laser sintered nylon, created using the Cell Cycle configurator	100
5.4	Rally Fighter	102
5.5	Hack Chair	105
6.1	Personalised AM hearing aids	117
6.2	Invisalign orthodontic aligner	118
6.3	Cranio-maxillofacial titanium implant	120
6.4	AM Titanium mandible replacement	120
6.5	Personalised prosthetic fairings by Bespoke Innovations	121
6.6	Future Factories Icon pendant range	123
6.7	Dildo generator software	125
6.8	Nervous System – Cell Cycle software	126
6.9	Digital Forming's platform	127
7.1	UK Government policies focusing upon 'personalisation'	135
8.1	Professional interactome design	154

8.2 Interactive computer model of human metabolism and other
 biological interactions 159
8.3 ICT component architecture for integrated (model-based)
 patient care with MIMMS 165
9.1 Elizabeth Sanders (2008) evolving map of design
 practice and design research 173

Contributors

Guy Bingham is a Senior Lecturer within the Design School at Loughborough University, UK. He is an internationally recognised researcher in Additive Manufacturing and a leading authority in the Design implications. His research includes over 30 publications and several landmark Additive Manufactured artefacts including footwear, sports personal protective equipment and garments.

Kath Checkland is a Professor of Health Policy and Primary Care in the Centre for Primary Care at the University of Manchester, UK, and works as a family doctor in a small practice in rural Derbyshire. Her research focuses upon the impact of UK health policy on the NHS. She qualified as a GP in 1991, and her subsequent academic career was fuelled by a desire to understand more fully the factors affecting the care the NHS can provide. Personalisation in healthcare arose as an important issue in one of her research projects, leading to her contribution to this volume.

Conor Farrington is a Research Associate at the Cambridge Centre for Health Services Research (CCHSR), University of Cambridge School of Clinical Medicine, UK. His research draws on social theory to explore and understand user experiences of new medical technology in the fields of diabetes, cardiovascular disease, and mental illness. He also works on the societal, philosophical, and aesthetic implications of new technologies such as wearables and wider movements such as Big Data, the Internet of Things, and Quantified Self.

Tom Fisher is a Professor of Art and Design Research in the School of Art and Design at Nottingham Trent University, UK. His academic background combines Art History, Design and Sociology and he has led research funded by the AHRC on industrial heritage, innovation in relation to new textile technologies and for Defra on sustainable clothing. He is a member of the Design Research Society Council and leads the Special Interest Group OPEN (Objects, Practices, Experiences, Networks). His current research seeks to deepen connections between Design and research in the human sciences by focusing on skills in material practices.

Olga Golubnitschaja has studied journalism, biotechnology and medicine. She is the co-founder of the theory of individual patient profiles, author of more than 300 publications in predictive, preventive and personalised medicine. She has been awarded a National/International Fellowship from the Alexander von Humboldt-Foundation, the highest prize in medicine, and the Eiselsberg-Prize, Austria. She is secretary-general of the EPMA (45 countries, www.epmanet.eu), editor-in-chief of the *EPMA Journal* (BMC, London), book series editor of 'Advances in Predictive, Preventive and Personalised Medicine' (Springer) and European representative in the EDR-Network at the NIH/NCI (http://edrn.nci.nih.gov/). Prof. Golubnitschaja is also an advisor and evaluator of projects dedicated to personalised medicine at the EU-Commission in Brussels, NIH/NCI, Washington DC, USA.

Marko Kapalla graduated in 1994 at the Faculty of Natural Sciences, Comenius University in Bratislava, Slovakia, where he received a MSc degree in Biochemistry. In 2001 he earned an academic degree 'RNDr. – Rerum Naturalium Doctor' in Physical Chemistry, and in 2014, at the Faculty of Medicine of Comenius University, he earned a PhD in the field of Normal and Pathological Physiology. He is co-founder and CEO of Negentropic Systems where he develops progressive laboratory information systems for PPPM. He is one of the founding members of EPMA, member of the EPMA Board of Directors, and associate editor of the *EPMA Journal*.

Tony Kent is a Professor of Fashion Marketing at Nottingham Trent University, UK. His research is centred on interdisciplinary approaches to marketing and design, focusing on brand image and identity in retail stores, and more recently the convergence of physical and virtual environments. He has a further interest in research methodologies and their application across disciplines. He was Principal Investigator on an AHRC-funded research project, 'Metamorphosis of Design Management' examining the relationship between education, research and industry in this field. He is a Member of the Chartered Institute of Marketing, Fellow of the Royal Society of Arts, Fellow of the Higher Education Institute, and sits on the Committee for the Marketing Special Interest Group of the British Academy of Management and on the research committee of the International Foundation of Fashion and Textiles institutions (IFFTI).

Richard Kettley is a Research Fellow at Nottingham Trent University, UK, working on a project with Nottinghamshire Mind Network. He completed his four-year MSc in Person-Centred Psychotherapy at the Sherwood Psychotherapy Training Institute in October 2013. He has worked as a counsellor at ISAS, Bilborough College, Nottingham Trent University, MIND, and in a senior guidance role at George Watson's College in Scotland. Richard has developed and delivers training material in using Interpersonal Process Recall methods in research with vulnerable people at the Sherwood Institute. Richard has previously worked for many years in a variety of educational settings.

Sarah Kettley is a Reader in Relational Design within the Product Design subject area at Nottingham Trent University, UK. She is interested in how networks of things can be designed for networks of people, and her research interests include craft theory, design for mental health and wellbeing, and design anthropology. She is a council member of the Design Research Society, and convenes the tentSIG special interest group in tangible, embedded and networked technologies. Her practice-led research resulted in the first user-centred application of the ubiquitous computing platform Speckled Computing in 2005. She recently led the EPSRC project, An Internet of Soft Things.

Iryna Kuksa is a Senior Research Fellow in Art and Design at Nottingham Trent University, UK. In her research, Iryna investigates the challenges and opportunities encountered by scholars, practitioners and educators in using immersive virtual environments and in applying 3D visualisation as research methodology. Iryna's recent book *Making Sense of Space: The Design and Experience of Virtual Spaces as a Tool for Communication* examines a variety of physical and virtual locations and their applicability to be used for performance practices; analysing how they influence our emotions, ways of communicating with one another, and our ability to be creative. Iryna's broad research interests enable her to make creative and inventive connections between various areas of knowledge, identifying exciting research questions and methodologies.

Heinz Lemke teaches and supervises research on Computer Assisted Medicine at the Technical University of Berlin, Germany, and is also Research Professor of Radiology at the University of Southern California, USA. He is Strategic Advisor on Research at the Innovation Center Computer Assisted Surgery (ICCAS), University of Leipzig. During the last 25 years he was also Visiting Professor at universities in USA, Japan, China, Egypt and Switzerland. Since 1983, Heinz Lemke has been organiser of the congress series Computer Assisted Radiology and Surgery (CARS), editor-in-chief of the *International Journal of CARS* and executive director of the International Foundation for CARS.

Rachel Lucas is a psychotherapist working with both long-term clients and in brief solution-focussed settings. Rachel trained on the MSc in Person Centred Psychotherapy at the Sherwood Psychotherapy Training Institute and completed her research in 2014. She is currently working on a research project at Nottingham Trent University, UK, which partners with MIND, looking at ways to support mental health difficulties through the use of smart textiles and experiential workshops. Rachel previously worked in textile design and couture embroidery in both the USA and the UK.

Jon Oberlander holds a Chair in Epistemics in the School of Informatics at the University of Edinburgh, UK. He is currently director of the University's Data Technology Institute, and co-director of its Centre for Design Informatics. His research lies at the intersection of computational linguistics and cognitive science, and aims at getting computers to talk (and write) like individual people. He has a long-standing interest in personalisation via natural language generation, particularly in the field of cultural heritage. This has led to work on context-sensitive interpretation and navigation in virtual and physical museums, and to projects exploring human–robot interaction.

Matt Sinclair is a Lecturer in Industrial and Product Design, having joined Loughborough Design School at the end of 2012. His research investigates how digital fabrication technologies enable the increasing involvement of the consumer in the design and manufacture of their own products, the implications for the role of the professional designer, and how brands and manufacturers manage the resultant complexity. This, together with his teaching, is grounded in an understanding of professional practice established through more than 20 years' experience as an industrial designer, design manager and creative director.

Amy Twigger Holroyd is a designer, maker, writer and researcher. Through her knitwear label, Keep & Share, she has explored the emerging field of fashion and sustainability since 2004. Her work has been featured in many books and publications, from *Vogue* to *Fashion Theory*. In 2013 Amy completed her PhD at Birmingham Institute of Art and Design, investigating amateur fashion making – which she describes as 'folk fashion' – as a strategy for sustainability. She is a Senior Lecturer in Design, Culture and Context at Nottingham Trent University, UK.

Foreword

Personalisation = profiting from the fact that all people are different

"Businesses are profiting much too little from the fact that all people are different." This mantra by a successful fashion entrepreneur summarizes very well the appeal of personalization as a corporate strategy: creating business models around heterogeneities among the preferences and needs of your customers. But this understanding is applicable far beyond the domain of for-profit companies. Personalization is equally, or even more important in non-profit organizations, public administration, education, or healthcare.

Still, it is remarkable how much conventional "mass production" thinking continues to dominate our perception of the world. We talk of customer segments, market clusters, or user personas – all concepts that are built around the idea of finding the common denominator of a group, instead of focusing on the things where people are different. In manufacturing, we still focus on ramp-up, scalability, and market share, again concepts from a world dominated by mass production, and not mass customization. And also as consumers or citizens, we often think how we can fit a general trend, how we have to adapt to an existing solution, and how we can meet the expectations of our peers. We are uncomfortable with neighbors that are different and live a different life style as we do. We all want personalization, but do so little to reach this objective!

Current digital technological developments, however, are making personalization the new standard. Consider, for example, additive manufacturing (colloquially: 3D printing), a technology that breaks with the established laws of economies of scale and provides customized products without a cost penalty. Smart, connected products, based on Internet of Things technology, allow the continuous adaption of designs and services to individual, context-specific user needs. Data analytics allows us to explore our inner self and helps us to match existing offerings to our personal needs, overcoming an old truth in personalization that people don't know what they personally want and require.

At the same time, new technologies also challenge personalization and ask us to consider how privacy and personalization relate to each other, how personal recommendations balance between one's own interests and those who provide the recommendations, and why we still like to hide in the crowd and share mass experiences on a large scale. The debate on personalization has just begun.

This is why this edited volume is such an important book. The editors did an astonishing job in bringing together various disciplines and perspectives on personalisation in a coherent framework, helping us to better understand the diversity and plurality of this topic. While a mass-produced, hence standardized, book on personalization seems to be an oxymoron, I am very sure that you will develop your very own, individual perspective and "take away" from the research and experiences presented in this volume!

Frank T. Piller,
Professor of Management, RWTH Aachen University, Germany
Co-Founder, MIT Smart Customization Group, MIT, USA

Introduction

Design and personalisation – by a person or for a person?

Iryna Kuksa and Tom Fisher

Rationale

Personalisation is rapidly permeating our everyday lives. From advertising to healthcare and from clothing to architecture – most services and products can be tailored to suit particular needs and preferences. Where does it leave designers when consumers specify their products? Do personalised health services deliver value to the tax payer? To grasp the implications of the personalisation of objects, services and experiences, requires a clear understanding of both what we expect 'personhood' to be, and of the potential enhancements, and threats, personalisation may bring to it. This is a matter of deciding the scope of the subject. Drawn narrowly, it appears to be a largely technical matter with instrumental objectives – to increase sales, to maximise clinical effectiveness; to give users a better experience. But the range of commercial, political and community interests that emerge around personalisation, and the range of academic and professional disciplines to which it is relevant, indicate that if we are to fully acknowledge the implications of personalised designs, such a narrow scope will not do. Reviewing a number of current instances of personalisation, a principle emerges related to the relative agency of 'persons' in different scenarios. Broadly, personalisation is either done *by* a person, or *for* a person and through this distinction it is possible to delineate some of its implications.

Nowadays, mass customisation, personalisation and co-creation (MCPC) strategies commonly aspire to turn customer heterogeneities into opportunities to profit, implying the question whether this 'co-creation' (open innovation and user innovation) should influence our view of mass customisation and personalisation. Many companies state that customers don't just prefer a personalised experience – they expect it (Deloitte Research 2011), which undoubtedly affects approaches to managing the design of both material and 'immaterial' products, and therefore the use of information technologies and the data they collect. 'Co-production', 'co-research' and 'co-design' are the buzzwords of today, with communities and collective 'grass-roots' informal engagement with technologies identified as crucial sources for innovation. The antecedents to this can be found in Pine's work on 'mass customisation' (Pine 1993) that challenged the 'one-size-fits-all' assumption of conventional mass production, emphasising the importance of information for both businesses and consumers. Latterly, and coming from a different direction, 'inclusive design' has made understanding and addressing the needs of all consumers increasingly mainstream (Clarkson et al. 2003). Although initially aimed at those excluded from a meaningful interaction with a product due to age or disability, it implies getting all users involved in all stages of the product development, prompting emerging business models that aim at meeting individual needs most effectively. How this proposition is going to be achieved on a larger (mass-produced) scale remains to be seen.

Even in the age of Industry 4.0, most of the major manufacturers do not offer mass customisation of their products. The reason being that most consumers are perfectly happy to buy standard merchandise or allow the company to customise the goods on their behalf. Nevertheless, the process of customisation is becoming increasingly important for the consumer, sometimes even more important than the end product itself. A good example here is the Adidas Sport Performance store in Paris, which is also called Mi Adidas innovation centre. It opened in October 2006 to provide every customer with a personalised shopping experience fit for an elite athlete and has been popular with purchasers ever since. Another example is Mymuesli, which is the first company to offer customised organic muesli for buying internationally. The customers can not only create their preferred mix of oats, fruits and nuts, but also name their customised products and suggest new ingredients for their muesli outside the company's offered range. Pacif-i, however, takes the idea of personalisation one level up. This company promises to change parenting forever by offering its customers a 'smart' pacifier with integrated Bluetooth technology and an app, which allows parents to monitor their babies' temperature and record medication intake from a smartphone. This development highlights the current tendency across manufacturers to become business eco-systems by attempting to integrate the Internet of Things in their products and services. The goal here is to offer the consumer a personalised experience through, for example, customised travel planning apps (e.g. Moovel), smart and responsive running shoes (e.g. Adidas) and connected cars (e.g. BMW). However, what is still needed are open business platforms – not company-specific ones – to embrace a full spectrum of options personalisation can offer.

Furthermore, the increasingly open sharing of personal data creates fears and uncertainties, which exist in tension with the concept of 'personalising' public service provision. In the context of neoliberal assumptions about the virtue of marketising public services, public institutions face the impulse to both protect individuals' sense of agency, and to share their data. The health IT sector, for example, is being transformed by big data, aiming to tailor individual clinical programs for every patient and designing devices to create personalised fitness routines and treatment plans. But the issue of data accessibility colours many such initiatives, raising questions about who should have the right of access to such sensitive information (health providers, patients or all) and how it should be regulated. Our online identities, patterns of behaviour and purchasing history, our digital 'fingerprints', are easily traceable and may stay 'out there' forever.

While targeted advertising and tailored 'smart' content aims at personalising our experiences, while we are watching we are also being watched by 'smart' spies that compromise our privacy. Targeted advertising stalks every Internet user, but the question of whether consumers really want to see it remains largely unanswered. Companies aim to reduce customers' reactance to potentially intrusive marketing activities by improving perceived consumer control, allowing them to personalise the degree of intrusion. However, it remains to be seen whether, as consumers of information, we are actually in control of our privacy.

In this book, we argue that the scope of a full discussion of personalisation must include bottom-up innovation by communities of practice that engage with technologies in new ways. It must acknowledge the commercial interests involved as the principle of personalisation plays out in public service provision, and the political background against which this takes place. It must recognise the implications for individuals' sense of agency of the personalisation of virtual experiences. It must inspect the specifics of the technologies that can bring personalisation about – but a key point is that the personalisation phenomenon does not reduce to these technologies, or any of these other factors. Its consequences exist in the relationships between them. This volume, therefore, points to some of the challenges that arise in design for personalisation, looking into how organisations (and individuals) relate to their 'target' groups, examining how their ownership is designed, and exploring how design-led social innovation may influence our 'personalised' experiences of the world around us.

We aim to find out what exactly constitutes personalisation and how similar (or different) it is from customisation practices. Defining this term proved to be not very straightforward. There is no general agreement in the little existing literature of what personalisation actually means. This is mainly due to knowledge of the subject being distributed across a number of disciplines, but also because of the fluid nature of this term. If one Googles personalisation, the first few hits come from the field of health and social care provision, in which personalisation is about achieving choice and control in many ways and in different settings, including basic needs; and about the dignity and well-being of the individual (Social Care Institute for Excellence website). When talking about fashion or product manufacture, personalisation is often referred to and/or interchangeable with mass customisation. The classic definition of mass customisation was offered by Tseng and Jiao in 2001 who state that it corresponds to 'producing goods and services to meet individual customer's needs with near mass-production efficiency' (p. 685). Customisation is about modifying a product (or sometimes a process), often choosing from a set of options according to individual (personal or business) requirements. Personalisation, on the other hand, is about a person as a stable entity, with 'bespoke' being at its extreme end. It is often physiologically determined like an individual hearing aid or a personalised artificial limb, or increasingly emotionally led like putting one's name or a photograph on a T-shirt. In some categories, it is impossible (and unnecessary) to distinguish between the two notions; for example, in the area of targeted advertising. Thus, the purpose of this book is to identify a 'phenotype' for personalisation, in order to find the way to characterise this phenomenon without creating rigid terminological boundaries. This is particularly important in the day and age of the Internet of Things and Industry 4.0 when an entire new dimension of personalisation and customisation applications are emerging. So, as Professor Frank Piller, one of the world's leading experts on mass customisation advised the editors of this volume: 'just customize your definition as it is valuable for you' (personal correspondence, May 2016). And we will attempt to do exactly this.

The structure of the book

Personalisation is an emerging field of scholarly interest and, as mentioned above, the current knowledge on this subject is widely dispersed. This book is the first of its kind. It brings various disciplines and viewpoints on personalisation under one umbrella in an attempt to synthesise the existing scholarship, as well as structure and define this nascent field. There are three parts to this volume: Part I 'Personalising consumption, retail and digital spaces'; Part II 'Personalising communication, marketing and manufacture'; and Part III 'Personalising health'. Each part contains three essays on the topic discussing particular instances of personalisation and its effects on different fields of knowledge and professional practice.

Part I: Personalising consumption, retail and digital spaces

An intersection is emerging between material spaces and immaterial technologies in the design of consumers' experiences. In retail, for example, a range of technologies from Internet to radio frequency identification (RFID) are facilitating the personalisation of shopping. Driven by consumer demand and competition, customisation and co-creation have become increasingly significant to fashion brands not only through the personalisation of physical products, apparel, and accessories, but also through their distribution and the location of the customising activity. This shift from mass to individual fashion means that nowadays any customer can not only borrow someone else's personality (through, for example, customising a famous footballer's T-shirt), they can also influence the perception of what constitutes fashion (or a particular brand or product) by creating new personalised communication tools such as fashion blogs. Further, the concept stores of fashion brands have evolved from goods-centred to service-centred locations focused on the experience of the brand. Their increasing use of interactive technologies, and omnichannel communication and distribution, has led to a higher level of personalisation. There is a shift towards using virtual reality as a platform for new intelligent virtual store designs (such as intel.com/retailsolutions), in order to understand and analyse the existing retail landscape and store performance, but also to enrich the merchandising arsenal following fast-changing consumer behaviours and preferences. Furthermore, wearable technologies and smart garments are on the rise to collect our biometric data (mainly health and fitness information), personalising the way we exercise, our lifestyle choices, but also promising to be able to detect the presence of cancer in a human body in the near future (CancerDetectingClothing.com).

This movement of virtual and real retail spaces towards personalisation resonates with recent art practice and research that focuses on how art interventions may affect, and potentially personalise, our engagement with public space and everyday objects. The works of Turner Prize-winning artist Mark Leckey presented at 'The Universal Addressability of Dumb Things' exhibition in De La War Pavilion and elsewhere in 2013, is a good example of the artist's reflection on the effects of personalisation brought by new technologies to inanimate objects. Until recently, however, there has been little research done on, for example, measuring the impact public art has on various aspects of social life. According to Gheorghe (2010), most previous studies were concerned with 'local evaluations of effects on the participants in the reception of specific works of public art' (p. 325). From the 2000s, however, the emphasis shifted towards the 'new genre public art' at the heart of which lies the participation and collaboration of community representatives in creating artworks (Kwon 2005; Lacy 1995). This approach to art-making aspires not only to facilitate 'social change' within participating communities, but also to influence and reconfigure public policies. Zebracki et al. (2010) synthesise other studies (e.g. Jancovich 2011; Hall 2003a, 2003b; Bell et al. 2012; Hall and Robertson 2001) to identify the following claims about the contribution made by public art to urban spaces: (1) *physical-aesthetic*: aimed at enhancing aesthetic quality and improving the attractiveness of a place to encourage better use of the public space; (2) *economic*: focused on providing marketing and place-promotion opportunities and encouraging public–private partnerships; (3) *social*: directed at addressing community needs and dealing with social exclusion by revealing fundamental social contradictions or undermining dominant meanings of urban space; and, finally, (4) *cultural-symbolic*: aimed at boosting awareness of local history, promoting cultural and civic identities, and at contributing to local distinctiveness. There is, however, little empirical evidence to support these claims.

The relevance of this analysis of public art to personalised design becomes clear when it is seen alongside design strategies that resemble those found in fine art. These are adopted in personalised retail spaces and some contemporary design professionals seek to use 'critical design' practice to raise the profile of current cultural, social and political issues, particularly those that derive from technologies. Critical design de-stabilises habitual ways of engaging with things, requiring any individual encountering such an object to 're-make' it for themselves. Professionals who use this design practice, frame it as an affective and provocative agent, which prompts them to ask more questions than they answer through design, stimulating the production of knowledge (Malpass 2011). Aligned to this, design-led social innovation seeks to provide a set of skills, methods and tools for communities to address a variety of issues including crime, social exclusion and social inequalities. Public participation in such practices enables designers to produce solutions tailored to resolve issues that arise in a particular spatial or community setting.

In this part of the book, Tony Kent examines personalisation (and customisation) from the fashion industry and design point of view. His chapter 'Personalisation and fashion design' looks into the origins of personalisation, the issues of ownership, identity and its relationship with the designer, fashion brand and the consumer. The latter, for example, had acquired a considerable influence not only on fashion design, but also on the location of personalising activities. The chapter discusses the emergence of the technology and media savvy 'prosumer' (the term derived from 'production by consumers') who informs popular fashion trends and engages directly with the production process through co-designing and co-creating practices. Such developments have resulted in the individualisation of the mainstream fashion industry, but more importantly, in personalisation of customer shopping experiences.

The following chapter – 'Making it mine: personalising clothes at home' by Amy Twigger Holroyd – investigates personalisation in the context of amateur fashion making and small-scale craft. The argument here is that personalisation in this field constitutes a continuum – the process of evolution – which could be equally rewarding and disappointing (for example, if the maker lacks the relevant technical or, in fact, creative skills). The personalisation and re-personalisation of garments has a long history, with the majority of clothes in the past made to fit an individual body and to create a unique style. The chapter draws on personal experiences of several individuals, presenting a compelling case study on how the reworking of existing garments could create alternative prospects for personalisation and exciting metadesign opportunities for amateur makers, in order to address the issues of longevity and sustainability of personalised garments.

Part I concludes with Conor Farrington's chapter 'Wearable technology as personalised fashion: empowering or oppressive?' It looks into the rise of wearable technologies and their 'invasion' of the fashion world. The chapter draws extensively on critical theory and the work of Adorno, Habermas and Benjamin to address challenges our society is facing from the passive (e.g. data collection) and active (e.g. user aesthetic intervention) aspects of personalisation introduced by wearable technologies and smart garments. It examines the characteristics of personalisation through the lens of utopia (empowerment of a person through greater self-knowledge and heightened sense of individuality) and dystopia (intrusion of privacy and misuse of data), which create a paradox within digital and aesthetic cultures. The issues of empowerment and oppression through personalised fashion are also discussed and conclusions are drawn on how personalisation can influence emancipatory social change and new techniques of governmentality.

Part II: Personalising communication, marketing and manufacture

New 'smart' technologies offer a dimension of personalisation in particular product types, especially in clothing. Body scanning technology and seamless garment production techniques promise personalised wear in the near future. Initiatives that have already taken shape (e.g. Mi Adidas and Fila Adatto) enable the customers to personalise sports shoes in terms of colour, materials and even a personal logo or a name tag. These applications were introduced not only to test consumer demands, but also to experiment with new manufacturing processes. 'Walk in, get scanned, learn about your feet and walk out with a pair of custom-fit Fila Adatto shoes' is the description of what a potential purchaser can achieve while using an interactive kiosk in Fila flagship stores (Boër and Dulio 2007).

Indeed, the emergence of smart technologies is transforming approaches to the design and manufacture of new products, which can now be personalised or even co-created by the end users. 3D printing, for example, has enabled the 'publishing' of not only utility items, but also art and sculpture, changing the ways contemporary designers and artists conceive new ideas and think about future projects. While some futurists argue that 3D printing technology is moving towards desktop size, which may permit direct digital manufacturing from one's home office; others remain less optimistic (Barnatt 2014). Of course, customisation is nothing new as people could always modify and personalise products they purchased to serve their individual purposes. But the difference nowadays is that with access to the relevant technology people with no skills or specialised training could make an utterly new product from scratch, market it and sell it, which could challenge existing business models and marketing techniques.

Along with the benefits of personalisation, such innovations generate challenges in how consumers navigate knowledge to make informed and relatively quick decisions about what they want. Web 4.0 enthusiasts predict that intelligent software agents (such as Siri – an application for iPhone OS, or avatars) will enhance the intuitiveness of navigation, acting as communication interfaces and providing active, personalised assistance. They will be able to learn a user's preferences and interests, make suggestions, function with minimal supervision, customising their assistance to each participant (Kuksa and Childs 2014). Personalised applications for mobile phones are already pervasive, and many businesses endeavour to go mobile first, including the option of social media sharing. This inevitably raises the issue of privacy and personal data, an area in which legislation lags behind. Current research on privacy benchmarks in mobile application design seeks to promote responsible business practice by focusing on how to inform users whether an app's developer has allowed it to use illegal personal data (Kuk 2014). However, protection against this personalisation 'for' a user by an intelligent product, will take some time to implement.

In his chapter 'Who is really in control? Pitfalls on the path to personalisation and personality', Jon Oberlander looks into personalised interaction between machines and humans, arguing that there are a number of ethical reasons for developers to refrain from designing 'too personalised' NLP (natural language processing) systems. The reason here is that if such systems possess 'personality', the natural reaction of the user would be to project human-like qualities upon them and treat them as accountable moral agents. This could lead to humans assigning much more autonomy to the machines than they actually have and, consequently, expecting them to be responsible for decision-making processes. The chapter poses two important questions of whether personalisation automatically implies personality, or whether personality automatically implies personalisation. To answer these, the author examines such notions as de-personalisation and re-personalisation and their potential for developing future intelligent computer systems.

In the following chapter, 'What will designers do when everyone can be a designer?', Matt Sinclair scrutinises the complex and multi-faceted phenomenon of the 'Maker Movement' and the consequences it causes to the relationship between designers and the end users. He argues that the boundaries between professional and amateur design practice are becoming increasingly blurred, changing the way the design work is conventionally understood. The chapter examines the benefits and constraints that mass customisation, crowdsourcing, open and opened design present amateur designers who attempt to personalise their products, challenging the assumption that digital fabrication will ultimately change all industrial design practice. It hypothesises that the future of design depends on the ability of a maker to act as designer and manufacturer at the same time, which is given by an easy, unfacilitated access to mass production technology.

The final chapter by Guy Bingham, 'The history and application of additive manufacturing for design personalisation', discusses the advances, technical constraints and implications of additive manufacturing (AM) technologies that are most commonly known as 3D printing. It presents seven case studies derived from medical healthcare and consumer goods manufacturing sectors, including web-based platforms. The chapter emphasises the ever-growing interest in and enthusiasm for the personalisation of consumer products, but also highlights current technical and skill limitations to generating personalised 3D manufacturing data. It argues that although additive manufacturing solutions are steadily maturing, the effective interaction with the technology is yet to be reached.

Part III: Personalising health

Today, personalisation is placed firmly in the centre of social policy in the UK (Hall 2011) and Europe. Its supporters assume that individuals are aware of their specific needs and being able to satisfy them brings a desirable autonomy – personalised clothing or footwear may indeed be more valuable to its owner than items that are just the same as all the others. However, assuming that this principle applies in the same way to all instances of personalisation is contradicted by the occurrence of the negative consequences of, for example, the 'automatic' personalisation of mobile apps that harvest personal data. Increasingly, users of public services are treated as consumers and an assumption that personalising those services (such as healthcare) will therefore bring unalloyed benefit is evident in their design. 'Fetishising the "personal" or individual in a collectively funded service brings many risks and may further entrench undesirable inequalities' (Checkland 2014). This 'fetishisation' may derive more from political drives to marketise services than a concern for service users – in a medical setting they may not feel capable of making such choices. The prevention of disease by predictive diagnosis emphasises the importance of risk stratification in order to personalise healthcare regimes on the basis of risk patterns (Golubnitschaja 2014). While this approach is underpinned by a discourse of increased choice, empowerment and responsibility (Department of Health 2007), it exists in a particular relationship to issues around the provision of personalised public health services. Along with new medical technologies such as antenatal imaging and genetic screening, this approach to personalising healthcare changes everyone into a potential patient – it pathologises states of health in which actual illness is absent. Predictive medicine in effect makes everybody sick by definition. Antenatal imaging 'constitutes the fetus . . . as a patient' (Verbeek 2011, p. 25).

This is not to say however, that particular treatments may not be usefully adapted to deal with variations in ability. Designing services and responsive modes for diverse populations with large in-group variation in terms of physical, cognitive and perceptual abilities (Brown 2014) may bring direct benefit to individuals with particular personal needs, for example, in teaching which is implemented according to the learners' abilities. The aim here is to reverse the logic of the educational system from the disability point of view, balancing the level of challenge for each learner, to ensure a sense of achievement and progress (Standen 2014).

At the heart of this part of the book is personalised service design and its applications in medical and healthcare settings. Kath Checkland starts the discussion in her chapter 'The 4 Ps: problems in personalising a public service (a personal view of personalisation in the NHS)' by pointing out the discrepancy in opinions amongst politicians (and medical professionals) on promoting and implementing the 'personalisation' agenda within the English NHS. She argues that existing social disadvantages and inequalities in our society play a key role when it comes to a patient's ability to make an informed choice of what personalised treatment or self-directed service they may require. The chapter looks into the recent rise of the 'personalised storytelling' (i.e. personal anecdotes and patients' accounts) adopted by the government and other policy makers that are now widely included in White Papers, analysing the impact this approach has on limited NHS resources.

The next chapter, 'Designing for personalisation in predictive and preventive medicine' by Olga Golubnitschaja, Heinz Lemke, Marko Kapalla and Tony

Kent, presents a somewhat opposing point of view on personalised medical care. The argument here is that the healthcare costs across the Western world are spiralling due to a variety of factors including the population's increasing life expectancy. To address this issue, the authors propose a novel approach to healthcare delivered by predictive, preventive and personalised medicine (PPPM) centres. They state that predicting a patient's predisposition to a disease using new and emerging technologies (through, for example, population screening, health risks identification and stratification of patients for optimal therapy) can not only reduce medical costs, but also change the (arguably) imbalanced disease-oriented healthcare philosophy towards a patient-centred alternative.

Part III concludes with the chapter entitled 'Towards a person-centred approach to design for personalisation' by Sarah Kettley, Richard Kettley and Rachel Lucas, which discusses a person-centred approach (PCA) to design within healthcare provision and psychology, attempting to address a current lack of theoretical context. The authors argue that PCA may help medical professionals in adopting relevant modes of practice and provide them with an attitude-, rather than technique-led framework when pursuing holistic participatory projects. They also share insights into how PCA can be integrated in participatory design when working with mental health communities and its impact on the participant (patient)–researcher relationship when the participant is given more autonomy in defining the matters of concern.

Conclusion

Personalisation is now, indeed, ubiquitous and we encounter it at some level on an everyday basis. What is crucial, however, is that we have enough knowledge of this new paradigm to understand it, to adjust to it, to make it serve us and to be aware of its potential consequences for our relationship with designed things, services and each other. Alongside the consequences of using personalised applications in product manufacturing and healthcare provision, technology also facilitates production of language-using platforms (such as smart trainers) that may communicate to users personally helping them to acquire new knowledge, or change their behaviour. There are some concerns, however, that if such systems are given personalities and human voices, there is a danger that users may start attributing social agency and moral qualities to them – relating to them and having feelings for them. It is entirely possible to have personalisation without personality. The current technological developments imply a distinction in principle between instances when personalisation is done by an individual – where they are able to determine their relationship with a product or service – and cases where personalisation is, in effect, provided for an individual. This distinction between personalisation *by* and personalisation *for* a person has different permutations in different cases, but may be a useful way to move towards a typology of personalised design.

The above examples, however, do not mean that all these innovations serve only humanity and overlook other species. Recently, field biologists have started using 'personalised' electronic tracking devices to study the behaviour of wild, free-ranging animals. Miniature tags containing video cameras, radio transmitters or physiological sensors are attached non-permanently to the animal, to collect detailed biological data (Rutz et al. 2012). For ethical reasons, and since the purpose of these technologies is to study natural, undisturbed behaviour, devices are manufactured to be as small and lightweight as possible. Pioneering efforts are being made in this field, to move away from a 'one-size-fits-all' strategy towards complete customisation (Rutz et al. 2007; Sinclair 2014), which is exactly what is happening in the 'human world'. Researchers tailor units to suit every individual animal captured, ensuring that safe limits are never exceeded, and that data are strictly comparable across subjects. There is hope that such technologies will be able to help humanity to win the desperate fight to save endangered species and tackle the world-wide problem of poaching and illegal trade of animal parts. So, personalisation may go beyond the human person.

We hope that this book begins to identify the dimensions of the phenomenon and typologies within it by investigating specific instances of personalised designs, their consequences for users, and for society.

Acknowledgement

This chapter is based on a preliminary study published in CENTRIC 2014 conference proceedings. The editors thank all contributors to the book and also speakers at the Design and Personalisation Symposium, which took place on 20 February 2014 at Nottingham Trent University, UK.

References

Barnatt, C. (2014) 3D Printing and Personalisation. *Presentation for the Design and Personalisation Symposium*, NTU, February 2014.

Bell, S., Morse, S. and Shah, R. A. (2012) Understanding Stakeholder Participation in Research as Part of Sustainable Development. *Journal of Environmental Management* 101: 13–22.

Boër, C. R. and Dulio, S. (2007) *Mass Customization and Footwear: Myth, Salvation or Reality?* London: Springer.

Brown, D. (2014) Design and Personalisation in the Context of Human–Computer Interaction, Disability and Rehabilitation. *Presentation for the Design and Personalisation Symposium*, NTU, February 2014.

Checkland, K. (2014) Personalisation and Health: A Critical View. *Presentation for the Design and Personalisation Symposium*, NTU, February 2014.

Clarkson, P. J., Coleman, R., Keates, S. and Lebbon, C. (2003) *Inclusive Design: Design for the Whole Population*. London: Springer.

Deloitte Research (2011) The Changing Face of Retail. http://www.deloitte.com/assets/Dcom-Germany/Local%20Assets/Images/06_CBuT/2013/CB_R_store_of_the_future_2013.pdf.

Department of Health (DoH) (2007) *Putting People First*. London: HMSO.

Gheorghe, C. (2010) Theories and Uses in Common: Responses of Art in the Public Sphere. *META: Research in Hermeneutics, Phenomenology, and Practical Philosophy* 2(2): 316–327.

Golubnitschaja, O. (2014) Advanced Healthcare Tailored to the Person: What Is Beyond the Issue? *Presentation for the Design and Personalisation Symposium*, NTU, February 2014.

Hall, E. (2011) Shopping for Support: Personalisation and the New Spaces and Relations of Commodified Care for People with Learning Disabilities. *Social & Cultural Geography* 12(6): 589–603.

Hall, T. (2003a) Art and Urban Change. Public Art in Urban Regeneration. In A. Blunt, P. Gruffudd, J. May, M. Ogborn, and D. Pinder (eds) *Cultural Geography in Practice*. London: Arnold, pp. 221–234.

Hall, T. (2003b) Opening up Public Art's Spaces: Art, Regeneration and Audience. In M. Miles (ed.) *Cultures and Settlements: Advances in Art and Urban Futures*. Bristol: Intellect, pp. 49–57.

Hall, T. and Robertson, I. (2001) Public Art and Urban Regeneration: Advocacy, Claims and Critical Debates. *Landscape Research* 26(1): 5–26.

Jancovich, L. (2011) Great Art for Everyone? Engagement and Participation Policy in the Arts. *Cultural Trends* 20(3–4): 271–279.

Kuk, G. (2014) Can Android Induce Responsible Practice in Privacy by Design through Featuring Apps? *Presentation for the Design and Personalisation Symposium*, NTU, February 2014.

Kuksa, I. and Childs, M. (2014) *Making Sense of Space: The Design and Experience of Virtual Spaces as a Tool for Communication*. Oxford: Chandos/Woodhead.

Kwon, M. (2005) Public Art as Publicity. In S. Sheikh (ed.) *In the Place of the Public Sphere? On the Establishment of Publics and Counter-publics*. Berlin: b_books. Available from: http://eipcp.net/transversal/0605/kwon/1149418119.

Lacy, S. (ed.) (1995) *Mapping the Terrain: New Genre Public Art*. Seattle, WA: Bay Press.

Malpass, M. (2011) Critical Design and a History of Marginalised Practice. *Design History Society Annual Conference: Design Activism and Social Change*. Barcelona: Universitat de Barcelona.

Pine II, B. J. (1993) *Mass Customization: The New Frontier in Business Competition*. Boston, MA: Harvard Business School Press.

Rutz, C., Bluff, L. A., Weir, A. A. S. and Kacelnik, A. (2007) Video Cameras on Wild Birds. *Science* 318: 765.

Rutz, C., Burns, Z. T., James, R., Ismar, S. M. H., Burt, J., Otis, B., Bowen, J. and St Clair, J. J. H. (2012) Automated Mapping of Social Networks in Wild Birds. *Current Biology* 22: R669–R671.

Sinclair, M. (2014) The (New Industrial) Revolution Will Not Be Televised. *Presentation for the Design and Personalisation Symposium*, NTU, February 2014.

Standen, P. (2014) The ViPi Educational and Pedagogical Framework. Internal Project Report.

Tseng, M. M. and Jiao, J. (2001) Mass Customization. In G. Salvendy (ed.) *Handbook of Industrial Engineering, Technology and Operation Management* (3rd ed.). New York: Wiley, pp. 684–709.

Verbeek, P-P. (2011) *Moralizing Technology: Understanding and Designing the Morality of Things*. Chicago, IL, and London: University of Chicago Press.

Zebracki, M., Van Der Vaart, R. and Van Aalst, I. (2010) Deconstructing Public Artopia: Situating Public-Art Claims within Practice. *Geoforum* 41: 786–795.

Websites

Cancer Detecting Clothing, www.CancerDetectingClothing.com

De La Warr Pavilion, http://www.dlwp.com/event/mark-leckey

Intel Corporation, www.intel.com/retailsolutions

Jason Horowitz, https://sekati.com/work/fila-adatto-kiosk

Social Care Institute for Excellence, http://www.scie.org.uk/socialcaretv/video-player.asp?guid=edff5119-2c47-4f20-b212-ed55b7a384a6

Mymuesli, https://uk.mymuesli.com/

Part I
Personalising consumption, retail and digital spaces

1 Personalisation and fashion design

Tony Kent

Introduction

The aim of this chapter is to explain personalisation in the context of the fashion industry and its implications for design. Personalisation, and more particularly customisation and co-creation, have become increasingly significant to fashion brands both through their products, apparel and accessories, their distribution and the location of the customising activity. In this respect, online and offline channels create further opportunities for interaction and engagement, blurring the boundaries between virtual and physical worlds and the opportunities for personalisation. These themes of consumer engagement embrace fast fashion and also slow fashion, multiple retailers and high fashion designers. In this context, the chapter will explore the dimensions of personalised fashion and its implications for design in an uncertain and complex environment.

Driven by consumer and media interest, fashion has become increasingly visible in contemporary society. Crane (2012) summarises its four dimensions, first as a form of material culture related to bodily decoration. It can communicate perceptions of an individual's place in society. It can be symbolic, for example, through uniforms, and in defining, albeit ambiguously, gender and sexuality. Second, fashion can be a kind of language in which clothing styles function as signifiers, distinguishing styles, and fashion from fads. Meanings of some types of clothing tend to be stable and singular, such as men's suits, while others are constantly changing and plural, for example, T-shirts and blue jeans.

Third, fashion can be understood as a system of business organisations that create, communicate and distribute it to consumers. Indeed, fashion pervades the consumption system as a whole (Firat et al. 1995). Consequently, fashion consciousness concerns not only clothes, but also 'every other (re)presentable aspect of consumption that can be rendered as an image-producing act' (p. 50). Finally, the social effects of fashion can be seen in the ways in which personal and social identity, of belonging and difference, are expressed and shaped by clothing and accessories. This dimension is closely related to discussions of fashion and its place in modern and postmodern individuality (Lipovetsky 1994). For Twitchell (1999), fashion provides opportunities for emblematic display, exhibitionism in the sense that individuals plan their clothing, but also decor and other consumption-based badges as a strategy for fitting into their targeted aspirational niche of personality and social status.

The concept of personalisation, who is undertaking the personalising and its location contributes to and is formed by this complexity. Personalisation, its origination and ownership, can be found in the creativity and activity of the designer, fashion brand and the consumer. These dimensions are increasingly integrated in co-creative and co-productive engagement and processes. Fashion designers engage with subject matters such as identity, sexuality and gender and their communication through fashion dress, shows, and media. They seek inspiration from an eclectic diversity of sources including history and historical dress, different cultures, politics, economics, and technology (Matharu 2010). Their creativity is diffused through the system and its networks, where it is interpreted or appropriated for retail markets and ultimately recycled into street fashion. From the perspective of the fashion designer, personalisation is inherent in their designed collections, and through exposure to, and commentary by, the fashion and social media.

Designers and fashion labels, which have to be considered together, are identified by a personal style. In this sense, personalisation distinguishes the designer, the label and the brand with a consistent and recognisable identity. Notably, brand personality has a significant place in creating and maintaining a strong identity. The fashion designer can have a long-standing association or be consciously introduced to transform or reinvent the brand. Ralph Lauren epitomises the tradition of American sportswear, in which designer and brand are closely identified, while Chloé sought a new design direction by appointing Stella McCartney to re-create the brand. Personalisation can be manifested in a specific approach to design; Yamamoto's style has consistently reflected his interest in shape and the folding of material. It may be defined by a single item and media exposure: Givenchy's black dress worn by Audrey Hepburn in the film *Breakfast at Tiffany's* epitomised the understated, refined elegance of his designs. More generally, British designers have demonstrated a 'rebellious spirit', and Belgian designers a 'gritty and perfectionist attitude' while maintaining distinct and varied styles (Matharu 2010, pp. 34–5). In these descriptions the sense of personalisation connects designer, events and places in contrast to the consumption of design, which has become increasingly placeless and ubiquitous.

The designer, the fashion label and brand are influenced, albeit in varying degrees, by their location: the places where designers work, present their collections and communicate through the media. The major fashion cities each demonstrate characteristics built around their fashion system, infrastructure and cultural heritage, which determine and maintain a distinctive style. They host fashion weeks for designers to present their collections twice yearly, typically for spring/summer and autumn/winter seasons. These serve a number of functions, such as demonstrating changes of style, materials and details, launching new designers, developing collaborations, and communication and promotion. A designer-led perspective essentially informs the relationships evident in these communities. However, other types of relationship between fashion producers and consumers are discussed in the next section.

Fashion and personal identity

Personalisation does not lie exclusively in the domain of the designer or brand. From a consumer perspective, changes in consumption hold implications for fashion design and its location. Fashion expresses personal identity in the sense that the style of the products that people purchase, use and display 'says something about who they are' and serves as an indication of their social identity along with other aspects of their lives.

An awareness of consumers' needs for self-identity and image form an important driver for personalisation. Twitchell (1999) demonstrates how fashion communicates personal identity both to others and to oneself. This can take the form of public display, from shopping bags to clothing, branded by names and visible logos such as Lacoste's alligator and Ralph Lauren's polo pony (p. 167). The connection between fashion and personal identity takes the form of individuals discovering their identity or identities through a process of understanding and interpreting their own responses to the various styles that are brought to their attention. Nevertheless, there remains a state of tension in the construction of identity: between this desire to be different and creative, and safe, easy acts of dressing. There is an ambiguity in fashion between innovation and conformity, revealing and concealing, which influences individual approaches to clothes (Woodward 2007).

Theory developments in hedonic consumption and consumption experiences (Holbrook and Hirschmann 1982; O'Shaughnessy and O'Shaughnessy 2002) have contributed to a new awareness among producers of consumer identity. More macro, cultural perspectives of consumer behaviour conceptualise the consumer as a socially connected being with the focus on consumption (Belk 1995). Further, the essential activity of consumption may not be the actual selection, purchase or use of products but the imaginative pleasure seeking to which the product image lends itself and a desire for novelty (Campbell 2012). Such postmodernist perspectives on consumption explain a preference by individuals to avoid commitment to a specific identity and to remain free to experiment with different identities (González 2012). This reflects the development of subcultural, intellectual, and personal differences among consumers and the extent to which such heterogeneity appears in the variety of unique offerings available to their consumption experiences (Firat and Dholakia 1998).

Diversity and pluralistic openness has contributed to marketing-related trends toward the creation of unique offerings targeted at finely segmented groups of consumers. The essence of differentiated segmentation as a marketing strategy can be viewed as one hallmark of postmodernism (Holbrook 1999). In a consumer-driven world, consumers may find the potential to become a participant in its customisation, by immersing themselves as an object into the world of objects, instead of trying to maintain a privileged and detached position from an object (Firat et al. 1995). The 'customising' consumer takes elements of market offerings and crafts a customised consumption experience out of these.

Individual fashion, through a proliferation of choice is evident in eclectic and street-fashion styles, and stands in contrast to the organisation of directed or co-ordinated fashions by fashion designers, their intermediaries and media commentators. An increasing appetite for technology has led to the emergence of the 'prosumer' – someone who demands superior products, that might once have been the preserve of professionals or experts, even for a hobby or leisure activity. Consequently, the role of the designer and fashion design has changed, as consumers have become more engaged in informing and co-creating fashion (Holbrook 2001). Multiple consumer identities are enabled by greater variety provided by the growth in fashion retailing, more specialisation and faster fashion. A move from producer-led to consumer-led fashion has resulted in the individualisation of mass-produced and standardised fashion.

Fast fashion

These organisational and individual perspectives on personalisation are evident in the tensions of fast fashion. While designers continue to present seasonal collections, fashion retailers have moved towards shorter, non-seasonal periods in order to respond to new trends or looks. Fast fashion is defined by affordable prices achieved by sourcing from low-cost producers and the use of quick-response supply chains, which enable frequent changes to collections and colourways to maintain originality and style. For example, a leading multiple retailer Zara, can bring new designs to market in less than four weeks.

Consequently, fast fashion has a hedonic purpose, where consumers expect fresh and fashionable offerings, and expectations of frequency and scarcity are reflected in an urgency to buy before the look sells out. With this approach to fashion, there is an absence of ties to the personality of a single stylist or a specific place in a global culture of fashion and brands. Fast fashion enables eclectic personal identity building that combines many different elements that are temporary and unstable. Retailers have been able to exploit original designs and designers, and in this way create competitive space. Zara, H&M and TopShop have successfully engaged with limited collaborations and concepts of mass exclusivity.

More broadly, 'masstige' enables consumers to enjoy the perception of luxury by combining mass-produced lines with an additional element of prestige, typically through design and branding. H&M through designer capsule collections create time-bound moments of luxury, and introduce scarcity into abundance. Social media provide access to extensive commentaries and images from blogs to designers' runway shows and fashion events. The results of mixing and matching to create individual style preferred by many consumers is reflected elsewhere in the personalisation of their lives. As such, retailers as fashion intermediaries enable consumers to create their own style in a world that is globally interconnected, regionally differentiated and personally individualised all at the same time (Light 2014).

Fast fashion enables consumers to create their own identity and multiple identities. It is eclectic, provides access to new ideas and products, and focuses on availability and affordability. Consequently, design is driven by speed and accuracy of interpretation for specific consumer markets, and less concerned with originality. Indeed, multiple media enable fashion to be disseminated so quickly and with so many interpretations that looks and styles follow on so fast from each other that the designer collection is replaced by consumer 'mash up'. Not surprisingly, brand logo often creates the point of distinction in a process where fashion brands are designing for the consumer to personalise.

Service-dominant logic

The availability of fashion and the opportunity to engage with the materiality of fashion and its images, has contributed to a diversity of personalising and customising activities. The opportunities for participative individualisation are increasingly significant to fashion brands through their products, apparel and accessories.

From a goods-dominant perspective of the fashion system, suppliers produce products and customers buy them. Market exchange in this view is concerned with transactions, and commoditised outputs based on mass production (Pine and Gilmore 1993; Lusch and Vargo 2014). With service-dominant logic (S-DL), customers engage in dialogue and interaction with their suppliers during product design, production, delivery and consumption. Such interactions are defined by co-creation, to describe customer–supplier dialogue and interaction and recognise the micro-competences of individuals and households (Schembri 2006). S-DL suggests that value starts with the supplier understanding customer value-creating processes and learning how to support customers' co-creation activities. Thus, the customer 'always being a co-creator of value' is a key foundational proposition of this logic (Vargo and Lusch 2014; Payne et al. 2009).

Effectively, S-DL extends the concepts of relationship building. A service-centred view of marketing sees a continuous series of social and economic processes and a learning process in which to identify or develop core competences: fundamental skills and knowledge that represent potential competitive advantage; identification of other entities (potential customers) that could benefit from these competencies; and cultivation of relationships that involve customers in developing customised, competitively compelling value propositions to meet financial needs. It also requires marketplace feedback by analysing financial performance from exchange to learn how to improve the firm's offering to customers and improve the firm's performance. The dominant logic of S-DL is 'the application of specialized competences (knowledge and skills), through deeds, processes, and performances for the benefit of another entity or the entity itself'

(Vargo and Lusch 2014, p. 40). Interaction, integration, customisation and co-production are hallmarks of this service-centred view.

Four elements condition the co-production process: First, control and the variable domain of experience. Second, temporality, a recognition that the meaning and value of the brand changes over time in response to changes in the ambient cultural environment and evolution of consumer goals, for example, the value of retro brands. Intergenerational contexts show that brands' propositions can become emblematic signs of family continuity. At a more micro level, firms 'can invoke consumers' repertoires of memories through their brand communication to imbue their consumption with a sense of continuity and connection to the past' (Arnould et al. 2006, p. 98). Finally, the existence of multiple customers links brands to other people.

These elements of SD-L and consumer culture theory are reflected in human-centred design approaches. Meroni and Sangiorgi (2011) distinguish twenty-first-century design from the predictability of the twentieth century, with its focus on the development and production of objects. Designing process and outcomes have become increasingly influenced by unpredictable factors, characterised by a social economy with a variety of actors and motivations that tie in with the ongoing dynamics of social innovation. Objects of design turn into a process of design, something that occurs over time, and an activity to achieve results. Service designs are entities in the making, whose final characteristics will emerge only in the complex dynamics of the real world.

Customisation

Organisational responses to changes in consumption and consumer identity, and the ascendancy of services and experiences, were partly realised by customisation. Lean production, agile manufacturing, mass customisation and customisation recognised the need for producers to respond to individual needs and accordingly adapt products and processes. These functions were subsequently extended to customerisation, which aims at tailoring a product to the needs of specific customers while delivering the desired product quickly and at low cost (Wind and Rangaswamy 2001). Later, instant customerisation was advanced as a manufacturing paradigm to realise the synergies between customisation, minimal customer lead-time, and low cost. When designing or redesigning a product, process, or business unit, each approach should be examined for possible insights into how to serve customers best. In some cases, a single approach will dominate the design. More often, however, there is a need for a mix of approaches to serve the business's particular customers (Gilmore and Pine 1997).

Mass customisation is defined as 'the mass production of individually customized goods and services' (Anderson 1997, p. 4), specifically aligning customised design and manufacture with mass-production efficiency and speed. It was explained as a new paradigm characterised by not only customisation, but also variety through flexibility and quick responsiveness (Pine et al. 1993, p. 34).

The approach offers the capability for individually tailored products or services on a large scale. It shares the logic of micromarketing and is widely regarded as an approach that can align increased customer satisfaction with higher profitability. In this context, mass customisation provides the facility to 'manufacture unique versions of a product in economically efficient lot sizes of one' (Holbrook 1999, p. 63).

Focusing on the customer, however, is both an imperative and a potential problem. In their desire to become customer-driven, many companies have resorted to inventing new programmes and procedures to meet individual customer's needs. Readily available information technology and flexible work processes permit them to customise goods or services for each customer in high volumes at low cost. However, many managers have discovered that mass customisation itself can produce unnecessary cost and complexity (Zipkin 2001).

Mass production implies uniform products, whereas customisation has connotations of small-scale crafts. However, mass customisation can only be realised through unique operational capabilities. The continuing development of electronic commerce and other technologies can reduce constraints on the system. In this respect 'disruptive innovation', of which 3D printing is a good example, provides new business models for individualised production (Baillie and Delamore 2011). Only certain industries can meet these conditions, but the fashion industry has shown that it is well placed to adapt and fulfil them from both consumer and producer perspective (Zipkin 2001).

Mass customisation in fashion

From a fashion perspective mass customisation can be further explained as the large-scale marketing of designer labels (Smith 1997). As Skov (2002) demonstrates, the emergence of mass-customised designer labels in the 1990s would have been difficult to achieve without access to global manufacturing networks. Skov takes the example of Hong Kong's garment industry since the 1960s. While it originally gained entry to Western markets by manufacturing long production runs of standardised items, it later specialised in shorter runs for all market segments, including multiple retailers and designer labels. With the increase in industrial flexibility, the organisation of labour and technology inevitably grew more complex. Factories that used to work on two or three styles at any one time may now work on three hundred, and they may accept orders down to a few dozen items. Such changes allow fashion designers the means to respond to new ideas and creative directions, while fuelling the dynamics of fast fashion and the micromarket of the individual.

Piller and Müller (2004) stress the importance of understanding customers' wants: that they are not buying individuality but rather purchasing a product or service that fits exactly to their needs and desires. Mass-customisation concepts, based primarily on the promise of customisation itself, are more likely to fail. Customers 'don't want choice. They want exactly what they want' (Pine 1993, p. 14). In the case of sports footwear, customers have exact wants for a distinctive style. By contrast, non-sports footwear brands offer their customers fit, comfort, higher functionality, and lower costs of ownership, before style.

Mass customisation offers individual solutions to customers' design requirements rather than products, and in this respect sports brands have been particularly successful. Decoration provides a controllable entry point to customisation, a route taken by the Converse brand, where customers can specify an individualised design and wait while a neutral-coloured canvas sneaker is colour sprayed to order. The process provides opportunities to engage the customer, add value and provide a unique service. NIKEiD offers an online customisation tool that enables consumers to create their own shoe from a limited series of designs. In this case, sports shoes for different activities can be customised from a larger number of components. The aim and appeal of the service is directed towards matching the footwear with what the customer likes: the customer is the designer and the shoe is the customer's identity. Adidas's adiVerse virtual footwear wall customises the product experience and helps guide the consumer to their perfect shoe, or alternatively, lets them browse the entire range of products, with each rendered in real-time 3D. The experience is defined by the use of technologies; not only the systems to visualise individual designs, but also multiple LCD touch screens that use facial recognition to detect a customer's gender. These approaches demonstrate the significance of the brand and designer label in determining the interaction with the consumer. In this relationship, a 'selection of options' process distances the designer.

Personalisation

Trends in co-creation and customisation by the producers and consumers of fashion are evident in sportswear, casual wear – notably T-shirts – but also in luxury products. These have been amplified by other personalisation initiatives in the twenty-first century. Government and organisational policies have focused on the individual across a wide spectrum of functions and services, for example, social care. The use of technology in health services to afford greater personalisation extends to wearable technology in or on clothing, with many recent developments designed to help monitor individual health and wellbeing. Personalisation in this context is about empowering individuals, designing with their full involvement and designing specifically to meet their own unique needs.

Consequently, there is a growing customer expectation for the personalisation of customer experiences that reflect personal needs, attitudes and situations. Connecting with customers has to be in a manner that suits them in order to achieve the highest possible customer value and protect the relationship between customer and provider (Davey 2014). This is evident in enduring forms of personalised fashion, in made-to-measure clothing to suit the customer's requirements and, increasingly, the design of bags and accessories to which the application of initials and motifs are applied. These personalising activities are particularly evident in luxury fashion brands that enable the customer to engage with the design process.

Within luxury fashion, Prada's approach returns to the tradition of 'bespoke' and the heritage of distinctive personal associations. Bespoke tailoring arose from describing the cloth customers picked out in advance for their suits. The cloth then became 'spoken for' or 'bespoken' typically for men's suits, and as demonstrated by London's Savile Row tailors, both material and tailoring became important elements of personalisation. The implications for design extend further than this, and contrast with mass customisation through a focus on limited production capacity, in small batches or limited editions combined with a respect for the traditional skills of craftsmen and artisan production methods (Higgins 2012). Increasingly 'bespoke' has become more widely used in menswear under the influence of celebrity demand – specifically from Hollywood – for different specifications of suits. In general, men have become more knowledgeable and sophisticated in their choices and needs, to which fashion brands have responded: Gucci opened their first men's flagship store to provide their most comprehensive menswear range, including a dedicated area for the Gucci made-to-measure programme (Kansara 2014).

There is clearly a spectrum of personalising approaches, from surface treatments that add the customer's name or initials to more complex co-creative engagement with the consumer. Louis Vuitton launched its personalised Mon Monogram service in 2010, while Hermès created Custom Silk Corner the following year to allow customers to make their own version of its scarves. In leather goods and stationery, Anya Hindmarch and Smythson provide bespoke services. Luxury watchmakers, for example, Jaeger-LeCoultre and Chopard, seek to expand their sales while preserving exclusivity, by making watches to order with anything from diamond stars to fully personalised shapes and decorations. It is notable in the context of co-creation that established watch brands insist on controlling the final design of the customised piece. Fundamentally, personalisation of appearance is essential to being seen as different from the crowd (Kansara 2014).

Personalisation, bespoke and customisation are increasingly important facets of the luxury experience, and retailers, too, can facilitate this aspect of luxury fashion. Harrods in-store bespoke event, Made with Love, which was dedicated to customisation, provided a platform for brands ranging from Gucci to La Perla to offer their bespoke services (Cochrane 2014). Personalisation as an in-store experience is evident in Burberry's One to One iPad application, which allows in-store sales staff to build and maintain customer profiles complete with global transaction histories and visual wardrobes for each individual shopper.

Given the trend for personalisation in the luxury sector, it would appear that there is scope for more mid-market fashion retailers to fill a gap in the market for consumers who aspire to own a designer brand but can't afford the premium prices. The most obvious opportunity is to offer a service to embroider the customer's initials on to their bags, in order to persuade them that they can have a product similar to a luxury one, but for a more affordable price (Mintel 2011). This option is already evident in the monogramming services introduced into both Topshop and Whistles. In other respects, personalisation has succeeded in the everyday wear of T-shirts and sportswear: anyone can – literally – personalise their favourite football team shirt with their own name. The next stage in the evolution from customisation to personalisation may see further opportunities for customer-driven fashions. 3D printing in-store, has a clear application for customer creativity in the specification of personalised accessories (Cochrane 2014). More specifically, the Yr digital printing service, found in Topshop and Topman describes itself as the 'world's first all-over print fashion brand . . . [for customers to] curate and create one-off high-quality garments in minutes' (www.yrsto.re). The idea of curation of the garment demonstrates the sense of ownership and distinctiveness, something to be looked after over time.

All these features are in keeping with Arnould et al.'s (2006) discussion of the conditions for co-production. However, customisation and personalisation not only change the customer's decision-making process, but also the post-purchase phases, where communicating and relationship building through production, delivery and ownership are significant elements of personalisation.

Fashion design and the Internet

The rapid development of online connectivity, versatility, and computing power has generally extended the opportunities for personalisation. Location in this context increasingly concerns the multichannel mediation of fashion – online, offline and mobile – and the possibilities for interaction with the consumer. By allowing access to customer information to provide consistent, timely and relevant individualised interactions, the processes of personalisation can increase customer loyalty and lifetime value (Jackson 2007).

Mobility and shifts in the distribution of fashion intelligence (Crewe 2013) extend the boundaries of co-creative fashion design. Style trends that are available on instant online runway shows, through fashion bloggers, and celebrity endorsements inspire new design. Online connectivity and communication using targeted data by brands offers new forms of engagement and personalisation. New designs can be co-created as virtual garments, through online postings and feedback, at every level of design complexity up to eveningwear designs.

However, personalisation is not only about communication, whether it is exclusively concerned with information, or integrated with other products or services. It must adapt so that it can 'anticipate relevant intent' of customers at the right time and at the right place. In other words, it needs to create a personalised offer that anticipates how customers' needs are changing. While 'big data' provides information to enable personalised products and services, personalisation generally involves people to create personal relationships and provide services. Digital technology provides brands with the opportunity to forge a personal relationship with every customer (Marketing Week 2012), which gives rise to the concept of personalisation not as a thing, but rather as *a way of doing things*.

These qualities are evident in online fashion brands. Net-a-Porter, a leading fashion retailer, has used a combination of surveys and behavioural data to offer each customer an individualised experience. The company can match new products around designers that the customer has previously signed up for or bought, and also products it thinks customers might like. For instance, a shopper in Paris who has bought Lanvin might be interested in Givenchy handbags, while a Stella McCartney customer in Texas might be shown blouses from Equipment. Burberry uses techniques such as landing page customisation, search re-marketing, dynamic display re-marketing and targeting in social platforms using real-time data insights (Sherman 2014). Typically, these personalised approaches lead to improved results. Style advice enables people to ask questions about specific looks and purchasing decisions. They can acquire personalised style advice from 'fashion insiders' ranging from junior stylists to bloggers who are free to suggest products from any e-commerce site. A growing number of affordable fashion sites offer consumers personalised product selections and customised shopping recommendations picked by 'celebrity stylists'.

One implication of online connectivity is that fashion design can be extended to use available information and material to support socialisation and collaboration in small and large-size communities, and to generate an interest in user-generated content (Ardissono et al. 2012). In recent years, online innovation communities have gained popularity in attempting to involve enthusiastic consumers in a company's development processes. Innovation community members may be invited to contribute to development activities such as generating and evaluating new ideas; elaborating, evaluating or challenging concepts; and creating virtual prototypes. Thus, they may generate valuable propositions and solutions, positive word-of-mouth, and collective commitment towards new offerings (Gebauer et al. 2013). In this context, co-creation can be applied to making and the functionality of patterns or materials: a technical pattern is easy to share and allows more technical discussion about its shape and cut for a more comfortable fit.

Moreover, communities of consumers can exist outside the organisation. 'Collaborative consumption' is characterised by swapping, sharing, bartering, trading and renting, having been reinvented by technologies and peer-to-peer marketplaces (Botsman and Rogers 2011). This form of 'social shopping' is particularly suitable for fashion and the re-positioning of the designer in a world of relationships rather than things (Baillie and Delamore 2011) as younger consumers, in particular, exchange ideas, seek advice and approval. Still more distributed forms of co-creation can be found in crowdsourced design platforms. These are all facilitated by the convergence of physical and virtual worlds: the provision of new ways to access a fashion designer's knowledge and skills, and new environments for co-creative processes and their communication.

While online access provides new opportunities to share knowledge and information of fashion, in another respect it presents new opportunities for a more literal form of personalised fashion through body scanning technologies. These have existed for some time as store-based facilities, usually owned by a third party such as Bodymetrics, a leading producer of commercial body scanners. However, the devices have failed to scale up, as tailoring products specifically for individuals creates an expectation of an absolutely perfect fit. This can be problematic in a mass market; Levi's introduced a body scanner for in-store customers, which scanned the body and sent the data to be manufactured into a pair of jeans to exactly fit the body shape. However, a fundamental problem lay in customer expectations: customers were disappointed if the garment was just 5 mm out of alignment (Stuart 2013). The need for personal measurements is more acutely felt when purchasing online. Individual body scanning through mobile phone or computer cameras, and the recording of accurate body size information, will enable fashion design to be more accurate and accessible. It will further allow consumers to co-create designs with more confidence, as they will have control over their precise sizing data in the process of designing.

Slow fashion and participatory design

The discussion up to this point has focused on the producer and consumer, and the design processes involving co-production and co-creation. However, an alternative view of fashion design and its personalisation sees consumers as users in which the designer takes a different role. Co-design defines this collective creativity across the whole span of a design process. Broadly, it refers to the creativity of designers and people not trained in design working together in the design development process (Sanders and Stappers 2008). It gathers insights into users' needs, allowing ideas to feed into concept design and product development (Baillie and Delamore 2011). More profoundly, co-designing value propositions that can support value creation processes requires a deep, long-term development partnership (Keränen et al. 2013).

Co-design has its foundations in the participatory design movement, which sees designers creating solutions with people from the community and recognises that local value chain actors can leverage local knowledge. It can also lead to innovations that may be better adapted to the context and be more likely to be adopted, since local people have invested resources in their creation (IDEO, 2008). These approaches directly counter the expert-centred approach and actively blur distinctions between researcher, practitioner and user. They are guided primarily by practical concerns, are sometimes explicitly grounded in stakeholders' ways of knowing, and are often aimed at building local capacity and catalysing change (Harder et al. 2013).

These approaches are evident in the *slow fashion* vocabulary of small-scale production, traditional craft techniques, local materials and markets, which challenge fast fashion's obsession with mass production and globalised style. It emphasises making and maintaining actual material garments, and re-finding earlier experiences of fashion linked to active making rather than watching (Fletcher 2010). Slow fashion demonstrates new priorities for the fashion sector, such as greater resourcefulness, the fostering of traditions, skills and new technologies; the creation of meaningful work; and improved social and ecological quality (Fletcher 2010). A focus on craft but also the adoption of new technologies can create new, and extend the life of, existing clothes and accessories. Slow fashion garments can create 'emotional durability' or, in other words, a personal connection with the wearer, which will ensure its longevity and may even result in it being passed on to the next generation (Pookulangaraa and Shephard 2013).

Consequently, the slow approach offers some alternative ways of addressing issues of fashion design and sustainability at a relatively local level by activating the potential for personal connection to garments to increase their longevity. It offers collaborations that challenge existing hierarchies of 'designer', 'producer', and 'consumer', and provides agency, especially to women. Slow fashion engages with the reuse of materials in ways that question the notion of fashion being concerned exclusively with the 'new'. By focusing on the materiality of fashion it questions the primacy of image, defining 'fashion' with making, clothes and identities, rather than only with looking (Clark 2008). Individual personalisation has, in many ways, been evident in the adjusting and changing of the size and shape of clothes, for example, children's clothes handed down through families and the adaptation of worn-out clothes – personalisation through transforming as distinct from repairing. These qualities demonstrate the micro-specialised competences previously proposed in S-DL.

The implications for slow fashion design firstly concern co-design methods that encourage empathy in designers with an aim to improve a person's experience of the object to be designed. The main way to implement this approach is by engaging all stakeholders in the process, and creating a space of participatory culture. With co-design, generative techniques are employed to use the creativity of the participants in order to enable them to be aware of their own experiences, and to express them in a creative and supportive environment (Bush 2014). A range of shared tools emerges that people can use to communicate with designers, and with it a language through which they can imagine and express their ideas and dreams for future experience (Sanders and Stappers 2008). These lead to design proposals that can serve as starting points for designers and/or design teams. Consequently, the role of the designer moves from translator to facilitator, in which the designer offers appropriate tools and expert knowledge to the participants in the co-design process (Bush 2014).

Second, this participative approach references a fundamental principle of service design: to find a balance between what designers should try to fix and what is to be left free (Meroni and Sangiorgi 2011). These may be seen and evaluated differently in each project and the design culture of its proponents, in which the human component of service is seen as a value to cultivate. The role of the designer in this context is as an actor able to listen to users and facilitate the discussion about what to do. Usually, the user is seen as an individual, aware and informed, active in proposing but passive in action. By contrast, communitarian or individual service encounters and the user as a bringer of capability typify this approach.

A final insight into slow fashion design draws on design for experience, considering not the only the aesthetics of things but the aesthetics of personal experiences. User needs include the emotional, spiritual, social, aspirational and cultural aspects of their relationship with products. This approach sees design as a process, and this, too, requires designing more closely with people as active partners, as 'direct contact brings empathy with users to design teams and positively influences the quality of the product concepts they produce' (Sleeswijk et al. 2011, cited in van Rijn et al. 2011, p. 65).

Conclusion

This chapter has assessed the dimensions of the personalisation of fashion design, moving from personalisation by 'one', the designer, to personalisation by 'many', the engagement of the community with slow fashion. It can be argued that personalisation of fashion lies in the hands of the designer and indeed this is true in part; fashion design reflects the designer's personality and individual style and interests. However, as the definitions of fashion and in particular fashion systems demonstrate, personalisation extends beyond the boundaries of the designer and into a broader system of intermediaries and consumers. The growth of consumption and the increasing significance of the consumer in the producer–consumer relationship from the 1980s are reflected in changes towards individuality and individualisation. From different theoretical perspectives, this development is a central component of postmodernism but also micromarketing: a focus on the individual and the means to individualise.

The response to individualism is seen in the use of different terms that define design ownership and agency and their application in fashion design. However, these are used with a lack of precision that in many ways is a cause and outcome of a diversity of discourses. Customisation and, more specifically, mass customisation tends to reflect a producer-led approach to distinctive products. A standard product or garment is customised to the consumer's requirement. Colloquially, personalisation covers some of the same ground but literally can be taken to personalise a garment or accessory and tends to be used by luxury brands and designer labels. Clearly, the application of a monogram to a standardised product could also be described as customisation. However, the designer's attention to craftsmanship and small-scale production, the brand and the environment in which it is experienced, is a further contributory factor to personalisation. Bespoke both refines the individualisation but also introduces a stronger element of co-creation.

The implications for designers of collaborating with users are evident in the different platforms for co-creation and co-design. The designer-led world of luxury fashion is distinguished from that of the fast fashion of mass consumption and the slow fashion movement of engagement with communities of users. Each of these presents a different perspective on design and the participation between designer intermediaries such as retailers and customers.

While fast fashion appears to offer the least opportunities for personalisation, it offers considerable opportunity for consumer-led individualisation seen most distinctively in street fashion. More knowledgeable, technologically enabled and skilful consumers combine with brands and producers to individualise fashion both online and in-store. Consequently, the personalisation of fashion will be increasingly nuanced as it expands through the dimensions of time and location, the individual and organisation.

References

Anderson, D. M. (1997) *Agile Product Development for Mass Customization: How to Develop and Deliver Products for Mass Customization, Niche Markets, JIT, Build-to-Order and Flexible Manufacturing*. London: Irwin.

Ardissono, L., Kuflik, T. and Petrelli, D. (2012) Personalization in cultural heritage: the road travelled and the one ahead. *User Modeling & User-Adapted Interaction*, 22(1/2), 73–99.

Arnould, E. J., Price, L. L. and Malshe, A. (2006) Toward a cultural resource-based theory of the consumer. In R. F. Lusch and S. L. Vargo (eds) *Service Dominant Logic of Marketing: Dialog, Debate and Directions*. New York: Sharpe, pp. 91–104.

Baillie, J. and Delamore, P. (2011) E-co-creation for fashion. Conference paper presented at the *Mass Customisation and Personalisation Conference*, November, San Francisco, CA.

Belk, R. W. (1995) Studies in the new consumer behaviour. In D. Miller (ed.) *Acknowledging Consumption*. London: Routledge, pp. 53–94.

Botsman, R. and Rogers, R. (2011) *What's Mine Is Yours: How Collaborative Consumption Is Changing the Way We Live*. London: Collins.

Bush, P. (2014) Therapeutic jewellery: crafting wellbeing. Paper presented at the 'Theorising Personal Medical Devices' Symposium. University of Cambridge.

Campbell, C. (2012) The modern western fashion pattern, its functions and relationship to identity. In A. M. González and L. Bovone (eds) *Identities through Fashion*. Oxford: Berg, pp. 9–22.

Clark, H. (2008) SLOW + FASHION – an oxymoron – or a promise for the future . . . ? *Fashion Theory: The Journal of Dress, Body & Culture*, 12(4), 427–446.

Cochrane, L. (2014) Made for you: Prada's customised shoes and the rise of personalised fashion. *The Guardian*, Fashion Blog, 30 July.

Crane, D. (2012) Introduction. In A. M. González and L. Bovone (eds) *Identities through Fashion*. Oxford: Berg, pp. 1–8.

Crewe, L. (2013) When virtual and material worlds collide: democratic fashion in the digital age. *Environment and Planning A*, 45(4), 760–780.

Davey, N. (2014) *Personalisation: How to Build a Successful Strategy*. Available at My Customer, http://www.mycustomer.com/feature/experience-marketing/personalisation-how-build-successful-strategy/. Accessed 12 December 2014.

Firat, F. and Dholakia, N. (1998) *Consuming People: From Political Economy to Theatres of Consumption*. London: Routledge.

Firat, F., Dholakia, N. and Venkatesh, A. (1995) Marketing in a postmodern world. *European Journal of Marketing*, 29(1), 40–56.

Fletcher, K. (2010) Slow fashion: an invitation for systems change. *Fashion Practice*, 2(2), 259–266.

Gebauer, J., Fuller, J. and Pezzei, R. (2013) The dark and the bright side of co-creation: triggers of member behavior in online innovation communities. *Journal of Business Research*, 9, 1516–1527.

Gilmore, J. H. and Pine II, B. J. (1997) The four faces of mass customization. *Harvard Business Review*, 75(1), 91–101.

González, A. M. (2012) Fashion, image, identity. In A. M. González and L. Bovone (eds) *Identities through Fashion*. London: Bloomsbury.

Harder, M. K., Burford, G. and Hoover, E. (2013) What is participation? Design leads the way to a cross-disciplinary framework. *Design Issues*, 29(4), 41–58.

Higgins, C. (2012) British menswear, leading the way! 'Heritage' in premium British menswear: innovations, providing solutions towards a more sustainable future? *Fashion Colloquia*, London: University of the Arts London. Available at http://process.arts.ac.uk/content/british-menswear-leading-way. Accessed 10 January 2017.

Holbrook, M. B. (1999) Higher than the bottom line: reflections on some recent macromarketing literature. *Journal of Macromarketing*, 19(1), 48–74.

Holbrook, M. B. (2001) The millennial consumer in the texts of our times: evangelizing. *Journal of Macromarketing*, 21(2), 181–198.

Holbrook, M. B. and Hirschman, E. C. (1982) The experiential aspects of consumption: consumer, fantasies, feelings and fun. *Journal of Consumer Research*, 9, 132–40.

IDEO (2008) *Human Centre Design Toolkit*, 2nd edn. Available online from https://www.ideo.com/post/design-kit. Accessed 10 January 2017.

Jackson, T. W. (2007) Personalisation and CRM. *Journal of Database Marketing and Customer Strategy Management*, 15(1), 24–36.

Kansara, V. A. (2014) Stores still critical to wooing men, but leaders re-wiring for digital age. *Fashion 2.0 Intelligence*. 24 June 2014. Available at www.businessoffashion.com. Accessed 20 December 2014.

Keränen, K., Dusch, B., Ojasolo, K. and Moultrie, J. (2013) Co-creation patterns: insights from a collaborative service design tool. In *Proceedings of the Cambridge Academic Design Management Conference*. Cambridge: University of Cambridge.

Light, L. (2014) Brand journalism: how to engage successfully with consumers in an age of inclusive individuality. *Journal of Band Strategy*, 3(21), 121–128.

Lipovetsky, G. (1994) *The Empire of Fashion: Dressing Modern Democracy*. Princeton, NJ: Princeton University Press.

Lusch, R. F. and Vargo, S. L. (2014) *Service-Dominant Logic. Premises, Perspectives, Possibilities*. Cambridge: Cambridge University Press.

Marketing Week (2012) 11 October 2012, p. 7.

Matharu, G. (2010) *What Is Fashion Design?* Mies: RotoVision.

Meroni, A. and Sangiorgi, D. (2011) *Design for Services*. Aldershot: Gower.

Mintel (2011) *Consumer Attitudes towards Luxury Brands, UK*, November 2011. London: Mintel.

O'Shaughnessy, J. and O'Shaughnessy, N. J. (2002) Marketing, the consumer society and hedonism. *European Journal of Marketing*, 36(5/6), 524–47.

Payne, A., Storbacka, K., Frow, P. and Knox, S. (2009) Co-creating brands: diagnosing and designing the relationship experience. *Journal of Business Research*, 62(3), 379–389.

Piller, F. T. and Müller, M. (2004) A new marketing approach to mass customisation. *International Journal of Computer Integrated Manufacturing*, 17(7), 583–593.

Pine II, B. J. (1993) *Mass Customization: The New Frontier in Business Competition*. Boston, MA: Harvard Business School Press.

Pine II, B. J. and Gilmore, J. H. (1999) *The Experience Economy – Work is Theatre and Every Business a Stage*. Boston, MA: Harvard Business School Press.

Pine II, B. J., Bart, V. and Boynton, A. C. (1993) Making mass customization work. *Harvard Business Review*, Sept/Oct, 108–116.

Pookulangaraa, S. and Shephard, A. (2013) Slow fashion movement: understanding consumer perceptions – an exploratory study. *Journal of Retailing and Consumer Services*, 20(2), 200–20.

Sanders, E. B.-N. and Stappers, P. J. (2008) Co-creation and the new landscapes of design, *CoDesign*, 4(1), 5–18.

Schembri, S. (2006) Rationalising service logic, or understanding services as experiences? *Marketing Theory*, 6(3), 381–392.

Sherman, L. (2014) A customised experience for each shopper? *BusinessofFashion.com*, 8 December.

Skov, L. (2002) Hong Kong fashion designers as cultural intermediaries: out of global garment production. *Cultural Studies*, 16(4), 553–569. Available at: http://www.tandfonline.com. Accessed 12 December 2013.

Stuart, R. (2013) *An Analysis of the Antecedents to and Dimensions of Consumption Experience in Fashion Stores*. Unpublished PhD Thesis. Manchester: University of Manchester.

Smith, P. (1997) Tommy Hilfiger in the age of mass customization. In A. Ross (ed.) *No Sweat: Fashion, Free Trade and the Rights of Garment Workers*. London: Verso, pp. 249–262.

Twitchell, J. B. (1999) *Lead Us into Temptation: The Triumph of American Materialism*. New York: Columbia University Press, Wheatley.

van Rijn, H., Sleeswijk Visser, F., Stappers, P. J. and Özakar, A. D. (2011) Achieving empathy with users: the effects of different sources of information. *Codesign*, 7(2), 65–77.

Vargo, S. L. and Lusch, R. F. (2004) Evolving to a new dominant logic for marketing. *Journal of Marketing*, 68(1), 1–17.

Wind, Y. and Rangaswamy, A. (2001) Customerisation: the next revolution in mass customisation. *Journal of Interactive Marketing*, 15(1), 13–32.

Woodward, S. (2007) *Why Women Wear What They Wear*. Oxford: Berg.

Zipkin, P. (2001) The limits of mass customisation. *Sloan Management Review*, 42(3), 81–87.

2 Making it mine

Personalising clothes at home

Amy Twigger Holroyd

Introduction

This chapter discusses personalisation in the context of amateur fashion making – the domestic knitting and sewing of clothes – and considers the motivations and experiences of those making and wearing personalised homemade garments. This topic emerges from my doctoral research, which explored the relationship between homemade clothes and sustainability, and more specifically investigated the potential of reworking knitted garments from the wardrobe (Twigger Holroyd 2013). This research was, in turn, informed and inspired by my practice as a designer-maker of knitwear with several years' experience of running workshops and participatory projects with amateur makers in a range of settings.

To start, I will define personalisation in terms of clothing, and set the scene by outlining the history and recent resurgence of domestic textile crafts. I will then describe the methodology used for the research, which involved a combination of making-based participatory activities and semi-structured interviews. Drawing on the insights gained from these activities, I will profile the opportunities for personalisation afforded by both the creation of new garments and the less familiar activity of reworking existing items. A number of fascinating themes emerge when reflecting on personalisation and homemade clothes; I will focus on two areas. First, I will discuss the skills that an amateur maker must exercise in order to personalise an item, and the ways in which professional designers can support this activity. Second, I will explore the mixed meanings associated with the homemade and consider the appeal, and danger, of uniqueness in dress; these factors affect the experience of wearing personalised clothes. I will conclude by briefly discussing the implications of personalisation for longevity and re-use.

Personalisation and clothing

The concept of personalisation in terms of clothing is deceptively slippery; among the various definitions of it that could be adopted, I have chosen *the making, or intentional alteration, of a garment for a known individual*. In this chapter

I am particularly focusing on amateur makers who undertake such projects for their own enjoyment and satisfaction. The creation of personalised items is not the sole preserve of the homemade, of course; tailors and dressmakers provide made-to-measure clothing as a professional service, as they have done for centuries (Ross 2008). In recent years, clothing companies have started to offer premium services that produce unique garments for individual customers; new menswear label Alton Lane, for example, uses 3D body scanning technology to facilitate the creation of bespoke tailored suits (Gayomali 2014), while companies such as Adidas and Pringle use digital platforms to support customers to create personalised products through the selection of particular patterns, colours and materials (Adidas 2015; Pringle of Scotland 2015). All of these processes sit in stark contrast to the usual situation, which sees garments being mass produced in standard sizes by the thousand and sold through high street shops in a distinctly impersonal process.

I am concerned not only with activities that produce new items of clothing, but also with processes that personalise existing items. Although any mass-produced garment will gradually become associated with its wearer over time, transforming from a generic product into a much more personally significant possession, I suggest that we should not consider this process to be personalisation unless it involves an intentional material alteration. I do not see the 'breaking-in' of shoes, therefore, as personalising them: although these objects physically change – gradually becoming shaped to the wearer's feet, and also reflecting the unique patterns of their gait – such changes are a by-product of the process of wearing, rather than a consciously staged intervention. Similarly, I would not include within the scope of personalisation the individual patterns of wear that occur as jeans adapt to a wearer; I would, however, include the deliberate act of shrinking raw denim jeans to fit an individual by wearing them in the bath. Likewise, I would include alterations that use sewing to adapt a newly purchased garment to better fit a person's body, or to alter or enhance the style.

If a maker were to rework a damaged or degraded garment from their wardrobe and somehow change it in the process, as in the examples of re-knitting that I will profile later, I would consider this as personalisation of the item. If they were to repair the garment in a way that aimed to restore it to its former state, however – using, to borrow terminology from Sennett (2008), a 'static' rather than 'dynamic' repair – I would not. If an existing garment were to be dynamically reworked not for a known individual, but rather for general sale – as is the case with the Remade range of upcycled items sold by UK charity Traid (Warren 2012) – I would, again, not consider it to be personalised; although the item itself would be unique, it would not have the direct link with a prospective wearer that I consider to be essential for personalisation.

These examples help to illustrate the scope of personalisation in clothing; they also serve to highlight various factors which differentiate them. We can see that in some cases personalisation takes place during the initial making process, while in others it is an intervention that takes place later; in the examples involving commercially produced clothing, personalisation may be supported by the designer or retailer, or may be an independent act undertaken by the wearer. Furthermore, these examples demonstrate that the personalisation of clothing falls within two broad categories: creating a personalised fit for an individual body, or creating a personalised style for an individual sense of identity. These aspects of personalisation may occur separately, or together. Each could be said to operate on a sliding scale of intensity: a 'mildly' personalised item would be made or altered to suit the needs or tastes of the wearer, yet could also be viably used by many other people, while an extreme case would be created for an individual wearer, to the likely exclusion of others.

Amateur fashion making

The domestic activities of making clothes and adapting existing garments were formerly much more widespread than they are today; it was only during the twentieth century that it became usual for us to wear standardised massproduced garments. Writing about the situation in Britain in the 1930s, for example, McDowell (1997) explains that the vast majority of women were able to sew their own clothes; while middle-class women would be making new items for themselves to wear, working-class women were more likely to be mending and adapting secondhand clothing to fit. During the Second World War, rationing led to an increase in this inventive adaptation; Breward (2003) reports that following the war, many more people embraced ready-made clothes, which had improved in quality. Thus in Britain, as in other industrialised countries, sewing clothes at home shifted from an integral element of domestic activity in the 1950s to a creative hobby during the 1960s. Participation declined from this point, as more women took up paid employment and adopted alternative ways of spending their valuable leisure time (Emery 2014). We can see a similar pattern in knitting: it had been a widespread domestic practice in the first half of the twentieth century and during the Second World War, but transformed into an optional leisure activity in the decades following the war (Black 2012).

It is widely acknowledged that there has been a resurgence of interest in amateur fashion-making practices in the last 15 years or so (Myzelev 2009; Bratich and Brush 2011; Hall and Jayne 2015). This revival has involved an increase in levels of participation; while trustworthy and transparent statistics demonstrating this increase are scarce, articles in the mainstream press regularly cite rises in sales of equipment and materials, along with other indicators such as making-related Internet searches and craft book publications (Lewis 2011; Lewis-Hammond 2014). The UK Craft and Hobby Trade Association recently reported that 3.5 million people in the UK make their own clothes with a sewing machine, 433,000 of whom started sewing only in the last year (Lewis-Hammond 2014). The UK Hand Knitting Association (2015), meanwhile, suggests that there are now 7.5 million knitters and crocheters in the country. Alongside this increase in participation we can observe a shift in the cultures of sewing, knitting and mending; Hackney (2013: 170) describes a 'new energy' at work, meaning that 'the crafts [...] have changed beyond all recognition in recent years'. Although, in my experience, the majority of amateur fashion making happening today involves the production of new items, there has also been a revival of interest in using sewing to rework existing pieces, with various books and blogs inspiring makers to see this as an exciting and accessible opportunity for creativity.

Various theories are in circulation regarding the cause of the resurgence of fashion making, with many pointing to the global financial crisis and the ensuing period of austerity as prompting a renewed interest in craft (Hall and Jayne 2015). While this may be part of the explanation, I would agree with Luckman (2013: 254) that the revival is 'largely a response to a number of bigger, longer, economic, industrial and cultural shifts around the economic base model *vis-à-vis* production and manufacturing in particular'. As she argues, these shifts involve a re-evaluation of the impersonal practices of mass production and an increased interest in the potential of small-scale craft. The recent growth of amateur fashion making has undoubtedly been assisted by the connective power of the Internet. As Bratich and Brush (2011: 242) describe, 'the knitting circle now meshes with the World Wide Web'. Online platforms, blogs and social media are providing opportunities for makers to connect as never before, sharing their projects, patterns and problems and providing mutual support (Kuznetsov and Paulos 2010).

Methodology

This chapter draws on my previous research, in which I investigated amateur fashion making as a strategy for sustainability; as I have explained, this topic emerged from my experience of facilitating various knitting workshops and projects. This work brought me into contact with scores of amateur knitters, and the conversations I had with them revealed that the practice of making clothes at home involves an array of fascinating problems, issues and opportunities. I recognised that the complex nature of this practice brought into question the assumption – which I had frequently encountered – that amateur fashion making is straightforwardly positive in terms of sustainability. I set out to explore the lived experience of making and remaking clothes at home, in order to build a more nuanced view of the ways in which this activity might contribute to a sustainable fashion system.

I explored this topic through the prism of a specific design-led challenge, investigating the potential for reworking existing items of knitwear using knit-based skills, techniques and knowledge. Although these re-knitting processes would have been an integral part of knitting practice in the past, activity has declined significantly and much of the relevant tacit knowledge has been lost; I sought to use my design practice to develop methods of re-knitting that are appropriate to the knitted garments in our wardrobes today. Because I intended that the processes would be used by knitters to rework their own garments at home, I recruited a group of six amateur hand knitters with whom to test the techniques. These participants were aged between 43 and 66 at the time of the project, and all female – reflecting the fact that knitting is a hobby predominantly adopted by women (Office for National Statistics 1997). The majority had previously attended one of my skills-based knitting workshops, and all were motivated to take part by the opportunity to explore new ideas.

The project was built around a series of four-day-long practical workshops, in which we tested the re-knitting processes; activity at the early sessions involved structured explorations of particular techniques and short design-related exercises, while the project culminated in each participant reworking an item of knitwear from her own wardrobe. These sessions were audio and video recorded; I transcribed every recording and used thematic coding and a constant comparative method (Robson 2011) in order to analyse the data. By capturing the participants' thoughts before, during and after the workshops, I was able to examine the ways in which their attitudes to re-knitting changed as the project progressed. The participants linked the activities we were undertaking with their previous making projects and aspirations for the future; thus, I was also able to investigate their broader experiences of making clothes. The workshops were preceded by individual semi-structured interviews and two evening 'knitting circle' discussion sessions, which provided further data relating to the participants' attitudes and prior experiences.

The workshop method was complemented by additional data, gathered via a drop-in knitting activity that I facilitated at a number of UK music festivals (Latitude, Green Man, End of the Road and Port Eliot) each summer from 2009 to 2012. This free activity provided a space for festivalgoers to sit and knit; projects took different forms, but in each case the completed pieces of knitting were left on display, growing in number as the festival progressed. I invited participants to leave comments on small cardboard tags attached to the knitting; while these often related to the memories evoked by the activity of making, at the 2012 events many responded to my prompt to 'share your feelings about wearing homemade clothes'. Over the period of four years, I gathered over a thousand responses, providing valuable insights into attitudes to making and homemade clothes from a large number of respondents.

During the course of my doctoral research and practice, I had come into contact with four women who sew their own clothes. I requested to interview them in order to extend the scope of my research to include sewing, and to consider how this practice might differ from knitting. These interviews, and the tags from the drop-in knitting activity, were transcribed and coded using a similar approach as for the workshops; all of these accounts have enriched my understanding of amateur fashion making. In the rest of this chapter, I will use the term 'participants' to refer to the knitters who took part in the re-knitting project and 'interviewees' to refer to the sewers I interviewed.

Making new garments

Let us now look in more detail at the two different modes of personalising homemade clothes I have identified, starting with the more widespread and familiar process of producing new items 'from scratch'. Using my definition, introduced earlier, we could say that all homemade clothes are personalised because they are made for a known wearer, bearing in mind their aesthetic and stylistic preferences and body shape. Indeed, my research shows that many home sewers and knitters are motivated by the ability to create an entirely unique garment to a personal specification; many of the positive responses to the prompt about homemade clothes at the drop-in knitting activity mentioned uniqueness and originality. Part of this appeal is the ability to create an item in your preferred combination of colour, fabric and style; one of the research participants described wanting to make her own clothes because 'what I'm wanting is just something that looks a little bit different, a bit more individual'. One of the interviewees demonstrated a similar attitude: 'Why would I make anything that looks shop-bought? I want to make stuff that doesn't exist anywhere else.' Another benefit of domestic making is the opportunity to create items that are personalised in terms of fit. This can have a powerful impact on the wearer's sense of wellbeing, as Rushmore (2015) describes: 'As my skills grew, I started making clothes that actually fitted me well for the first time in my life, and my body image started shifting in parallel. [. . .] the feeling of abnormality and exclusion began to lift'.

Most homemade garments are produced using pre-designed patterns; these tools can vary from 'quick and easy' options to 'couture' projects requiring a high level of skill. Knitting patterns provide instructions in the form of written, and sometimes graphically represented, code, while sewing patterns combine full-size shaped pattern pieces with step-by-step guidance. Although these resources are invaluable in guiding makers through what is – even for a simple garment – a relatively complicated procedure, they introduce a degree of standardisation to the process of making, which could be seen as a barrier to personalisation. This standardisation partly relates to fit; patterns are typically offered in standard size ranges, just like the ready-made clothes on the high street. It also relates to style; although patterns have long offered choices in terms of styling, 'so that the sewer could choose various options and features, giving her a role to play in the design of the garment' (McLean 2009: 78), these options are often limited to an alternative neckline or sleeve length (Figure 2.1). While the choice of materials is a prime opportunity for personalisation, meanwhile, I am aware that some makers decline to stamp their individuality on a garment in this way, aiming instead to produce an exact replica of the original sample as photographed for the pattern. Bearing all of these factors in mind, it can be argued that many makers following patterns are producing items that are barely personalised; in fact, we might conclude that these garments differ from mass-produced clothing only in terms of the context in which they are made.

Anyone with experience of making their own clothes, however, will know that the use of patterns does not, in fact, lead to identical outcomes; homemade items will inevitably bear the hallmarks of the maker's individual technique. Furthermore, most makers do seize the opportunity to pursue personalisation

Figure 2.1 Design variations offered by sewing patterns.
Source: Amy Twigger Holroyd.

through the choice of materials; one of the interviewees suggested that sewers 'bring themselves' to a pattern when selecting fabric for their garment. Furthermore, makers frequently venture beyond the options offered in terms of size and style; Szeless (2002) suggests the term 'unorthodox home dressmaking' to describe the ways in which home sewers adapt patterns themselves. Knitters, similarly, alter pre-designed patterns: it is common for a different yarn to be used to that recommended, and more experienced knitters might choose to use alternative stitches or to vary elements of the design.

Makers are also able to alter patterns to create a custom fit, adapting the standard sizes offered to suit their individual needs – either before starting work, or while the project is in progress. One of the participants described altering the neck shape, sleeve length and body length of a knitted jumper, explaining: 'I'll take ninety per cent of this pattern, and I'll just do the bits that I want, so that I know I'll wear it and be comfortable in it'. For those willing to put in the time and effort, a toile (sample garment) can be made to test the fit, with any changes transferred to the pattern and subsequently the final garment. Alternatively, makers can choose to work more independently, creating garments without the aid of pre-designed patterns; this opens up the options in terms of personalisation. Drafting a pattern using your individual measurements creates a more personalised fit than altering a standard pattern, just as originating your own design allows you to pursue a personal vision to a greater degree than would be possible when tweaking an existing style. As we will see later, however, this challenging activity requires both creative and technical skills, and many makers lack confidence in their abilities.

Reworking

The reworking of existing garments offers an alternative opportunity for personalisation. As I have explained, this activity is less prevalent than the practice of producing new items of clothing. Thus, in order to discuss the potential for personalisation through reworking, I will draw on the experiences of the research participants as they engaged with the activity of re-knitting for the first time.

Before embarking on the group workshops, I first developed a range of relevant re-knitting techniques that I could explore with the participants, gathering knowledge from an array of knitting books and combining them with my own ideas. While doing so, I realised that the resources I would produce to share these techniques would need to be quite different to a normal knitting pattern, with its linear format and narrow set of options. Every item of knitwear in our wardrobes has a different combination of characteristics in terms of gauge, structure, yarn, colour, shape and condition, and when we rework an item we must take these characteristics into consideration. Thus, it would be impossible to produce conventional patterns for re-knitting; instead, I aimed to create flexible methods, or 'treatments', that could be adapted to suit the specifics of any particular item. Each treatment is highly flexible in terms of scale, aesthetic and finish; these processes can be used in countless ways to personalise an item of knitwear. The fit of a garment can be altered, as can the aesthetic; the alteration may be highly visible or rather more subtle.

Although re-knitting offers the same benefit in terms of personalisation as making new – the opportunity to create a unique item to suit your own needs and preferences – the fact that this activity is not more common suggests that these benefits are not readily apparent to makers. This was certainly the case with the research participants: despite having the practical skills needed to rework existing items through knitting, they had not previously considered doing so. They were intrigued by the possibility of transforming their clothes in this way, but were generally unsure about what form this transformation could take. One of the participants, for example, suggested at the outset of the project: 'I can't see it, I can't visualise, I can't imagine what you would do. I'm not very imaginative in that way.' Another said that any customisation process she had attempted in the past 'just never looked right. It was never good enough that you'd want to wear it. It was a lot of effort, and the result was unsatisfactory.' At the workshops, however, the participants quickly embraced the techniques I had developed and responded positively to their potential. Following the project, it was apparent that their view of knitting had expanded, and that they were now considering re-knitting as an option for other items in the wardrobe. One participant described having 'a large pile of knits waiting for new futures'. Another explained: 'I think I've realised that knitting the garment is not the end of the journey. [. . .] it can always become something else'.

The projects completed during the research demonstrated the flexibility of the re-knitting treatments: two of the participants replaced sections of the sleeves of their cardigans, while two others re-knitted the trims of their items, one adding pockets along the way. One participant converted a jumper into a cardigan and another reshaped an oversized item, adding new trims and repurposing the waste fabric into pockets. Of the six items, two were originally homemade and four were mass produced. Each of the garments had an identifiable problem: three had holes and two were not a good fit, while one was simply felt to be too boring to wear. In fact, analysis of the discussions that took place at the workshops revealed that it was precisely these problems that prompted the participants to consider personalisation; 'perfect' items seemed to discourage intervention, while garments that were considered to be deficient in some way were perceived as 'open' and ripe for alteration. The participants successfully overcame the various problems associated with the garments, personalising the items in the process by designing alterations that suited their own personal aesthetic. They were pleased with the transformed items, and enjoyed wearing them. It was evident that the participants would not contemplate reworking just any damaged or deficient garment, however; an item needed to offer the prospect of a positive outcome, and had to be perceived as sufficiently valuable to expend the necessary time and effort in reworking it. Within the participant group, this sense of value variously related to emotional attachment, an expensive or high-quality fibre, a garment in too good a condition to discard, and a homemade item representing a great deal of embedded effort.

Reworking reframes making as an ongoing, cyclical process, rather than a one-off event that brings an item into being; this has potentially powerful implications in terms of personalisation. Our needs and preferences, of course, change over time; if we are able to alter a garment to meet these preferences once, then we can – in principle – do so again and again. While our needs may change in terms of obvious factors such as size and fit, it is important to note that changes will also relate to intangible factors such as identity. Indeed, the evolving context of fashion is such that changes in dress are required in order to maintain a consistent sense of identity (Roach-Higgins and Eicher 1995); thus, in order for a personalised garment to remain relevant and appealing to its owner, it may need to be reworked – re-personalised – at intervals throughout its life. This is precisely what happened in the case of the participant who felt that her cardigan was too boring to wear (Figure 2.2); although she had knitted this item for herself some years before and had enjoyed wearing it for a while, she now felt it did not reflect her identity. By updating it to correspond with her current preferences (Figure 2.3), she was able to change the meaning that she perceived in it. Through reworking, personalisation can become a process

Figure 2.2 Hand-knitted cardigan in the early stages of transformation, with samples.
Source: Amy Twigger Holroyd.

Figure 2.3 The same cardigan after re-knitting, with samples and calculations.
Source: Amy Twigger Holroyd.

of evolution, albeit one that is limited by the characteristics of the physical garment and the ability, and attitude, of the maker.

Design and metadesign

Having considered the opportunities for personalisation offered by making and reworking, we can now consider two themes that arise when reflecting on this topic. The first theme is design: we will look at both the design skills that a maker needs to exercise in order to personalise an item, and the role of the professional designer in providing frameworks and materials that support amateurs to undertake this design activity – a task described by de Mul (2011) and others as 'metadesign'.

As I have described, the majority of making projects are guided by pre-designed patterns; makers can amplify the potential for personalisation by deviating from these instructions in various ways, or work more independently to originate their own designs. Either way, makers wanting to create unique garments must develop a vision for their item, and couple this with a strategy for how to execute it: thus, they require both creative and technical design skills. The technical skills are arguably more accessible: makers can learn how to draft their own patterns, for example, via workshops, books and online resources. As described earlier, as part of the re-knitting project I developed practical resources that could be used by the participants to plan the alterations to their garments: step-by-step instructions, technical advice and stitch patterns that could be adapted to the particularities of each individual item. The participants used their tacit knowledge of knitting – gained primarily through the use of conventional patterns – to make sense of these resources in relation to their garments, considering technical issues and evaluating the complexity of various proposed solutions.

My experience of producing the re-knitting resources highlights a central challenge faced by the metadesigner: how much to limit the options offered by the frameworks they create. As I experimented with the re-knitting techniques, I realised that some processes involved several technical variables; in combination, these variables generated a staggering number of combinations, many of which were awkward to knit or produced a messy-looking result. De Mul (2011: 37) proposes that the metadesigner must restrict such options in order to help the user; as he explains, 'the designer's task is to limit the virtually unlimited combinational space in order to create order from disorder'. I wanted to edit the options available in order to remove those that were unsatisfactory, and to prevent the user from becoming overwhelmed. I felt that it was important, however, that the treatments remained flexible in both technical and aesthetic terms; I intended that makers would use the resources I developed to create personalised designs that reflected their taste, rather than my own. As such, the priorities of my metadesign project were very different to those of a commercial personalisation platform, such as the Adidas and Pringle examples discussed earlier; in such contexts the options offered are much more restricted. Users are able to vary specific elements according to set options – such as selecting the colour of a component from a limited number of choices – in order to keep users' creations within manufacturing-related and aesthetic boundaries set by the brand.

Let us now turn to the creative skills required when developing individual making projects. In my experience, these skills feel more alien to many amateurs; all of the participants in my research project were attracted by the idea of feeling more creative in their craft activities, but had not felt confident enough to attempt to design their own items previously. As one of the participants commented at the start of the project: 'It's a scary thing to be creative, when you've got nobody anywhere giving you a nod that you're on the right line'. In the project, I sought to create a supportive environment that would enable the participants to design for themselves. The design exercises that I integrated into the early workshops, which involved gathering inspirational materials and exploring colour, helped them to gain confidence in specific design-related processes. More holistically, the project as a whole created a permissive space in which they felt 'allowed' to explore their creative ideas.

Two elements of the project proved to be particularly important in creating this supportive space. The first factor is experimentation: developing the habit of sampling different ideas and being willing to make mistakes. As a trained designer, I find that experimentation is key to developing an appropriate and appealing solution, and also one of the most enjoyable parts of the design process. However, as one of the participants suggested, 'There's no culture for ordinary knitters of playing around'. Furthermore, from my conversations with makers I am aware that many fall into the trap of expecting a garment to turn out exactly right on the very first attempt, becoming discouraged if it does not. I encouraged the participants to experiment from the outset of the project, and it was striking how quickly they shifted their thinking and practice. The second factor is peer support: the participants worked collaboratively, discussing their projects in pairs and small groups. Their design ideas developed through discussion, evolving and becoming clearer with each iteration. When the participants reflected on their experiences of designing, they felt that these conversations and the support of the others in the group had been particularly important. As one participant commented: 'I love the collaboration bit of it, chatting about it, the exchanging of ideas'. Another made a similar point: 'I need to feed off other people, I think, to get ideas, and then to gain confidence in my ideas, I suppose'. When we dress we anticipate the gaze of others, and imagine their appraisals of our clothing choices (Kaiser 1997). This consideration is essentially a concern for the opinions of the people around us; in this project, the knitters were able to get 'a nod' from a number of trusted peers throughout the process of personalising their garments.

Wearing personalised clothes

So far, we have focused on the experience of creating personalised clothes; let us now discuss the experience of wearing them. As we have seen, the prospect of wearing a one-off item, uniquely tailored to the individual's needs and preferences, is a significant motivation for many of those who choose to make their own clothing. Franke and Schreier (2010) describe how self-designed or customised products are perceived as being more valuable by their creators; domestic making could be seen as an amplified version of customisation, which strengthens attachment and a sense of value. I have spoken to many makers who have successfully created one-off items for themselves, and wear these garments with great pride. However, I have also come across a multitude of stories that indicate that homemade items do not always fulfil their promise and may fail to become the wardrobe staples their creators had hoped. One response from the drop-in knitting activity to the prompt about wearing homemade clothes epitomises this problem: 'Often disappointed: they never quite match up to how I imagined and hoped them to turn out!' This disappointment partly stems from the fact that achieving a high-quality fit and finish is a difficult task, requiring skill and care. It is also down to the tendency, common amongst makers, to be hypercritical of things we have created ourselves. One of the interviewees has observed this tendency when teaching sewing to others: 'Learners can get so stressed out. They're looking through the magnifying glass at what they've done.' Beyond these concerns relating to the materiality of personalised garments, though, I would argue that the misgivings we feel about wearing these items often relate to the mixed meanings associated with homemade clothes in contemporary culture.

Homemade clothes are frequently portrayed in a negative light; Turney (2004) describes domestic textile crafts being 'frequently the butt of jokes' and seen as 'old-fashioned, requiring little skill or design flair'. Luckman (2012) identifies a lingering association between the homemade and poverty, which she traces back to the Depression in the 1930s and the post-war desire for mass-produced goods. New perceptions of sewing and knitting as creative and aspirational practices are emerging, however, through the vibrancy and diversity of contemporary textile making culture; these fresh perceptions reframe homemade clothes as eminently desirable items. A positive, even romantic, attitude to the homemade is reflected in the comments gathered at the drop-in knitting activity, which included terms such as 'made with love', 'quality', 'comfortable', 'original' and 'satisfying'. The image of homemade clothes in the public perception, therefore, is rather muddled: old-fashioned and indicative of poverty on one hand, alternative and aspirational on the other. When we dress we anticipate what those around us will think of our selections; as Dant (1999: 107) explains, 'wearing clothes is social in that what people wear is treated by those around them as being some sort of indicator of who they are'. When we wear our homemade items, we are aware that they may be perceived in a negative light, and this can have an impact on our sense of identity. No matter how much our personalised clothes may delight us and meet our personal requirements, their appeal has the potential to be tainted by the cultural meanings which, far out of our control, circulate in society.

Consideration of the social experience of dressing leads us on to a further issue related to homemade clothes: uniqueness. Clothes connect the individual with others in society; this connection is shaped by the dynamic processes of identification and differentiation. First identified by Simmel (1904), identification, or conformity, describes a need to belong and carries a sense of solidarity, whereas differentiation, or individualism, describes a need to feel unique. Uniqueness is a self-correcting process, so when individuals start to feel too similar to others they will find ways to reassert their individuality, and vice versa (Snyder and Fromkin 1980). Thus, although uniqueness in dress is generally considered to be desirable, if our clothing is *too* different, it will cease to perform that crucial role of connecting us with others.

Originality is often thought to mean not being influenced in any way – not imitating others. But, if originality becomes an ultimate goal, and one consistently pursues it, one loses the most valuable means of growing as a person – the possibility of imitation, the process that is so essential to the development of the self in the first place (Csikszentmihalyi and Rochberg-Halton 1981: 190).

Shop-bought items – even those offering a degree of personalisation – have been 'validated' by a chain of professionals, providing reassurance that the item is desirable and appropriate; it will not have strayed far from the path of normality. Conversely, a personalised homemade item represents, and displays, the decisions of a single person and thus has the potential to be unwittingly transgressive of social norms. This is especially the case in situations where the maker has deviated significantly from a pre-designed pattern, originated their own design or used 'open' resources such as those that I developed for re-knitting. Although makers may derive great satisfaction from the process of designing and making a unique item of clothing, they have much less assurance that their garments will be positively received in the outside world, compared to a shop-bought alternative. This danger can be overcome, to some extent, by integrating peer support into the design process, as was the case in the re-knitting project.

Personalisation, longevity and re-use

To round off this exploration of personalising clothes at home, I would like to return to the topic of sustainability, and in particular the issues of longevity and re-use. I have frequently come across the assumption that homemade clothes are particularly emotionally significant, and therefore more likely to be kept and worn over an extended period. There is evidence to support this argument; Mugge et al. (2005), for example, identify active personalisation as a route to product attachment and longer product lifetimes. However, this relationship is not as simple as it might appear; emotional significance is not exclusive to homemade or personalised items, and – as I have explained – many homemade garments do not turn out as hoped, and are therefore never worn.

Furthermore, there is a flipside to the connection between personalisation and longevity: should we reject our personalised items, they may be less suitable for re-use than more generic garments. Consider, for example, traditional Eastern modes of dress, which involve a wrapped sheet of fabric; this garment adapts to the wearer through the act of wrapping, and could be handed on to wearers of any shape and size. In contrast, the ultra-personalised couture garment, made to fit one individual, is far less likely to find a subsequent wearer. Similarly, we may find it difficult to re-use one-off items that have been created to suit a very individual sense of identity. Thus, we must conclude that personalising clothes at home has unpredictable results in terms of longevity and re-use, and therefore sustainability: while the garments we physically shape to meet our needs and preferences may hit the spot and remain in use for many years, we run the risk of creating anomalies that will struggle to find their place in contemporary fashion culture.

Conclusion

In this chapter I have examined processes of personalisation in the context of fashion, and specifically amateur fashion making. Sewing and knitting offer various opportunities for personalisation, even when patterns – which initially appear to standardise activity – are used; clothes can be personalised in terms of both fit and style, and with varying degrees of intensity. The ability to create a one-off item, specifically catering for the individual's unique preferences, is frequently mentioned as a motivation by people who choose to make their own clothes at home. While this activity most commonly involves the creation of new items, existing clothes can also be personalised; through this process deficient garments, which are seen as 'open', are renewed and altered to suit the maker.

Although personalisation has the potential to be intensely satisfying, the experience of making and remaking unique clothes at home is not always positive; these activities require a mix of creative and technical skills, and makers are sometimes disappointed with their finished projects. Furthermore, when we consider the important social function of fashion it becomes evident that uniqueness in dress carries dangers: if taken too far, it can interfere with the connections we make with those around us. Personalisation can also cause problems in terms of re-use: the more closely an item is tailored to suit the preferences of one individual, the less likely it is to find another home, should it be discarded.

Given the growing popularity of making, it is important that we develop our thinking about the contemporary experience of crafts such as sewing and knitting. While these practices offer many intrinsic benefits, there is a need to challenge the widespread assumption that personalised homemade clothes are automatically successful and straightforwardly sustainable. By exploring the characteristics of current practice we can build up a much more detailed picture of amateur fashion making and its relationship to the mainstream fashion system. This understanding can then be used to inform future metadesign initiatives that seek to support amateur makers in their own creative activities.

References

Adidas (2015) *Adidas: customise*. Available at: http://www.adidas.co.uk/customise (accessed 10 October 2015).

Black, S. (2012) *Knitting: fashion, industry, craft*. London: V&A Publishing.

Bratich, J. Z. and Brush, H. M. (2011) Fabricating activism: craft-work, popular culture, gender. *Utopian Studies*, 22(2), 233–260.

Breward, C. (2003) *Fashion*. Oxford: Oxford University Press.

Csikszentmihalyi, M. and Rochberg-Halton, E. (1981) *The meaning of things: domestic symbols and the self*. Cambridge, UK: Cambridge University Press.

Dant, T. (1999) *Material culture in the social world: values, activities, lifestyles*. Buckingham, UK: Open University Press.

de Mul, J. (2011) Redesigning design. In B. van Abel, L. Evers, R. Klaassen and P. Troxler (eds), *Open design now: why design cannot remain exclusive*. Amsterdam, The Netherlands: BIS Publishers, pp. 34–39.

Emery, J. S. (2014) *A history of the paper pattern industry*. London: Bloomsbury.

Franke, N. and Schreier, M. (2010) Why customers value self-designed products: the importance of process effort and enjoyment. *Journal of Product Innovation Management*, 27(7), 1020–1031.

Gayomali, C. (2014) Here's what it's like to step into a 3-D body scanner for a custom-made suit. *Fast Company*, 3 September. Available at: http://www.fastcompany.com/3035092/heres-what-its-like-to-step-into-a-3d-body-scanner-for-a-custom-made-suit (accessed 10 October 2015).

Hackney, F. (2013) Quiet activism and the new amateur: the power of home and hobby crafts. *Design and Culture*, 5(2), 169–93.

Hall, S. M. and Jayne, M. (2015) Make, mend and befriend: geographies of austerity, crafting and friendship in contemporary cultures of dressmaking in the UK. *Gender, Place & Culture*, prepublished 26 February 2015 as doi: 10.1080/0966369X.2015.1013452.

Kaiser, S. B. (1997) *The social psychology of clothing: symbolic appearances in context*, revised 2nd edn. New York: Fairchild.

Kuznetsov, S. and Paulos, E. (2010) Rise of the expert amateur: DIY projects, communities, and cultures. In *6th Nordic conference on human–computer interaction*. Reykjavik, 16–20 October. Available at: http://www.staceyk.org/hci/KuznetsovDIY.pdf (accessed 10 October 2015).

Lewis, P. (2011) Pride in the wool: the rise of knitting. *The Guardian*, 6 July. Available at: http://www.theguardian.com/lifeandstyle/2011/jul/06/wool-rise-knitting (accessed 10 October 2015).

Lewis-Hammond, S. (2014) The rise of mending: how Britain learned to repair clothes again. *The Guardian*, 19 May. Available at: http://www.theguardian.com/lifeandstyle/2014/may/19/the-rise-of-mending-how-britain-learned-to-repair-clothes-again (accessed 10 October 2015).

Luckman, S. (2012) *Locating cultural work: the politics and poetics of rural, regional and remote creativity*. Basingstoke, UK: Palgrave Macmillan.

Luckman, S. (2013) The aura of the analogue in a digital age: women's crafts, creative markets and home-based labour after Etsy. *Cultural Studies Review*, 19(1), 249–270.

McDowell, C. (1997) *Forties fashion and the new look*. London: Bloomsbury.

McLean, M. (2009) 'I dearly loved that machine': women and the objects of home sewing in the 1940s. In M. D. Goggin and B. F. Tobin (eds), *Women and the material culture of needlework and textiles, 1750–1950*. Farnham, UK: Ashgate, pp. 69–89.

Mugge, R., Schoormans, J. P. L. and Schifferstein, H. (2005) Design strategies to postpone consumers' product replacement: the value of a strong person–product relationship. *The Design Journal*, 8(2), 38–48.

Myzelev, A. (2009) Whip your hobby into shape: knitting, feminism and construction of gender. *Textile*, 7(2), 148–163.

Office for National Statistics (1997) *Social trends, 27*, London: Stationery Office.

Pringle of Scotland (2015) *Pringle deconstructed*. Available at: https://www.pringledeconstructed.com (accessed 10 October 2015).

Roach-Higgins, M. E. and Eicher, J. B. (1995) Dress and identity. In M. E. Roach-Higgins, J. B. Eicher and K. K. P. Johnson (eds), *Dress and identity*. New York: Fairchild, pp. 7–18.

Robson, C. (2011) *Real world research: a resource for users of social research methods in applied settings*, 3rd ed. Chichester, UK: Wiley.

Ross, R. (2008) *Clothing: a global history*. Cambridge, UK: Polity Press.

Rushmore, J. (2015) Sewing my clothes is an escape from fashion's dictates. I no longer hate my body. *The Guardian*, 3 August. Available at: http://www.theguardian.com/commentisfree/2015/aug/03/sewing-clothes-escape-fashion-dictates-no-longer-hate-my-body (accessed 10 October 2015).

Sennett, R. (2008) *The craftsman*. London: Penguin.

Simmel, G. (1904) Fashion. *International Quarterly*, 10, 130–155.

Snyder, C. R. and Fromkin, H. L. (1980) *Uniqueness*. New York: Plenum.

Szeless, M. (2002) Burda fashions – a wish that doesn't have to be wishful thinking: home-dressmaking in Austria 1950–1970. *Cultural Studies*, 16(6), 848–862.

Turney, J. (2004) Here's one I made earlier: making and living with home craft in contemporary Britain. *Journal of Design History*, 17(3), 267–282.

Twigger Holroyd, A. (2013) *Folk fashion: amateur re-knitting as a strategy for sustainability*. PhD thesis. Birmingham City University, UK. Available at: http://bit.ly/folkfashion (accessed 10 October 2015).

UK Hand Knitting Association (2015) *About us*. Available at: http://www.ukhandknitting.com/about-us (accessed 10 October 2015).

Warren, H. (2012) TRAIDremade: designing waste out of fashion. *The Ethical Fashion Source Intelligence*, 26 November. Available at: http://source.ethicalfashionforum.com/digital/traidremade-designing-waste-out-of-fashion (accessed 10 October 2015).

3 Wearable technology as personalised fashion
Empowering or oppressive?

Conor Farrington

Introduction

Few technologies are as personal, or as personalisable, as wearable technologies. Defined as technological devices worn on (or otherwise attached to) the body and/or clothing, the new generation of wearables – as distinct from older wearable devices such as glasses and prosthetics – enable their users to enact a number of new actions and capacities in addition to complementing or augmenting pre-existing technologies and agendas. Increasingly, wearables and smart garments allow for a considerable degree of personalisation, with regard to both data collection modalities and visible appearance. To date, medical and wellness applications for wearables have dominated, whether in terms of cutting-edge clinical trials of wearable medical devices or in terms of consumer-focused wearables enabling biometric and behavioural self-tracking. In terms of fashion, 'smart' garments and accessories – items incorporating electronic components and/or digital connectivity – are increasingly worn on account of their unique appearance and aesthetic functionalities. The Cute Circuit smart dresses worn at high-profile events by singers Katy Perry and Nicole Scherzinger are good examples of such apparel (see Figure 3.1). Smart garments are also increasingly utilised for their ability to collect data, as seen, for instance, in athletic outfits with the capacity to measure heart-rate, calorie counts, and distances travelled. The wearables market is growing quickly, with a strong boost from the recent release of the Apple Watch, and is forecast to reach $53bn by 2019 compared with $4.5bn in 2015 (Juniper Research, 2015). Consequently, it is likely that wearables will assume an ever more prominent role in the everyday technological landscapes of the future.

Recognition of the growing significance of wearables does not entail that their likely impacts are fully understood. As might be expected given the emergent nature of the wearable family of technologies, understandings of their cultural, sociological and philosophical implications have lagged behind the rapid rate of technical innovation. As is often the case with new technology more widely (Wyatt et al., 2000), debates surrounding wearables and smart garments tend to become polarised between utopian advocates in the technology world who emphasise positive aspects of their usage (e.g. capacities for personalisation, empowerment, and greater self-knowledge) and dystopian critics from outside the technology world who emphasise potentially negative aspects of their usage (e.g. surveillance and intrusion of privacy, digital addiction and corporate misuse of data). As such, current debates typically neglect the nuanced complexities that surround the use of technology in practice and the unpredictable outcomes that typically result from the introduction of new technologies (see, e.g. Orlikowski, 2000). Sociologists of technology have long recognised, for instance, that technology usage cannot straightforwardly be predicted from its design, since a given technology's affordances (such as functionalities and capacities) are always open to differential interpretation and use (Matthewman, 2011). More widely, the meanings given to particular new technologies, and thus their eventual role in cultural and social dynamics, are also unpredictable (Ulucanlar et al., 2013), not least because they necessarily accumulate through complex exchanges between new and existing technologies, specific individuals and groups, and wider (meso- and macro-level) societal developments and dynamics. Thus, attempts to understand the future impacts of wearables across multiple spheres of activity will need to balance utopian and dystopian polarities with theoretically informed, historically aware, and empirically grounded approaches that explore wearables usage in concrete settings.

This chapter seeks to deepen theoretical understandings of wearable technology by drawing upon the resources of Frankfurt School critical theory to explore wearable technologies and smart garments from the perspective of personalisation, understood in terms of the individual's capacity to modify aspects of their life in line with their own desires and contexts. More specifically, this chapter examines how personalisable aspects of wearable technology and smart garments can be considered as empowering and emancipatory, on the one hand, or dominating and repressive, on the other. It does so by focusing on a central paradox in dress and fashion, which arises from the nature of mass production in contemporary economies. We believe that we express our individual identities through personalised fashion choice, but since almost all accessories and items of dress are mass produced, we may, in fact, be expressing others' identities (e.g. designers, retailers, dominant celebrities) rather than our own. 'Personalised' fashion choice may thus be oppressive rather than empowering. Since wearable technologies are often highly visible, they should be considered under the rubric of fashion as well as that of technology; consequently, they are also subject to this paradox. However, the capacities for personalisation that many wearables offer may constitute a (partial) escape from this bind, as argued in the final part of the chapter.

Critical theory is a useful tradition when considering the empowering or oppressive character of wearable technologies because of its general focus upon human emancipation and flourishing and the dilemmas and challenges facing individuals in contemporary societies. Critical theory is a complex school of thought with many distinct branches, but its essence may be defined in opposition to what Max Horkheimer (in his 1937 essay 'Traditional and Critical Theory') termed 'traditional theory': positivist scientific theories characterised by formal conceptual schemes encompassing logically linked propositions based on (or testable against) empirical facts, and founded upon a paradigm of scientific knowledge as a theoretical representation of an independent domain of objects. As against this approach, Horkheimer denies the separation of theory and fact, and develops a Marxian and interdisciplinary view of critical theory as examining its own social and historical situatedness and seeking to further emancipatory ends by developing a critique of that same concrete setting: '[the critical theorist's] presentation of societal contradictions is not merely an expression of the concrete historical situation but also a force within it to stimulate change' (1999: 215). This critique of society has at its heart the critique of ideology, or systems of ideas that combine descriptive and prescriptive elements and thus link the worlds of political thought and action. Critical theorists see ideology as generating false consciousness by preventing individual agents 'from correctly perceiving their true situation and real interests; if they are to free themselves from social repression, the agents must rid themselves of ideological illusion' (Geuss, 1981: 3). Taking its cue simultaneously from societal wrongs and theories that seek to legitimise these wrongs, critical theory as a method of social thought develops a Weberian view of modern societies as rationalised, alienating, and reified. It seeks a form of reflection capable of first uncovering and then addressing the roots of the societal pathologies arising from capitalism by enabling human flourishing and freedom, while retaining awareness of the limits and social context of theorising itself.

The analysis proceeds by considering theoretical ideas from three key thinkers in the Frankfurt School critical theory tradition: Theodor Adorno, Jürgen Habermas, and Walter Benjamin. While these philosophers do not directly address issues of wearable or personalised technologies in their writings, their reflections on modern art and the fate of the individual in contemporary societies are nonetheless highly relevant to explorations of wearable technology in the context of fashion. Specifically, this chapter reconceptualises Benjamin's concept of the 'aura' surrounding artworks (including fashion items) in terms of notions of personalisation in the context of wearable technologies and smart garments, and in so doing salvages important ideas from the thought of both Adorno and Benjamin within a wider, Habermasian framework. This revitalisation of the concept of the aura sheds light on pressing questions of empowerment and oppression in light of wearable technologies. Before proceeding to consider these critical theory thinkers in turn, however, it is necessary to delve more deeply into notions of fashion choice and individual expression, which constitute the backdrop against which the empowering and/or oppressive aspects of wearable technology may be evaluated.

Fashion choice and individuality

The highly visible nature of many wearables and the explicitly aesthetic focus of many smart garments in particular (but also smart jewellery and other accessories), means that their uptake and impact will depend not only on their technological capacities, but also on their perceived aesthetic characteristics and appeal in the context of wider socio-cultural trends and dynamics. Consequently, the meeting point between wearable technology and fashion assumes considerable importance. This chapter adopts a broad definition of fashion as referring to both (a) the aesthetics and (b) the functionality of dress, with dress conceived (building upon Eicher and Roach-Higgins, 1995) as an assemblage of body modifications and/or supplements utilised by a person for specific functions and to communicate with other human beings through aesthetic means. This definition can thus be separated from the other primary meaning of fashion as (often faddish) change, and also from narrower definitions of dress that focus on the communicative aspects of clothing and accessories, sometimes at the expense of acknowledging the various functions that dress performs (e.g. protection from the elements and preservation of modesty, in line with societal norms). The etymological root of the term 'fashion' in the Latin *factio* (a making or doing) and the linked verbal meaning in English ('to fashion something' = 'to make something') also furnishes a useful allusion to the technological and agentially productive character of fashion artefacts, including new wearable technologies but also the vastly older technologies utilised for making clothing and accessories for tens, if not hundreds, of thousands of years.

The crossover between technology and fashion is highly relevant to the choice and use of wearables on aesthetic grounds, since the adoption of wearable technologies on this basis invokes long-standing notions of expressing and communicating individual identity through personalised fashion choice as well as newer agential possibilities arising from digital technologies. It is typically, if unreflexively, assumed that we express our individual identity by making personalised fashion choices of various kinds, especially choices relating to our visual appearance as expressed through the clothes and accessories we wear, our hairstyles, make-up, and so forth. Geczy and Karaminas (2012: 10) express this view as follows: 'We wear clothes, cover ourselves with an outer skin of codes and creations, in order for us to be seen how we truly are'. However, such notions are complex and contested owing to the mass-produced nature of many garments and accessories and the paradoxical character of the notion of expressing individuality by conforming to current, often society-wide trends and styles. Specifically, the fact that (bespoke couture aside) many individuals will wear the same garments and accessories as other individuals introduces a tension into the notion of expressing individual identity through personalised fashion choice, and raises the question of whether fashion designers should be considered as 'co-sender[s]' (with the wearer) of communicative messages arising from fashion choices (Barnard, 2002: 31). Semiotic accounts of fashion interpret communication and meaning as arising from (largely tacit) negotiations between designers, wearers and spectators of fashion choice, further reducing the agential capacity of the individual in terms of identity communication (Barnard, 2002). From this perspective, personalised fashion choice appears less empowering than it might intuitively seem.

The limits placed on individual expression through personalised fashion choice in contemporary societies can be overstated, and a number of countervailing tendencies can be identified. Each person wears clothing differently owing to idiosyncrasies of physique and gait, for example, as stated by Agee and Evans (1941; cited Hauser, 2005: 157) in a manner conforming to gendered linguistic mores of the period: 'Each man's garment [wears] the shape and beauty of his induplicable body'. Moreover, individual garments can be personalised with accessories and tailoring, and are likely to be perceived differently in different social and geographical settings, many of which may themselves be highly coloured by a given individual's identity, in interaction with others. Consequently, there is still some scope for individual expression despite the mass production of garments and processes of communal and intersubjective meaning construction. More fundamentally, it is also possible to question the assumptions of individualism and settled identity that (arguably) underpin notions of expressing individuality through fashion choice, and which can be linked to wider notions of neoliberalism and free market economics. It has long been recognised – e.g. by the sociologist Georg Simmel, writing in 1904 – that fashion choice can contribute productively to identity formation through the identification of the individual with wider social groups (Aspers and Godart, 2013), foreshadowing communitarian critiques of liberalism and neoliberalism. Nevertheless, Simmel also recognises the tension between 'adaptation to society and individual departure from its demands', such that individuals not only desire to be part of groups but also 'possess the desire to be, and to be considered as, apart from that larger whole' (1971; cited Barnard, 2002: 12). Consequently, a tension between the individual and wider societal pressures lies at the heart of fashion. This tension also animates the critical theory of Theodor Adorno, explored below.

Theodor Adorno and the 'culture industry'

Much of Adorno's work focuses in some way on the perceived crisis of the individual subject and the ways in which individuals tend to become isolated, de-sociated, and in a sense de-personalised in contemporary societies. Adorno allows that individuals in such societies have the capacity to personalise their lives, for instance through choice of leisure activities and forms of popular entertainment such as television, radio, and cinema. However, he sees this kind of personalisation as proceeding upon an illusory basis, and as concealing the ways in which mass-market interests subvert the creative potential of popular culture and render it a tool for the co-opting of individuals into consumerist agendas. The kinds of personalisation that then face the individual, both in terms of cultural choice in general and fashion choice in particular, are limited and disempowering in different ways.

Adorno is perhaps best known for the book *Dialectic of Enlightenment*, which he co-authored with Horkheimer and published in 1947 (Adorno and Horkheimer, 1979). In this book, and in numerous essays discussing themes in the cultural study of art, music and literature, Adorno elaborated a dark-hued view of modern society in which popular culture – or, to use the term that Adorno preferred, the 'culture industry' – plays a vital role in co-opting individuals into capitalist ideology as consumers during their leisure hours, in a similar way to the co-optation of individuals as workers by capitalist economics during working hours (Adorno, 1980, 1991). For Adorno, the everyday products of popular culture – Hollywood movies, newspapers, television and radio broadcasts – were not harmless entertainments but ideological blandishments with deleterious effects on social life and consciousness. He argued that popular culture did not (as its name implies) emerge autonomously and organically from the lives of individuals or communities, but was manufactured according to the 'interests of the producers and the exigencies of the market, both of which demanded the domination and manipulation of mass consciousness' (Witkin, 2003: 2).

Adorno distinguished between 'culture' and 'pseudo-culture', based on an opposition between an autonomous subjectivity at a critical distance from society and a dominated subjectivity that is manipulated by society. Whereas 'culture' helps to secure, however partially, a degree of agency, autonomy and authenticity for individuals (and thus a platform from which to resist and critique society), pseudo-culture jettisons this 'vital relation to living subjects' (Adorno, 1993: 23) and instead enables the assimilation of passive subjects within a dominating market system. Adorno was not claiming that individuals do not, in fact, desire to consume the standardised, fetishised, and de-personalised products of popular culture in a personalised manner, but rather that this desire was an illustration of a hidden societal pathology at work – a pathology, moreover, that is based on a concomitant 'pseudo-individualisation' replacing genuine individuals and moulding them instead into passive, alienated, and de-sociated masses characterised by false consciousness (Witkin, 2003). An analogy may be drawn here between individuals choosing fashion items in the mistaken belief that they are expressing their own individuality rather than the aesthetic and commercial agendas of others.

These reflections strongly influenced the kinds of culture and personalised cultural choices that Adorno saw as worthwhile and valuable in modern societies. More specifically, Adorno developed a highly rarefied notion of art, according to which even works that were apparently critical of society were vulnerable to co-optation by the culture industry (Beddow, 1994). In order to avoid this, culture had to 'preserve its social truth by its antithesis to society, through isolation' (Adorno, 1980: 28). Worthwhile autonomous culture, that is, was no longer generated through a basis in society and the lives of its members, but rather in opposition to it, and was characterised not by ready comprehensibility but difficulty (especially formal difficulty), obscurity, and inaccessibility: 'only the formalist work of art, inaccessible to the masses, resists the pressures towards assimilation to the needs and attitudes of the consumer as determined by the market' (Adorno, 1984: 40). Adorno saw the later, atonal compositions of Schoenberg and the plays of Samuel Beckett as examples of this kind of aesthetic, as opposed to the music of Stravinsky and the plays of Brecht, whose superficially challenging nature thinly masked their relative accessibility and thus reconcilability with the cultural mainstream. In the context of modernity and associated processes of urbanisation, fragmentation, and disenchantment, cultural works can no longer claim authenticity by means of links to organic communities and 'vital lives' lived within them, but only by highlighting precisely the lack of such autonomous sources for art and by reminding individuals of 'the uncomfortable fact that in this antagonistic and cruel world they are spiritually homeless' (Witkin, 2003: 61). The atonal music of the Second Viennese School was rejected by popular audiences, notes Adorno (1980), not because they were not understood but because they were, on the contrary, all too well understood as an expression of the anxiety and existential angst underpinning modern capitalism.

Culture thus becomes, as Witkin (2003: 60) puts it with regard to music in particular, 'two torn halves', with a fundamental divide, as Adorno has it, 'between incomprehensibility and inescapability' with no 'third way' in between (1991: 31). Artists can either produce faux works of art, tired and obsolete imitations of the past that co-opt consumers into the culture industry, or seek to produce genuine works of art which represent an authentic and original contribution and the possibility of a critique of society, but at the cost of being disconnected from society. In neither case, it seems, is there the possibility of a genuine connection with individuals and their lives in the context of their emergent, interactional and organic interrelations with each other and society. Personalised cultural choice thus confronts individuals with two unpalatable alternatives, which are both disempowering in different ways.

If fashion is allowed the status of art (on which see Geczy and Karaminas, 2012 and Hollander, 1993), an analogous bind could be elaborated with regard to dress and wearable technologies, with designers seen – somewhat schematically and for the sake of argument – as either slavishly following mass-market trends with off-the-peg garments and accessories, on the one hand, or embracing radical and innovative fashion by designing only the most challenging and unorthodox pieces for fashion show runway collections, on the other. It could be said, moreover, that the situation is yet more challenging for wearers of fashion than it is for designers, since the former must concede a considerable aesthetic responsibility for their appearance to the latter while still attempting to maintain the appearance of expressing individual identity through personalised fashion choice. Related to this issue, and in some ways specific to the fashion world, is the possibility of being seen as a 'fashion victim' – of having surrendered one's aesthetic autonomy to what can be seen as oppressive and exploitative forces (Barnard, 2002) – even if one chooses to wear, for example, a radical catwalk design on 'authentic' individual grounds. Even if this fate is avoided, the kind of individualism enabled by radical fashion choice is one that is explicitly disconnected from society, with implications for the kinds of empowering projects that can be envisaged and accomplished. Yet, on Adorno's terms, avoiding this problem by making fashion choices that echo dominant trends does not escape oppressive forces either. This is in effect an act of submission, an act of 'sacrificing one's life as an expressive subject in the delusion that identification with the machine [of capitalist society] would permit one both to escape the threat to oneself that it posed and, vicariously, to share in its power' (Witkin, 2003: 6). Thus, the expression of individual identity through personalised fashion choice, and the wider possibilities of emancipation open to individuals, appears to be placed into doubt in various ways whether one chooses mass market or avant-garde apparel. On this 'tragic' view, while our fashion choices – e.g. our choices of wearable technologies and smart garments – may seem to empower us through the expression of identity, they are instead likely to either facilitate the illusion of individuality or enable it in a limited, isolated, and thus potentially unproductive manner.

Jürgen Habermas, modernity, and authenticity

Habermas was a student of Adorno, but came to reject his and Horkheimer's pessimism as a misdiagnosis of the problems of modernity since the Age of Enlightenment. While Habermas concurs in many ways with Adorno's explication of the pathologies of capitalist societies and their negative implications for individuals, he offers a more positive reading of contemporary society in which individuals always have the potential to express their individuality in an authentic (and aesthetic) manner. Thus, while the commercial agenda of mass culture undoubtedly presses in upon individuals and seeks to determine their choices, it is always possible to resist what Habermas calls the 'colonisation of the lifeworld' without being forced to resort (as Adorno argued) to esoteric avant-gardism. Personalised fashion choice can therefore be seen as a potential source of empowerment, although Habermas also emphasises the unavoidability of the imperatives of economics and state power.

As Finlayson (2005: 10) remarks, much of Habermas's work can be read as an attempt to

> rescue the original idea of critical theory [that is, providing a critique of and remedy to modernity's troubles] by combining a more nuanced and justifiable history of the Enlightenment [than Adorno and Horkheimer's] with a more coherent model of social theory.

Since the 1960s, Habermas has built upon this general theoretical agenda, critiques of 'first generation' critical theory, and a shift from the philosophy of consciousness to the post-metaphysical, linguistic 'philosophy of intersubjectivity' in order to develop a sophisticated body of work that addresses a wide range of moral, social, political, sociological and philosophical issues. Habermas's critical theory embodies the aim of creating a social order that enables human flourishing and emancipation, with emancipation understood as the removal of barriers to freedom from need, ideological manipulation, and oppression (Habermas, 1984). In contrast with 'first generation' critical theorists such as Adorno, however, Habermas insists that such emancipation can only come about as the result of a genuine consensus between social actors rather than the stipulations of a class of enlightened leaders. The role of critical theory is not to proffer solutions *de haut en bas*, but rather to assume a role analogous to that of the psychoanalyst towards a patient, helping to reconstruct and explicate social 'pathologies' and potential solutions in conjunction with members of society and by drawing upon communicative resources that members of society already possess, with the final responsibility for reform and transformation resting upon society rather than the critical theorist (Finlayson, 2005).

Habermas proceeds from the standpoint of 'communicative action', or the notion that the most fundamental and meaningful form of social action takes place 'intersubjectively' (i.e. between actors) when they engage in linguistic communication oriented towards reaching shared understandings (Habermas, 1985). When engaging in communicative action, individuals utter speech acts which present 'criticisable validity claims' to moral rightness, factual truth, or personal authenticity, and explicitly or implicitly offer to provide reasons in support of these claims should his or her interlocutor request (or 'criticise') them. Thus, the inherent *telos* of language towards reaching mutual understanding, which we necessarily invoke whenever we engage in speech, creates an immanent, ever-present possibility of consensual and rational resolution of competing claims and the airing of criticisms of existing societal orders. Habermas argues that this kind of interaction raises the possibility of generating consensual social orders that depend neither on the threat of sanctions nor on shared traditions and values (Finlayson, 2005). Habermas contrasts communicative action with 'purposive-rational action', which he conceptualises as oriented towards success (i.e. the fulfilment of goals and objectives via means–end calculations) rather than reaching understanding. While purposive-rational action is necessary for the effective operation of societal systems and organisations, Habermas argues that only communicative action creates the possibility of generating the broad consensus upon which rests the possibility of social critique and reform. As such, communicative action assumes greater normative importance in Habermas's critical theory, although this is separable from the extent of communicative action present in any given context. Indeed, the gap between the ideal and the real in terms of communicative action is what gives the theory its critical bite.

In addition to classifying action as either communicative or purposive-rational, Habermas also situates these kinds of action in two distinct spheres of social life that he terms, respectively, 'the lifeworld' and 'the system' (Habermas, 1985). Habermas conceptualises the lifeworld as a concept for the everyday world we share with others, whose meanings and understandings provide an essential background for communicative action. While the lifeworld is characterised by communicative action, 'the system' is characterised by purposive-rational action. More precisely, the system is constituted by 'sedimented structures and established patterns' of purposive-rational action (Finlayson, 2005: 53), namely the 'steering mechanisms' (directing and coordinating mechanisms) of *money* and *power*, which respectively dominate and steer two key 'subsystems': modern economies and state administrations (Habermas, 1985). Money and power obviate the need to reach understanding through communicative action, and encourage agents to 'fall naturally [i.e. without a communicatively established normative consensus] into pre-established patterns of institutional behaviour' (Finlayson, 2005: 54). In a manner reminiscent of Adorno's treatment of the culture industry, Habermas emphasises that the aims and objectives embodied within the two subsystems are not always apparent to actors, who work nevertheless to realise them: '[M]oney and power . . . serve to hold together differentiated and self-steering systems of action, independent of any *intentional* effort, that is, attempts at coordination on the part of actors' (Nielsen and Habermas, 1990: 107).

In an ideal Habermasian society, the system and the lifeworld co-exist in an equilibrium characterised by a productive balance between purposive-rational and communicative kinds of action in both private and public spheres. Sociologically, however, Habermas argues that modern societies are typically characterised by the system's tendency to 'colonise' the lifeworld, with the subsystems of economy and state 'penetrat[ing] ever deeper into the . . . lifeworld' (1985: 367) and thus extending purposive-rational action into social spheres previously and/or ideally integrated through communicative action. Colonisation processes result in the bureaucratisation and 'monetarisation' (commoditisation) of increasingly large areas of social life, leading to impoverished public sphere debates, growing consumerism in the private sphere, and markets controlled by unaccountable decision-makers. Colonisation processes thus instigate a wide-reaching transition from a world of shared understandings and meanings to a situation in which the lifeworld is rendered visible and potentially problematic, and from a society in which communicative intersubjectivity is replaced by 'the instrumental habit of treating others as the means to one's ends' (Finlayson, 2005: 60).

The notion of the colonisation of the lifeworld demonstrates a certain kinship with Adorno and Horkheimer's pessimistic diagnosis of Enlightenment's reversion to myth, conformity and barbarity and the pathologies of modern societies. However, Habermas's critique of the *Dialectic of Enlightenment* emphasises that this work overlooks important kernels of communicative action that have always been present in cultural modernity and which form the basis for a constructive critique of modernity from within modernity, with the consequence that Adorno and Horkheimer overstate the impossibility of escape from the constraints of instrumental rationality (Habermas, 1979). The implicit universality and ubiquity of communicative action has important implications for areas of Habermas's neo-Kantian deontological theory of morality (confusingly termed 'discourse ethics') and, more importantly for the purposes of this chapter, his theory of 'ethics' understood as a 'conscious plan of life' based upon a *critical* appropriation of one's life history and societal traditions 'in the light of an authentic life project' (Habermas, 1993: 175–6). While morality involves seeking a consensus with a wider community about the rightness of morally binding norms, and pragmatic discourse involves seeking a consensus about truth, ethical discourse comprises instead an appeal for recognition of an authentic individual identity. Identity, on this account, is conceived of in performative, dramaturgical terms as a process of expressive ethical self-realisation in which both authenticity and sincerity are evaluated intersubjectively by others, beginning with questions such as who I am, who I would like to be, or how I should lead my life. The answers to such questions can be understood as providing the identity-constitutive basis upon which personalisation can proceed. On Habermas's account, the colonisation of the lifeworld in modern societies encroaches upon, but (contra Adorno) cannot entirely overcome, the potential for individuals to engage in ethical discourse and seek to establish and express authentic individual identities.

Aesthetics play an important, if somewhat neglected, role in Habermas's critical social theory as a part of communicative action (1984). Habermas recognises that the loss of freedom, meaning and identity identified by Adorno are pervasive features of modernity, but attributes this to the particularities of capitalism rather than universal logics of cultural and societal rationalisation, i.e. phenomena that necessarily accompany the transition from traditional to modern societies (Ingram, 1991). Habermas acknowledges the dual trends of cultural debasement and arcane avant-gardism that Adorno highlights, but insists on the continuing potential for aesthetic value by analogy with the ever-present possibility of staking ethical claims to authenticity. Art, for Habermas, is affective and non-propositional, and characterised in terms of structures of feeling rather than in terms of mimetic pictures of reality (Boucher, 2011). He sees art as making validity claims not regarding universal acceptability (as Kant had argued with regard to judgements of taste) but with regard to artistic truth, aesthetic harmony, innovative force, and worthiness (i.e. the artistic statement being made is worth telling) as well as authenticity (Habermas, 1985). As with ethical discourses more widely, art can voice problematisations of contemporary society and fulfil critical purposes by revealing socially silenced human needs, with critique understood not in Adornian/Hegelian terms of criticising a 'reified social totality in light of an image of human wholeness' (Boucher, 2011: 68) but rather in the Kantian/Weberian sense that art clarifies the interests and needs of individuals engaging in ethical debate and thus potentially augments their autonomy. As with ethical self-expression in general, artistic expression is challenged but not ruled out by the colonisation of the lifeworld:

> the . . . relegation of art to connoisseurs cut off from mainstream life, as well as its degradation to hedonistic entertainment, is not necessitated [in Habermas's view] by the 'inner logic' of aesthetic rationalisation, but by its subsumption under the commodity form.
>
> (Ingram, 1991: 85)

When applied to the fashion world, Habermas's ethical and aesthetic philosophy highlights the potential for individuals to express themselves through personalised fashion choice despite the oppressive tendencies of consumerist capitalism, and (contra Adorno) without necessarily embracing the esoteric and the avant-garde. While colonising imperatives of money and power are ever-present in modern societies, individuals can challenge and, to some extent, escape them by drawing upon the communicative and expressive potential that always exists in language, ethical discourse, and aesthetic activity, which can be mobilised through fashion choice (including the use of wearable technologies). Yet, Habermas's approach reminds us of the ironic character of such activity, of the 'insight that the structures within which the [aesthetically expressive] subject moves are always constraining in potentially serious ways, even when they appear on balance to be the most enabling ones available' (White, 1986: 427). Caution is thus required in order to avoid interpreting Habermas as replacing Adorno's excessive pessimism with excessive optimism.

Walter Benjamin: the aura redux

Habermas's notion of ethical and aesthetic self-expression, and his insistence that such self-expression is always possible despite the colonising imperatives of commodification and bureaucratisation, form the backdrop against which this chapter now considers Walter Benjamin's notion of the 'aura' and its disappearance in the art of modern societies. Benjamin saw the loss of the aura and the 'de-sacralisation' of bourgeois art as an empowering shift, and one that offered ordinary individuals the capacity to use art to express themselves rather than reproducing elite worldviews. While Benjamin saw the aura largely in negative terms, this chapter reconceptualises the aura in more positive, Habermasian terms in order to consider how personalisable wearable technologies might be thought to offer new possibilities for both empowerment and oppression.

Benjamin's quasi-magical notion of the aura is one of his major contributions to aesthetic theory and critical theory more widely. In his 1936 essay 'The Work of Art in the Age of Mechanical Reproduction', Benjamin describes some of the ways in which modern technologies such as photography and film have fundamentally altered the way in which we experience art. Before the invention of technologies that enable mechanical reproduction of works of art through, for example, photographs, moving film or audio recordings, each work of art was characterised by an 'aura' arising by virtue of the work's unique presence in time and place, the 'apparition of distance' between the work and its contemplator, and an authenticity based upon embeddedness in 'the fabric of tradition' (1968: 215). Friedlander (2012: 147) elaborates on the notion of an aura:

> The figure of an aura of light emanating from an object and surrounding it, making it slightly more than it is, suggests that there is a space of meaning that comes with the object and allows us to relate to it significantly.

To shed light on the aura, Benjamin, like Adorno and Horkheimer, reaches back into pre-history to emphasise the ritualistic origins both of art itself and traditional ways of experiencing it: 'We know that the earliest art works originated in the service of a ritual – first the magical, then the religious kind . . . This ritualised basis, however remote, is still recognisable as secularised ritual even in the most profane forms' (1968: 215). Secularised rituals, in this context, include the presentation of art in (formerly elite) spaces such as art galleries and opera houses, which sought to maintain the aura of art by emphasising organic and authentic aesthetic traditions. However, the aura of artworks is destroyed by mechanical reproduction (e.g. a photograph of a painting or a recording of a symphony), which bypasses such rituals and detaches the work of art from its unique tradition and situation in time and place. For Benjamin, technical reproductions offer new affordances compared with the original – e.g. enlargements of photographs or slow-motion film shots – and allow the enjoyment of art in a wide range of locations, achieved by substituting 'a plurality of copies for a unique existence' (1968: 214).

The consequence, claims Benjamin, is a 'tremendous shattering of tradition', which frees art from its long-standing dependence on ritual and creates new possibilities for those who create and experience art, arising from shock effects, the constant flows of sensory data perceived through distraction rather than concentration, and new combinations of different media. Far from decrying this loss of the aura in art, Benjamin sees this as an emancipatory and democratising shift, a recognition that a 'sense of the universal equality of things' has increased to the extent that 'it extracts [equality] even from a unique object by means of reproduction' (1968: 214), leading (he hoped) to a 'heightened degree of participation [in art] by the 'masses''' (Witkin, 2003: 51). The distance between the audience and the auratic work of art is destroyed, allowing all sectors of society to approach and appreciate art. Moreover, while art was originally valued for its aesthetic autonomy and its status as an end in itself, technical reproduction recreates art as a thing like any other, thus undermining the bourgeois claim to artistic specialism and 'requir[ing] an external criterion of value in terms of *function*' (Sigurdsson, 2001: 55). Substantively, Benjamin links the new mass media to notions of political change, and, with regard to the normative slant of his aesthetic theory, to 'the liberation of the masses from the exploitation and alienating powers of capitalism' (Sigurdsson, 2001). Thus, he states: 'the instant the criterion of authenticity ceases to be applicable to artistic production, the total function of art is reversed. Instead of being based on ritual, it begins to be based on another practice – politics' (1968: 215). Benjamin recognised the potential to use mass media for manipulative ends, and criticised both fascist and communist regimes thereby. But, as Witkin (2003: 53) notes, he also hoped that:

> the destruction of the aura of works of art and the falling back of the art object into ordinary consciousness liberated a critical and active imagination in which art would lose its exclusivity and become an instrument of the ordinary consciousness of ordinary people.

Inevitably, Adorno was heavily critical of Benjamin's work, which contradicted his critique of the culture industry (Witkin, 2003). While Adorno saw popular culture as, in effect, the opium of the masses, Benjamin saw rather the immanent possibility of democratisation and emancipatory progress; and while Adorno saw the formalism and inaccessibility of 'high' art as the principal source of aesthetic critique, Benjamin saw the same works as attempting to maintain the elite and disempowering notion of the aura. Both thinkers overextended their arguments, with Adorno lumping all popular culture together and implausibly dismissing the possibility of authentic artistic value in, for example, jazz, late Romantic music, and cinema, and with Benjamin exaggerating the emancipatory potential of post-auratic art and, more fundamentally, exaggerating the decline of aura and the impossibility of maintaining it in (e.g.) fascist film (Witkin, 2003; Sigurdsson, 2001). However, it is possible to revitalise the concept of the aura via notions of personalisation in the context of wearable technologies and smart garments, and with regard to important ideas from the thought of both Adorno and Benjamin within a wider, Habermasian framework.

This reconceptualisation proceeds from Benjamin's linkage of aura and authenticity. Recall Benjamin's definition of the aura as arising from authenticity, which is itself based upon embeddedness in 'the fabric of tradition' (1968: 215). Benjamin sees this as a disempowering phenomenon, since it is rooted in ritualistic and, subsequently, bourgeois traditions of elite experiences of art. However, the oppressive nature of the aura recedes if the aura is conceived of in neo-Habermasian terms as a phenomenon arising from expressions of individual authenticity through fashion choice. In this context, the relevant work of art is not a painting or a symphony but the individually-curated appearance of the individual as created through personalised fashion choice in line with an ethical/aesthetic project of self-formation, and the relevant notion of authenticity relates not to concerns of artistic provenance but rather to an individual's own history, character, and unique presence in time and space. The aura that arises from an individual's irreplaceability and uniqueness – from his or her 'personalised' existence – is thus not experienced in the first instance as disempowering (though see below), but, it can be argued, as a potentially empowering instantiation of individual authenticity.

Moreover, as the principal visual, textural, and technological medium through which individuals present themselves to the world, fashion assumes particular importance in processes of expressive self-disclosure, in effect transforming individuals into so many artists responsible for designing the 'wearable art' that clothes and characterises their bodies; thus, Hollander states that 'dress is a form of visual art, a creation of images with the visible self as the medium' (1993: 311). Particularly in modern societies characterised by the possibility of adopting a critical attitude towards tradition, the playfulness and ephemerality of fashion (in the alternative sense of fashion as change) offers strong resonances with what Habermas terms 'the unbounding of subjectivity' (1984: 235) resulting from a Baudelairean disenchantment with bourgeois cultural conventions and new-found awareness of the aesthetic as a distinct sphere of activity (White, 1986). Personalised fashion choice, including choice of wearable technologies on aesthetic grounds, can thus play a role in authentic self-expression even for individuals living in capitalist, consumerist societies.

Wearable technologies and personalisation

Within this broad framework, wearable technologies and smart garments assume a place of particular importance because of their unique capacities for personalisation. Two particular aspects of wearable technology are central here. It is important to acknowledge, first, that all clothing – indeed, all material objects – are modifiable in unique ways, such that each garment and accessory can, in a sense, be said to possess an aura. Benjamin himself recognised this in an earlier essay (his 'Little History of Photography') in which he discussed an aura 'that had seeped into the very folds of the man's frock coat or floppy cravat' (1931; cited Hansen, 2008: 340). As Hansen notes, the 'aura of objects such as clothing or furniture stands in a metonymic relation to the person who uses them . . . [and derives] from a long-term relationship with the wearer's physique' (2008: 340; also Hauser, 2005). This notion captures the first key aspect of personalisation as it relates to wearable technology – i.e. the passive notion of personalisation that arises from wearables and smart garments collecting data on their individual users. Users of such technologies thus possess not only the aura that surrounds every item of clothing that is worn and personalised through use, but also what might be termed an *augmented aura* – a heightened instantiated uniqueness in relation to position in time and space – precisely because the data thus collected are so specific to the individual and their unique position in time and space. (Everyone can wear a frock-coat or cravat and personalise it through their gait, but only one person can occupy a particular set of GPS coordinates.) Moreover, since the data offer new possibilities for action for both users and others, this 'passive' aspect of wearable technology may lead to, or otherwise enable, active forms of empowerment and/or oppression (see 'Concluding remarks').

A second key aspect of personalisation relates to active, or deliberate, personalisation, in which users intervene in the visual appearance of wearable technologies for aesthetic ends. This kind of intervention depends upon, but can be separated from, the prior act of making a fashion choice regarding which specific kind of wearable technology to utilise. Furthermore, it may overlap with passive personalisation in the case of devices with both personalisable appearance and data-collection capacities. In the active personalisation context, an augmented aura may also arise, but in this case from the use of digital or other interfaces to alter the appearance of a given piece of technology, such as the Cute Circuit Pink & Black dress shown in Figure 3.1. The 10,000 micro LEDs embedded in the dress's silk chiffon and organza fabric can be manipulated by users through a dedicated iPhone app (Q by Cute Circuit) in order to display different colours and animations, allowing the wearer to alter their appearance – to alter their self-expression – without changing their

Figure 3.1 Cute Circuit Pink & Black Dress.

Source: Wiki Commons (https://commons.wikimedia.org/wiki/File:Eiza_Gonz%C3%A1lez_ en_IDM_pasarelas.jpg?uselang=en-gb).

clothing. The dress can also be programmed to respond to Tweets in real-time, for example at fashion shows or other red carpet events, using the hashtags #makeitblack or #makeitpink.

Another example is the dbCHRONICLE™ bag from accessory designer Diana Broussard shown in Figure 3.2. Constructed from resin Plexiglas, the bag features an LCD screen with audio. The bag comes with a designer art video with music by David Lang[1] and motion graphics by Giovanni Locantore, but the user can also upload and play any two additional videos (including self-created videos) in line with the user's outfit, mood, and social context. Videos are uploaded via a USB cable, which also charges the bag. Additional affordances include the possibility of removing the black resin chain strap to carry the bag as a clutch. Broussard has described the design as adding a 'new dimension to self-expression by introducing motion to fashion with videos . . . a cool fly girl could play her favorite music video, a flashback to ghetto blasters on the city streets but this time in a high "TechLuxe" bag' (Broussard, 2015).

The affordances presented by pieces such as these offer users the potential to overcome the paradox of expressing individuality through mass-produced items, precisely because these 'mass-produced' items (in the sense that they are not individually tailored) offer unique and highly individual personalisation in terms of appearance, thus creating a form of individual, wearable modern art that creates unique augmented auras in turn. Pragmatically speaking, these affordances can be utilised for ethical self-expression (in Habermasian terms) in whatever

Wearable technology as personalised fashion 67

Figure 3.2 dbCHRONICLE(TM) bag.
Source: Designer.

artistic style the individual's personal circumstances and preferences might suggest, whether populist, arcane, or a post-avant-garde blend of the two, in addition to offering new social and interactional possibilities. They can also be used to convey critiques of society, for instance by displaying critical messages on a smart dress display, or (a further sense of personalisation) by altering the data collection modality of a given piece of wearable technology to further specific aims – e.g. collecting air pollution data in particular geographical areas. Thus, it is no longer necessarily the case that mass-produced fashion must destroy auratic art, as Benjamin's argument implies; nor is it the case that consumerist society forces a choice between populist and esoteric art and vitiates the potential for social critique, as Adorno claimed.

Concluding remarks: does wearable technology empower or oppress?

The reconceptualisation of aura outlined above suggests not only that individuals each possess a unique Benjaminian aura created through personalised fashion choice aligned with Habermasian processes of ethical self-expression, but also that wearable technologies can give rise to augmented auras through passive and active processes of personalisation. Some of the implications of this new theorisation for critical theoretical questions of empowerment and oppression have already been suggested. Most fundamentally, the act of self-expression through aesthetic means, and fashion choice in particular (including choice of wearables and smart garments), can be seen as an empowering aspect of – in Habermas's terms – ethical discourses within the wider remit of communicative action, and one with potential to enable social interaction and communication as well as critiques of society. The capacity for self-expression and related aspects of sociability is further heightened by the personalisable appearances of some wearable technologies, which offer not just augmented auras and a heightened sense of individuality, but a way out of the paradox of fashion choice (i.e. the challenge of expressing individuality through mass-produced garments) and the polarity identified by Adorno between populist and esoteric art, in addition to the possibility of displaying critical messages and images. A different kind of empowerment is offered by 'passive' personalisation, or the capacity of wearable technologies to collect unique data on an individual and her environment. This kind of data can enable projects of self-change and, in some circumstances, wider critical projects aimed at emancipatory social change. The example given above is that of collecting air pollution data with wearable sensors, which could be used to force policy changes in a given local area. In general terms, then, it seems clear that there are significant ways in which wearable technology might empower users in a variety of contexts.

Yet, as Habermas's analysis of contemporary societies reminds us, the immanent potential for communicative action is counterbalanced by the imminent threat of the system colonising the lifeworld. Corporations and others may access the 'personalised' data collected by wearable technologies, and subsequently use these data to target users with advertising, predict future health outcomes for insurance purposes, or monitor user performance in the workplace. In this sense, wearable technologies could introduce new techniques of governmentality (Foucault, 1991). In terms of aesthetics, the commercial interests of mass media are (as Adorno emphasised) both pervasive and powerful in contemporary societies, and may lead users of, for example, personalisable wearable technologies to personalise the appearance of their smart garments in line with wider (and potentially oppressive) cultural discourses and pressures. A related issue concerns the nature of the aura itself, which may, in some cases, become augmented to such a degree that it becomes disempowering for others. An obvious case is that of celebrities such as pop singers or footballers, whose charisma and appeal may lead their fans to think less of their own authenticity unless it is modelled on such role models. The singer Katy Perry is a particularly interesting case in this regard, since she makes frequent use of smart dresses in her appearances. Thus, there is always the possibility of the emancipatory potential shown by wearable technologies becoming subverted by tendencies towards cultural conformity and by hidden political, corporate, and social agendas.

The resulting picture is multifaceted: while considering wearables and smart garments as personalisable fashion choices allows for the emergence of individuality and emancipation in the shape of augmented auras, this takes place within a wider consumerist system in which the potential for domination is ever present; and while technology imposes uniformity of a certain kind, its affordances can also allow for the liberation of choice and expressiveness. Consequently, wearable technology constitutes a complex and ambivalent dimension within both digital and aesthetic cultures. The resources of critical theory offer a useful approach to fashion, both in terms of evaluating the wider issues involved in making fashion choices and in terms of conceptualising the novel phenomena and issues introduced by the use of wearable technologies and smart garments.

Note

1 Performed by So Percussion, published by Red Poppy Music, from the album *The Woodmans: Music from the Film*, courtesy of Cantaloupe Music.

References

Adorno, T. (1980) *The Philosophy of Modern Music*. New York: Seabury Press.
Adorno, T. (1984) *Aesthetic Theory*. London: Routledge.
Adorno, T. (1991) 'On the Fetish Character in Music and the Regression of Listening'. In J. Berstein (ed.) *The Culture Industry*. London: Routledge, pp. 29–61.
Adorno, T. (1993) 'Theory of Pseudo-Culture'. *Telos* 95, 15–39.
Adorno, T. and Horkheimer, M. (1979) *Dialectic of Enlightenment*. London: Verso.
Aspers, P. and Godart, F. (2013) 'Sociology of Fashion: Order and Change'. *Annual Review of Sociology* 39, 171–92.
Barnard, M. (2002) *Fashion as Communication*. London: Routledge.
Beddow, M. (1994) *Doctor Faustus*. Cambridge: Cambridge University Press.
Benjamin, W. (1968) 'The Work of Art in the Age of Mechanical Reproduction'. In H. Arendt (ed.) *Illuminations*. London: Fontana, pp. 214–218.
Boucher, G. (2011) 'The Politics of Aesthetic Affect – A Reconstruction of Habermas' Art Theory'. *Parrhesia* 13, 62–78.
Broussard, D. (2015) 'At Last, a Wearable You Will Want to Wear'. http://www.forbes.com/sites/chanderchawla/2015/08/17/at-last-a-wearable-you-will-want-to-wear/ [accessed 30 October 2015].
Eicher, J. B. and Roach-Higgins, M. E. (1995) 'Dress and Identity'. In M. E. Roach-Higgins, J. B. Eicher and K. K. P. Johnson (eds) *Dress and Identity*. New York: Fairchild Publications, pp. 7–18.

Finlayson, J. G. (2005) *Habermas: A Very Short Introduction*. Oxford: Oxford University Press.
Foucault, M. (1991) 'Governmentality: Lecture at the Collège de France, 1 February 1978)'. In G. Burchell, C. Gorden and P. Miller (eds) *The Foucault Effect: Studies in Governmentality*. Hemel Hempstead, UK: Harvester Wheatsheaf, pp. 87–104.
Friedlander, E. (2012) *Walter Benjamin: A Philosophical Portrait*. Cambridge, MA: Harvard University Press.
Geczy, A. and Karaminas, V. (2012) 'Fashion and Art: Critical Crossovers'. In A. Geczy and V. Karaminas (eds) *Fashion and Art*. London: Bloomsbury, pp. 1–12.
Geuss, R. (1981) *The Idea of a Critical Theory: Habermas and the Frankfurt School*. Cambridge: Cambridge University Press.
Habermas, J. (1979) 'Consciousness-raising or Redemptive Criticism'. *New German Critique* 17, 30–59.
Habermas. J. (1984) *Theory of Communicative Action Volume One: Reason and the Rationalisation of Society*. Thomas McCarthy (translator). Boston, MA: Beacon Press.
Habermas, J. (1985) *The Philosophical Discourse of Modernity: Twelve Lectures*. Cambridge, MA: The MIT Press.
Habermas, J. (1993) *Justification and Application: Remarks on Discourse Ethics*. Cambridge, CA: Polity Press.
Hansen, M. B. (2008) 'Benjamin's Aura'. *Critical Inquiry* 34(2), 336–375.
Hauser, K. (2005) 'The Fingerprint of the Second Skin'. In C. Breward and C. Evans (eds) *Fashion and Modernity*. Oxford/New York: Berg, pp. 153–170.
Hollander, A. (1993) *Seeing through Clothes*. Berkeley, CA: University of California Press.
Horkheimer, M. (1999) 'Traditional and Critical Theory'. In M. O'Connell (ed.) *Critical Theory: Selected Essays*. New York: Continuum Press, pp. 188–243.
Ingram, D. (1991) 'Habermas on Aesthetics and Rationality: Completing the Project of Enlightenment'. *New German Critique* 53, 67–103.
Juniper Research (2015) 'Wearables – Smart Chic or Smart Hype'. http://www.juniperresearch.com/press/press-releases/smart-wearables-market-to-generate-$53bn-hardware [accessed 21 October 2015].
Matthewman, S. (2011) *Technology and Social Theory*. London: Palgrave Macmillan.
Nielsen, T. H. and Habermas, J. (1990) 'Jürgen Habermas: Morality, Society, and Ethics: An Interview with Torben Hviid Nielsen'. *Acta Sociologica* 33(2), 93–114.
Orlikowski, W. R. (2000) 'Using Technology and Constituting Structures: A Practice Lens for Studying Technology in Organizations'. *Organ Sci* 11(4), 404–428.
Sigurdsson, G. (2001) 'Towards the Work of Art in the Age of Digital Simulation: Walter Benjamin Revisited'. *Literature & Aesthetics* 11, 51–73.
Ulucanlar, S., Faulkner, A., Peirce, S. and Elwyn, G. (2013) Technology Identity: The Role of Sociotechnical Representations in the Adoption of Medical Devices. *Social Science and Medicine* 98, 95–105.
White, S. K. (1986) 'Foucault's Challenge to Critical Theory'. *The American Political Science Review* 80(2), 419–432.
Witkin, R. W. (2003) *Adorno on Popular Culture*. London: Routledge.
Wyatt, S., Henwood, F., Miller, N. and Sorker, P. (eds) (2000) *Technology and In/Equality: Questioning the Information Society*. London: Routledge.

Part II
Personalising communication, marketing and manufacture

4 Who is really in control?

Pitfalls on the path to personalisation and personality

Jon Oberlander

Introduction

Machines can communicate with people, to offer them personal support, to help them learn, or to help change their behaviour. Natural language processing (NLP), or computational linguistics, is the sub-field of artificial intelligence devoted to building machines that use language flexibly to inform and interact with their users. This chapter sets out first to draw attention to some features of recent work on NLP – and specifically, natural language generation – that support personalised interaction between machines and humans. The focus is on personalised museum guidance, with examples drawn from our work on ILEX, the Intelligent Labelling Explorer. Then, it touches on methods that have been developed for investing NLP systems with personality. The discussion there focuses on the expression of opinions, and draws on our work on Critical Agent Dialogues. With this background in place, the chapter then explores some of the problems associated with personalisation and with personality, along with potential design solutions. Our findings show that the principal problem with personalisation is that systems can end up with too much *actual* autonomy; while the principal problem with personality is that systems may end up with too much *perceived* autonomy. The chapter concludes that there are ethical reasons why designers should develop NLP systems that can be made less (rather than more) personalised, and project less (rather than more) personality.

NLP and personalisation

Research in NLP has delivered a variety of systems. They can, for instance, take large amounts of natural language text or speech as input, and answer questions, or translate from one language into another. Like machine translators, summarisation systems take textual input and produce textual output. However, the 'translations' they produce are typically shorter versions of the documents they are given as input, containing only the most salient information. If we focus specifically on textual output, and therefore consider natural language generation systems in particular, there are several contexts in which

74 *Jon Oberlander*

they can be usefully deployed. This section of the chapter therefore introduces generation systems, and then goes on to describe our work on personalised museum guidance. It outlines the kinds of language problems that have to be addressed, by way of an example from ILEX, and then steps back to identify the way in which personalisation leads on to the topic of personality.

Natural language generation

In generation systems, a computer typically takes raw data from a database or some other computation system, and dresses up that content in words, using information about the dictionaries and grammars of natural languages – like English or Chinese. Language generation can also fruitfully be used wherever many documents, each with few readers, must regularly be produced to explicate rapidly varying sets of numbers. A classic example is in tailored weather reports or forecasts (Reiter and Dale 2000); or a more recent scenario involves the generation of instructions for individual users inside virtual environments (Koller et al. 2010). There has also been a considerable amount of work on possible uses of language generation in intelligent tutoring systems, which monitor a student's progress through a set of learning materials. These systems enter into dialogues with students to test their understanding, monitor the current state of their knowledge, and provide tailored advice in text or speech, in order to motivate them to learn more (see for instance D'Mello and Graesser 2012). Coaching systems can also be used in much less formal environments. For instance, there has been rapid growth in the uptake of tracking devices used by 'quantified self' enthusiasts. Devices include the Jawbone Up, the Nike Fuelband, and the Apple Watch. They provide streams of user-generated data, covering exercise or sleep or food consumption. These streams can currently be visualised to encourage reflection and motivate further exercise. It is easy to think of applications of natural language generation in this context; a simple system can produce verbal summary reports (Phan 2012) and a more sophisticated coaching system could tailor its advice for future user activity.

Generation as personalisation

Some of the work on natural language generation at the University of Edinburgh has explored a particular domain that is less formal than standard intelligent tutoring systems, and perhaps less obviously goal-driven than fitness coaching. The Intelligent Labelling Explorer (ILEX), and its descendents, tailor 'intelligent labels' for museum objects to take into account who is reading them, and what they have seen (and heard) before, thus reducing repetition, and allowing objects to be linked together via comparisons. ILEX was developed at the University of Edinburgh, in collaboration with the National Museums of Scotland (Hitzeman, Mellish and Oberlander 1997; Oberlander et al. 1998; O'Donnell et al. 2001). The development of the system was inspired by the observation that, irrespective of a visitor's educational level, some labels in museums are hard to understand, in spite of significant work by museum curators and educationalists.

The root of the problem is, of course, that the labels are impersonal. The people who write the labels don't know who's reading them: child or adult, dedicated expert or wandering butterfly, English or Greek visitor. And the writers also have to allow for the fact that the classic Victorian museum is random access: the label on a particular object may be the very first one that a visitor reads. So that label can't assume that the visitor has absorbed any information from any other object's label, however nearby it might sit. The upshot is that one label is written for many different audiences, and it ends up repeating a significant amount of information that can probably be found on nearby objects as well. The result is that anything new or remarkable about a given artefact may be buried in a sea of redundant detail.

But if a language generation system knows something about the person reading or listening to its words, it can personalise its output. It can tailor what it says, to take into account what that person is likely to know, or the time of day, or where they are sitting, or it can simply take into consideration what the visitor has already looked at. The intelligent labels generated by ILEX could draw connections between the current object and those others in the museum already seen. They effectively spun as coherent a story as possible out of random selections of artefacts; sometimes ILEX would surprise even its designers with the unanticipated connections it could draw between objects. This reflects the fact that ILEX was first and foremost a personalisation system: the computer chose what facts to present to users, meaning that users had no control of that process (beyond the important feature that they got to choose which objects were to be described). The contrast here is between this kind of system-initiated personalisation, and an alternative approach, which embraces user-initiated customisation. In the language of hypermedia researchers, ILEX was an adaptive system, rather than an adaptable one: it is intelligent and initiates the tailoring, so that the user does not need to specify how the system's output should vary (Brusilovsky and Maybury 2002). Later, we will return to the important contrast between the personalisation and customisation, and discuss their pros and cons in more detail.

An illustration

In generating intelligent labels, there are several linguistic problems that have to be solved by the system. For example, the problem of referring expression generation and the problem of comparison arise when the system chooses the best way of introducing various objects to the viewer and attempts to link together facts about the current and already seen artefacts. The issue here is that if important connections are not made, the user will be misled and, if irrelevant connections are established, the user will be confused. Furthermore, the problem of aggregation arises because information has to be presented to the user in forms that are easy to read, and which avoid the sheer repetitiveness

76 *Jon Oberlander*

of regurgitating a list of facts retrieved from a database. Finally, for current purposes at least, the system must connect the individual facts about an artefact to the more general information about the domain. Failure to do so may create the problem of generalisation. The final version of ILEX addressed each of these four problems as follows.

First, referring expression generation involves choosing the best way of picking out an object, using pronouns, nouns, determiners and adjectives. It is handled by a special component, which takes into account what has been said already, and what other real world items might be mixed up with the intended object, given a potential description. Thus, in Figure 4.1, 'this jewel' is used for the first reference to a brooch, and 'it' for subsequent references; but it would have been 'the Page brooch', if it was mentioned again after the reference to 'the previous item'. The anaphora component also chooses how to describe objects that have not yet been seen, as in the list of suggested links at the bottom of the page; notice that unseen objects are all indefinites ('a'), while known objects are referred to via definite descriptions ('the').

Second, comparison generation is handled by a sophisticated software component that allows the system to mention other objects in the description of the current one. By determining how all the objects in the database resemble one another along a variety of dimensions, the system can identify items that should be either distinguished from the current object, or which might help the user understand more about it. The development of this component hinged on an understanding of the psychology of comparison, as well as the relevant linguistic facts. For instance, we would typically only compare one object with another, reasonably closely related item, along a single, salient dimension (such as the materials from which they were made), rather than including all their

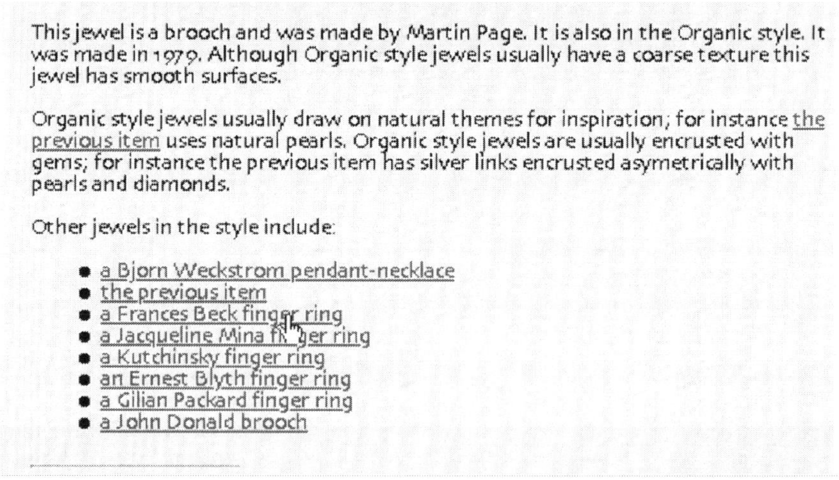

> This jewel is a brooch and was made by Martin Page. It is also in the Organic style. It was made in 1979. Although Organic style jewels usually have a coarse texture this jewel has smooth surfaces.
>
> Organic style jewels usually draw on natural themes for inspiration; for instance <u>the previous item</u> uses natural pearls. Organic style jewels are usually encrusted with gems; for instance the previous item has silver links encrusted asymmetrically with pearls and diamonds.
>
> Other jewels in the style include:
>
> - <u>a Bjorn Weckstrom pendant-necklace</u>
> - <u>the previous item</u>
> - <u>a Frances Beck finger ring</u>
> - <u>a Jacqueline Mina finger ring</u>
> - <u>a Kutchinsky finger ring</u>
> - <u>an Ernest Blyth finger ring</u>
> - <u>a Gilian Packard finger ring</u>
> - <u>a John Donald brooch</u>

Figure 4.1 Extract from a personalised web page generated by ILEX, the Intelligent Labelling Explorer.

similarities and differences. And we ultimately found it better only to compare the current object to ones recently seen, rather than potentially relevant items elsewhere in the collection, but as yet unseen, or seen long ago.

Third, the aggregation component revises the surface forms used to express facts about objects. Thus, the system outputs 'This jewel is a brooch and was made by Martin Page', rather than 'This jewel is a brooch. This jewel was made by Martin Page.' by using a set of re-write rules that determine which kinds of facts are best related together.

Finally, our system links facts to generalisations, as in 'Although organic style jewels usually have a coarse texture, this jewel has smooth surfaces'. As well as making the text read more fluently, this kind of connection directly serves the goal of introducing more general information about a domain, via links to simple facts about the current object.

The object to be described is always chosen by the user and the set of expressible facts is ranked regarding their relevance at this point in the discourse. Several parameters are taken into account in computing this ranking, including the interest, importance and assumed understanding of the facts. In addition, the types of rhetorical structures that the facts serve are taken into account (they can be linked by relations such as contrast or exemplification) and it is by using such moves that the system can opportunistically satisfy its goal of communicating high-level information. 'Although organic style jewels usually have a coarse texture, this jewel has smooth surfaces' is a good case in point: the current jewel is actually a counter-example to the generalisation, so the best way to introduce the generalisation is by using the rhetorical relation of contrast.

From personalisation to style

Descendents of this original ILEX system could generate text – and speech – in multiple languages, including Italian or Greek. For example, the Multilingual Personalised Information Object (M-PIRO) system provided not just extra languages, but also better authoring support, and more sophisticated user modelling (Isard et al. 2003; Androutsopoulos, Oberlander and Karkaletsis 2007). A specific point of difference was that ILEX offered only short-term, session-level user modelling: it knew which other objects had been seen during a single visit, and used this information in its tailoring. But it did not have any long-term, persistent representations of visitors, and hence if a person visited the system on two consecutive days, ILEX would treat them on the second day as if they had never visited the gallery before. M-PIRO addressed this limitation by exploiting a separate 'personalisation server', which provided a persistent record of a user's history, as well as their type (such as adult versus child). Although ILEX could support user types, this facility remained underexploited until M-PIRO provided a more principled separation of user models from the rest of the knowledge held in the system. With this in place, user models could be used both to help select what information to present, and also to control the relative complexity of language to be used in expressing it.

But when a system personalises its text to one user type or another, its language style or 'voice' can change too. For instance, we might decide that children should be presented with shorter sentences, and simple facts. By way of example, compare the following ways of expressing roughly the same content, from the M-PIRO system (Karasimos and Isard 2004). First: 'This exhibit is a stamnos. It was created during the classical period. It dates from circa 420 BC.' This (child-directed) version has no aggregation, and no comparison. Second: 'This exhibit is a stamnos. Unlike the previous vessels, which were created during the archaic period, this stamnos was created during the classical period.' This (adult-directed) version uses both aggregation and comparison. Such differences are driven by the need to personalise to the user, but they help project a different style on the part of the system.

Another, perhaps more subtle, aspect of linguistic style relates to the kinds of connective a speaker or writer uses to link together sentences in a discourse. In ILEX, because we were interested in building up complex discourses, we deliberately set out to use rhetorical structures such as exemplication, contrast or amplification. To make it easy to see when they had been deployed, we always used explicit cue phrases (like 'for instance', 'although' or 'indeed'). Thus, our system would generate sentences like this: 'Organic style jewels are usually encrusted with gems; for instance, the previous item has silver links encrusted asymmetrically with pearls and diamonds.' This complex sentence expresses two facts linked by the exemplification relation, using 'for instance' introduced by a semi-colon, and it also happens to include a low-frequency word, 'asymmetrically'. As a result, it has an unmistakeably academic tone.

The child–adult differences in M-PIRO's language draw attention to the fact that personalisation will give a system a tone of voice that reflects assumptions about its intended audience. The explicit marking of discourse structure in ILEX's language draws attention to the fact that – without having designed it intentionally – we had built a system that, by default, possessed an academic tone of voice. Taken together, it should be clear that language-using systems can project a kind of personality, whether we mean them to, or not.

Summarising this strand of work on language and personalisation, we conclude that natural language generation subsystems can provide personalisation features for computer systems, affecting the textual choices made by those systems. However, working with these systems reveals that they typically project a kind of personality, and it is to this issue that we now turn.

NLP and personality

The fact is that a relatively simple system for personalised museum guidance (ILEX) seems to have a personality and a slightly more sophisticated system (M-PIRO) may be able to shift its tone of voice, and let us consider some deeper questions about the relationship between human language generation and the individual differences between language users.

Personalisation and personality 79

The core idea is that different people express themselves differently, when given the same writing task. Even if they had exactly the same experiences one day, they would typically write about them in distinctive ways. A potentially powerful factor influencing the ways in which people express their selves lies in their personality. The most widely used model of human personality today describes its five main factors (Costa and McCrae 1992). People vary along the following dimensions, shown in Figure 4.2: how extravert they are; how emotionally stable or neurotic they are; how conscientious; how agreeable; and how open to new experiences they are. Work by Pennebaker and colleagues showed that individual differences along some of these dimensions led to measurable differences in language use. For instance, text from high extravert writers has been found to contain fewer negations, tentative words, and negative emotion words, and more social and positive emotion words (Pennebaker and King 1999).

In our earliest work, we explored how such differences between people affected their language choices when writing email (Gill and Oberlander 2002; Oberlander and Gill 2006); later on, we considered the language choices and personalities of bloggers (Oberlander and Nowson 2006; Iacobelli et al. 2011). With this approach, and given enough text from people of known personality, it is possible to achieve two quite different goals. On the one hand, we can train a machine learning-based system to take as input blog entries, and automatically classify the personalities of their writers. For instance, Iacobelli et al. (2011) report 84 per cent accuracy for estimating a user's openness to experience from their blog text. On the other hand, we can identify which words or phrases are characteristic of particular personality types. It is this second goal that leads to the results that are relevant to our current purposes.

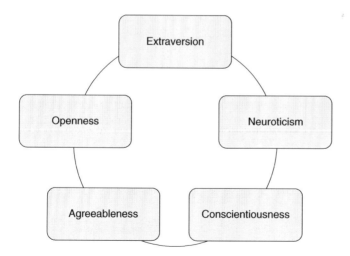

Figure 4.2 The Five Factor Model of personality.
Source: Costa and McCrae (1992).

One interesting finding was how good a diagnostic the use of punctuation is: multiple exclamation marks are associated with high neuroticism; ellipses are associated with high extraversion (Oberlander and Gill 2006). Other findings are by turns intuitively correct, reassuring, or puzzling. For instance, it seems intuitively correct that swear words appear more frequently in text written by high extraverts than in that written by low extraverts (Iacobelli et al. 2011); and it is perhaps reassuring that 'by the way' appears more frequently in text written by highly conscientious individuals than in that written by individuals with low levels of conscientiousness (Oberlander and Nowson 2006). But it is hard to understand why 'comment about' appears more frequently in text written by low agreeableness individuals than in that written by highly agreeable individuals (Iacobelli et al. 2011).

All these generated expressions are, of course, processed by hearers and readers, who form impressions of the personality of the language generator – be it human or machine. Language-using systems can therefore easily lead users to attribute social agency and personality to machines (Reeves and Nass 1996). Thus, it makes sense to consider whether it is feasible to exploit these results about individual differences in human language choice to help build systems that project a specific personality via their own language choices. Walker and her colleagues have carried out much relevant work in this area for over a decade, from Walker, Cahn and Whittaker (1997) to Walker, Lin and Sawyer (2012). In the latter case, for instance, the goal is to (semi-)automatically generate 'in-character' dialogue for virtual dramatic characters, based on pre-existing film dialogue. They extract features from dialogues in a corpus of film scripts, build models of types of characters, and then adjust parameters in their language generation system to produce utterances 'perceived as being similar to the intended character model'.

The linguistic resources described above led us to explore a specific scenario in this arena. The core idea is that people increasingly encounter computer-controlled agents in games, but these agents' dialogue capacities are still quite limited; equally, e-commerce solutions sometimes offer agents who can hold simple chat-based dialogues with customers, but again, the agents will become confused if people use unexpected language. One way to get around this problem is to have the user view a pair of computer agents talk (or text chat) to each other, rather than directly to the user. This way, there is no language exchanged that is too complex for the agents to understand. Although the user's experience is less interactive, they may still benefit from overhearing a scripted dialogue between the computer agents (van Deemter et al. 2008). In this context, it is worth exploring the idea that the two agents can project distinct personalities by selecting specific words or phrases when they have to express some propositional content. In the crAg project on Critical Agent Dialogue, we built pairs of agents who exchanged views about movies, and whose dialogue was read by human users.

When an agent wanted to say something as simple as 'The music was good', the language generation system would compute all the different surface realisations, which would allow this proposition to be expressed. We could provide

Personalisation and personality 81

Figure 4.3 Some possible ways of saying 'The music was good'.[1]
Source: Jon Oberlander.

literally thousands of variations for given propositions; selection among these variations was achieved by ranking them for their probability given a language model built from a collection of text from users known to possess a particular personality feature (Isard, Brockmann and Oberlander 2006). In our studies, the requisite language models were built from the text collections we had produced for the earlier work on personality classification. For 'The music was good', we can generate over 3,000 variants, taking into account various conversational markers. Among these, the variant preferred by the high neurotic language model is 'I have to say I thought that the music was really good'; as shown in Figure 4.3, this option is lower in the ranking offered by the low neurotic language model, whose top choice is 'I mean, I thought the music was really good'. Such differences are subtle, but they can add up when it comes to the impressions formed by users. Users viewing these agent dialogues could perceive at least some personality differences reliably (Gill, Brockmann and Oberlander 2012).

Summarising this strand of work on language and personality, it seems fair to conclude that people can definitely attribute personality to computer systems on the basis of textual choices made by those systems. Yet, while we may want agents in games to project particular personalities, there are some problems concerning both personalisation and personality, which we will address in turn.

Problems with personalisation

Thus far, in discussing personalisation, we have focused on the extent to which language generation can automatically tailor information presentations in the context of museum guiding. But the domain of personalisation is much broader in two ways. First, there are, of course, many other types of system that take advantage of personalisation. For instance, Internet searches are typically personalised, along with associated targeted advertising; so, too, are the recommendation services used to support product selection in e-commerce; and as well as the informal museum guiding we discussed above, there are more formal intelligent tutoring systems and other environments for e-learning. Second, considering this broader range of applications, it should be clear that personalisation can be achieved using mechanisms that do not rely on language choice per se. For instance, the placing of targeted advertising may not change the language used, but only the context in which an advertisement is shown. Similarly, recommendation-based services, like Amazon, record the products a user has been browsing through, and suggest other objects – that the user has not looked at – which 'People Like You' have looked at or bought. Yet, the verbal descriptions of those new objects are not explicitly linked to the objects the user has looked at previously.

That said, the broader range of personalised systems all depend on knowing something about the given user, which leads to both practical and ethical complications. The required knowledge could be elicited by asking users to fill in a questionnaire, or a profile page; or it could be captured simply by recording in the background what they do as they move around and behave naturally, online or indeed in the physical world. Either way, what is built is a user profile or user model; it is the notion of user models – particularly the persistent, long-term user models – that raises a problem for designers wishing to support personalisation. Judith Kay and colleagues have articulated very clearly four facets of the problem, all of which can ultimately be traced back to the fundamental difficulty: the lack of user control offered by standard user models. Lack of user control is at once a practical and an ethical concern. Kay and Kummerfeld (2012) argue that standard user models are problematic in terms of their privacy, invisibility, error and waste.

Regarding privacy, it is clear that user models contain personal information; yet 'the norm is that people can neither access nor control their user models . . . people appear to have become increasingly concerned about their privacy being compromised in personalised systems' (Kay and Kummerfeld 2012, p. 3). Turning to invisibility, the problem is that termed by Pariser (2011) as the 'filter bubble': it is often very difficult for users to tell if an interface is personalised, or if it is, what parts of it are; so personalised news services may filter out information with(out?) the user knowing it, while personalised search will give two users potentially very different results, unbeknownst to them. Errors in user models arise because they are usually built on the basis of inference from observed user behaviour, itself noisy, which will involve classifications and generalisations that are prone to introduce more noise. This is a problem because few personalised systems make it easy to edit out data errors or correct invalid inferences. Waste in user models is more of concern to system developers than users: essentially, users provide lots of data to multiple systems, but this information is rarely shared; so each system developer has to work out ways to acquire data that may already be in another system's user model. It is perhaps worth noting that any moves to reduce waste should not make worse existing problems over privacy. As Kay and Kummerfeld observe, these four problems with user models stem from the fundamental issue, which is the lack of user control over the personal information in their own models, and the tailoring that is licensed by those models. Bozdag and Timmermans (2011) have a similar analysis, noting that user models are problematic in eroding user autonomy, transparency and identity. Their concern over autonomy is closely related to the control and invisibility issues already noted, and their identity problem relates to the privacy issue. Their proposal for enhancing autonomy is, in effect, to enable user-initiated customisation to override system-initiated personalisation, and we will return to consider work in this tradition shortly. However, their transparency problem appears to add a new dimension. They note that a user 'cannot assert control in an opaque system, since he will not be well informed how the system works' (p. 11), and they argue against the view that users have a right to 'full and truthful disclosure of the underlying rules or algorithms governing indexing, searching, and prioritizing' (p. 11). Their concern is that 'it will be very difficult for an average user to comprehend the algorithm' (p. 11). They suggest instead that users should be shown the implications of the algorithms. Their proposal for enhancing transparency is then to allow users to see that personalisation is taking place, and which filters are in operation.

The general solution that Kay and colleagues have implemented and explored is known as 'scrutable user modelling'. For users to gain value from scrutable models, they have to put in real effort; such models are 'designed and implemented so that the user can study, or scrutinise, the way she works, to determine what information the user model holds, the processes used to capture it, and the ways that it is used' (Kay and Kummerfeld 2012, p. 4). There is much to be said for this design approach, for instance, in terms of tackling the invisibility problem by continuously showing that filters or other user model assumptions are in place. Scrutable user modelling thus already meets the design requirements discussed by Bozdag and Timmermans. But the transparency problem raised by the latter perhaps remains a concern: scrutiny is potentially hard work (just as understanding the underlying filtering rules is hard work). Telling someone that personalisation is occurring does help them, but it does not necessarily show them what its specific effects are, especially if many rules are simultaneously in play. A system may be so complex and subtle that giving those it affects access to it, or even just awareness of it, does not de-fuse its ethical implications.

In fact, there is an intuitive solution: de-personalisation. If a user can sign-out of a system, and see what it presents to an un-modelled user, then they can see in quite concrete terms what the effects of personalisation are. Such de-personalisation is always an option for services such as Google, where a user need only sign out of search or news to see what is on offer to a user without a user model. Alternately, and perhaps more vividly, we could try another idea: re-personalisation. If a user can be shown what would be seen by another user, with a very different user model, then they may get a richer impression of the effects of personalisation. Implementing such re-personalisation might be trickier than de-personalisation, but it is an idea worth exploring. If properly implemented, it might resonate with existing online practice, whereby some users construct their own fictional personas (Turkle 2011): if someone wants to present a new persona, it might be useful to see the world through that persona's filter bubble.

However, before moving on to discuss a rather different problem raised by personality in systems, it is worth dwelling on the pros and cons of user-initiated customisation (or adaptability) as another solution to the problem of system-initiated personalisation (or adaptivity). Bozdag and Timmermans propose customisation as a solution to the problem of autonomy, and it should be clear that if users correct errors in the type of scrutable user models discussed by Kay and Kummerfeld they are in effect customising their systems. Indeed, the idea of injecting customisation into personalised systems has already been explored by a number of groups (such as Ahn et al. 2007; Sundar and Marathe 2010; Tintarev and Masthoff 2012). Assuming that a personalised system is doing a reasonable job at meeting personal information needs, the emerging consensus is that adding customisation typically makes the system's results objectively worse; for instance, the news items are less suitable to the user, or product recommendations less satisfactory to them. However, by and large, users actually prefer the customised systems to the personalised but uncustomised version; it is plausible to maintain that this is attributable to the enhanced feeling of control or autonomy licensed by customisation. However, Sundar and Marathe observe an interaction between the preference for customisability and perceptions of privacy, which is moderated by level of expertise. They find that power users resort to customisation when privacy is perceived to be low, but accept personalisation when privacy is high; the reverse pattern holds for less experienced users. They conclude:

> A clear design implication is that interfaces have to feature different types or levels of customisation for users with different levels of expertise. Most users may respond favourably to tailored content, but experts need to be provided privacy assurances or the means to express their agency, whereas novices ought not to be burdened with calls for (customisation) unless encouragement is available in the form of privacy guarantees.
>
> (2010, p. 319)

To summarise the position for now: personalisation does raise problems in the form of inscrutable user models, but there are potential solutions. Customisation is one, although it introduces its own complications. De-personalisation and re-personalisation may be pragmatic and promising alternatives worthy of further investigation, and if so, it is likely that scrutable user modelling can ultimately support these too.

Problems with personality

In most of our own work on personality, we have assumed that this is simply a good thing: that we want users to treat machines as if they have some intelligence, a distinctive personality, and perhaps even something like moods or emotions. The field of affective computing is founded on the idea that there is value in building machines that detect and express emotions, moods, and personalities (Picard 2000). From a design point of view, Norman (2004) has suggested that emotional displays make machines more predictable for their human owners or users: the emotions provide a 'soft' signal of likely future behaviour on the part of the machine.

But against this, Bryson (2010) has argued that designers of intelligent systems step onto a slippery slope when they invest machines with social properties like personality. She makes several key claims: (1) Having servants is good and useful, provided no one is dehumanised; (2) A robot can be a servant without being a person; (3) It is right and natural for people to own robots; (4) It would be wrong to let people think that their robots are persons' (p. 65). Her primary concern is that we quickly move from thinking of machines as being social agents to thinking of them as moral agents. Against this, she argues that while robots or other artificial intelligences can certainly assist humans making decisions, it is wrong to consider them as decision makers themselves, because they are simply tools, and so the legal and moral responsibility for their actions will always lie with a human:

> Ordinarily, damage caused by a tool is the fault of an operator, and benefit from it is to the operator's credit. If the system malfunctions due to poor manufacturing, then the fault may lay with the company that built it, and the operator can sue to resolve this.
>
> (p. 69)

The point is this: if designers build systems that sound like, and look like, human beings, then users will tend to project onto them other human properties. Users will come to think of them as social agents, and then perhaps as moral agents, responsible for their own decisions. The latter belief, however ill-founded, might actually prove rather convenient for future system developers, who would prefer not to be held responsible for each and every error made by a language-using system. Thus, it is quite possible that such developers will be happy to see, and even encourage, the blurring of the line between human and machine agency.

So, given that we will continue to build language-using machines, we need to think rather harder about the role of personality. Perhaps we are wrong to consider that this is simply a good thing. There may be specialised niches where it is entirely appropriate, such as computer-controlled non-player characters in computer games. Yet, so long as there are places where personality is not appropriate, or should not be projected in case it gives rise to Bryson's hazard, there is an interesting problem. Earlier, it was noted that a personalised system (ILEX) appeared to project a particular 'academic' personality, thanks to its language choices. But that system was not actually designed to project a personality. So, even if system developers determine not to propagate personality when it is unnecessary or unhelpful, users may be unable not to infer the presence of a personality behind a communication.

What this indicates is that at least one of the solutions proposed above, addressing the personalisation problem, has no realistic prospect of success when applied to personality. Specifically, we suggested that de-personalisation could help show users how things might be if they moved outside their filter bubble. The analogous move here would be something like 'de-personification': switching off the personality of a language-using computer. Given what has been said already, there is arguably no such thing as no personality. Technically, however, it is perfectly feasible to turn off the mechanisms we use to project a personality, such as the selection of variants of utterances by ranking against a special personality-based language model. All we need to do is instead select the utterance variant that is made most probable by a general language model: one constructed by pooling together all the language from all the people with different personalities. Then we would simply be choosing the most average, most popular way of saying something. But this bland or average language choice might not have the desired effect. It still represents a personality, and one might speculate that it would be a particularly attractive one. From work on face perception, it is known that 'average' faces, created by compositing images of many individuals, are judged to be especially attractive. Perhaps the same effect would hold for average texts; against this, it may be argued that readers and listeners prefer some variation over total uniformity, so that if a language-using computer stuck too close to majority behaviour, people would disprefer it. Either way, de-personification on these terms still leaves the ghost of a personality in the machine.

In response, one might instead hazard an analogue of re-personalisation; here, it would be 're-personification': switching the language-using computer's selected personality for another one. Instead of striving for no personality, or the average personality, it would simply be calling up the wrong personality. By way of example, we could swap a patient, encouraging tutor personality with an impatient, critical one. Or a calm, warm healthcarer personality with an anxious, cold one. That kind of switch might be enough to undermine a user's view that the personality behind the machine represents a fixed, autonomous agent.

Indeed, it should be possible here to introduce a facility analogous to customisation: rather than substituting in random alternative personalities (some of which might be hard to distinguish from one another), we might do better to let the user actively choose which new personality they wish to interact with. Of course, an impatient, critical tutor might be rather less helpful for learners than the ideal personality: D'Mello and Graesser (2012) suggest as much when reporting on experiments with Affective AutoTutor. They adapted AutoTutor, an existing intelligent tutoring system, by enabling it to estimate a student's motivational status (for instance, engaged versus bored). They then projected either a supportive personality or an edgier, more critical one. The latter was never as effective as the former. However, experience with customisation suggests that the benefits in terms of the user's enhanced feeling of autonomy can outweigh the disadvantages of weaker learning progress. That said, it is plausible to suggest that user-initiated re-personalisation might need to be limited in its temporal scope: someone who deliberately chooses a bad teacher is certainly exercising their ability to control a system, but they may be undermining their own interests in the long term. And if the main point of re-personalisation is to convince users that the personality projected by the system is a programmable artefact, then this surely only requires a short-term demonstration anyway.

To summarise, the principal problem with personalisation was the loss of user control, with systems ending up with too much actual autonomy. Personality raises its own distinctive problem, albeit one linked again to user autonomy and control: here, the principal problem is that systems may be perceived to have more autonomy than they actually possess. People need to be reminded that even though systems with personality may be considered social agents, they are not moral agents, and they remain simply tools for human use. There is potential for a solution here, but there is less room for manoeuvre than for personalisation.

Conclusion

We have seen that natural language generation can provide personalisation features for a variety of useful intelligent computer systems, affecting the textual choices made by those systems. However, working with some of these language-using personalised systems revealed that they can unintentionally project a specific kind of personality. Subsequent work on systems designed to actively project personality confirms that people can definitely attribute personality to computer systems on the basis of systematic textual choices made by those systems. Yet, while we may want agents in games to project particular personalities, there are some problems concerning both personalisation and personality. On the one hand, personalisation does raise problems in the form of inscrutable user models, but there are potential solutions. Customisation is one, although it introduces its own complications. De-personalisation and re-personalisation are both pragmatic and promising alternatives worthy of further investigation, and it is likely that scrutable user modelling can ultimately support these too. On the other hand, personality raises a different kind of problem linked to autonomy and control: people need to be reminded periodically that computers are simply tools, and in this case, re-personification may be a more viable solution than de-personification.

There is a loose end, here, perhaps. It is natural to ask whether personalisation automatically implies personality, or whether personality automatically implies personalisation. In both cases, the answer must be no. A personalised web search engine does not appear to project much in the way of personality; and a computer game character with a distinctive personality may present exactly the same information to every user. The claim here is that it is not personalisation that invokes personality: it is language use. Consider a personalised online assistant, for search or recommendation or tutoring or guiding. If it uses language, then its language will project some personality, even if it is an average one. But a personality-rich language-using agent does not need to act as part of a personalised system. In such cases, a sophisticated agent will appear somewhat less intelligent if it persistently fails to adjust its utterances to suit its human user. But on balance, it seems as if you can take the personalisation out of language-using systems, but you can't take the personality out of them. Thus, as far as designing around the problems we have discussed, the news is mixed. For the classic Pariser filter bubble, we can pop the bubble by customisation, de-personalisation and re-personalisation; scrutable user models provide a suitable framework for further progress. But to pop the new 'personality' bubble, we currently have fewer resources at our disposal.

Note

1 Ranked by CrAg, the Critical Agents Dialogue system. There are over 3,000 ways of expressing this message. The ranking on the left is based on a language model built from text written by people with high neuroticism scores; the one on the right is based on a model built from text by people with low neuroticism scores. The variant ranked at the top on the left slips down the ranking on the right.

References

Ahn, J. W., Brusilovsky, P., Grady, J., He, D. and Syn, S. Y. (2007) Open user profiles for adaptive news systems: help or harm? In *Proceedings of the 16th International Conference on World Wide Web*, ACM, pp. 11–20.

Androutsopoulos, I., Oberlander, J. and Karkaletsis, V. (2007) Source authoring for multilingual generation of personalised object descriptions. *Natural Language Engineering*, 13, 191–233.

Bozdag, E. and Timmermans, J. (2011) Values in the filter bubble: ethics of personalization algorithms in cloud computing. In *1st International Workshop on Values in Design – Building Bridges between RE, HCI and Ethics*, pp. 7–15.

Brusilovsky, P. and Maybury, M. T. (2002) From adaptive hypermedia to the adaptive Web. *Communications of the ACM*, 45(5), 30–33.

Bryson, J. J. (2010) Robots should be slaves. In Y. Wilks (ed.), *Close Engagements with Artificial Companions*. Amsterdam: John Benjamins Publishing Company, pp. 63–74.

Costa, P. and McCrae, R. R. (1992) *NEO–PI–R Professional Manual*. Odessa, FL: Psychological Assessment Resources.

D'Mello, S. and Graesser, A. (2012) AutoTutor and affective AutoTutor: learning by talking with cognitively and emotionally intelligent computers that talk back. *ACM Transactions on Interactive Intelligent Systems*, 2(4), 23.

Gill, A. J., Brockmann, C. and Oberlander, J. (2012) Perceptions of alignment and personality in generated dialogue. In *Proceedings of the Seventh International Natural Language Generation Conference (INLG 2012)*, pp. 40–48.

Gill, A. J. and Oberlander, J. (2002) Taking care of the linguistic features of extraversion. In *Proceedings of the 24th Annual Conference of the Cognitive Science Society*, pp. 363–368.

Hitzeman, J., Mellish, C. and Oberlander, J. (1997) Dynamic generation of museum web pages: the intelligent labelling explorer. *Archives and Museum Informatics*, 11, 107–115.

Iacobelli, F., Gill, A. J., Nowson, S. and Oberlander, J. (2011) Large-scale personality classification of bloggers. In *Lecture Notes in Computer Science 6975, Proceedings of the International Workshop on Machine Learning for Affective Computing (MLAC2011)*, pp. 568–577.

Isard, A., Brockmann, C. and Oberlander, J. (2006) Individuality and alignment in generated dialogues. In *Proceedings of the 4th International Natural Language Generation Conference*, pp. 22–29.

Isard, A., Oberlander, J., Androutsopoulos, I. and Matheson, C. (2003) Speaking the users' languages. *IEEE Intelligent Systems*, 18, 40–45.

Karasimos, A. and Isard, A. (2004) Multi-lingual evaluation of a natural language generation system. In *Proceedings of the Fourth International Conference on Language Resources and Evaluation (LREC 2004)*, pp. 829–832.

Kay, J. and Kummerfeld, B. (2012) Creating personalized systems that people can scrutinize and control: drivers, principles and experience. *ACM Transactions on Interactive Intelligent Systems*, 2(4), 24.

Koller, A., Striegnitz, K., Gargett, A., Byron, D., Cassell, J., Dale, R., Moore, J. and Oberlander, J. (2010) Report on the second NLG challenge on generating instructions in virtual environments (GIVE-2). In *Proceedings of the 6th International Natural Language Generation Conference*, pp. 243–250.

Norman, D. A. (2004) *Emotional Design: Why We Love (or Hate) Everyday Things*. New York: Basic Books.

Oberlander, J. and Gill, A. J. (2006) Language with character: a stratified corpus comparison of individual differences in e-mail communication. *Discourse Processes*, 42, 239–270.

Oberlander, J. and Nowson, S. (2006) Whose thumb is it anyway? Classifying author personality from weblog text. In *Proceedings of the COLING/ACL 2006 Main Conference Poster Sessions*, pp. 627–634.

Oberlander, J., O'Donnell, M., Knott, A. and Mellish, C. (1998) Conversation in the museum: experiments in dynamic hypermedia with the intelligent labelling explorer. *New Review of Hypermedia and Multimedia*, 4, 11–32.

O'Donnell, M., Mellish, C., Oberlander, J. and Knott, A. (2001) ILEX: an architecture for a dynamic hypertext generation system. *Natural Language Engineering*, 7(3), 225–250.

Pariser, E. (2011) *The Filter Bubble: What the Internet Is Hiding from You*. London: Penguin.

Pennebaker, J. W. and King, L. (1999) Linguistic styles: language use as an individual difference. *Journal of Personality & Social Psychology*, 77, 1296–1312.

Phan, T. (2012) Generating natural-language narratives from activity recognition with spurious classification pruning. In *Proceedings of the Third International Workshop on Sensing Applications on Mobile Phones (PhoneSense '12)*, ACM.

Picard, R. W. (2000) *Affective Computing*. Cambridge, MA: MIT Press.

Reeves, B. and Nass, C. (1996) *The Media Equation: How People Treat Computers, Television, and New Media like Real People and Places*. Stanford, CA: CSLI Publications; Cambridge: Cambridge University Press.

Reiter, E. and Dale, R. (2000) *Building Natural Language Generation Systems*. Cambridge: Cambridge University Press.

Sundar, S. S. and Marathe, S. S. (2010) Personalization versus customization: the importance of agency, privacy, and power usage. *Human Communication Research*, 36(3), 298–322.

Tintarev, N. and Masthoff, J. (2012) Evaluating the effectiveness of explanations for recommender systems. *User Modeling and User-Adapted Interaction*, 22(4–5), 399–439.

Turkle, S. (2011) *Life on the Screen*. New York: Simon and Schuster.

Walker, M. A., Cahn, J. E. and Whittaker, S. J. (1997) Improvising linguistic style: social and affective bases for agent personality. In *Proceedings of the First International Conference on Autonomous Agents*, ACM, pp. 96–105.

Walker, M. A., Lin, G. I. and Sawyer, J. (2012) An annotated corpus of film dialogue for learning and characterizing character style. In *Proceedings of the International Conference on Language Resources and Evaluation*, pp. 1373–1378.

van Deemter, K., Krenn, B., Piwek, P., Klesen, M., Schroeder, M. and Baumann, S. (2008) Fully generated scripted dialogue for embodied agents. *Artificial Intelligence*, 172, 1219–1244.

5 What will designers do when everyone can be a designer?

Matt Sinclair

Introduction

> We, the people, the untrained majority, are the future of design. We have the tools and we will be the masters of our personal environments ... We're not dumb consumers, we're creative consumers ... We won't buy anything that isn't uniquely specified by ourselves.
>
> (McGuirk, 2009: 48)

When Justin McGuirk wrote the above in 2009, a contemporary discussion about the ability of non-designers to engage in design and personalisation activities was already well established. Originating in theories of participatory design and co-design, the debate had been re-energised by the possibilities emerging from new approaches to manufacturing provided by digital fabrication technologies such as laser cutting and additive manufacturing (to become known more popularly as 3D printing). Often referred to under the umbrella term of the 'Maker Movement', this stream of activity emerged among enthusiasts and hobbyists empowered by access to these increasingly low-cost technologies. The users of 3D printers by companies such as Makerbot and Ultimaker, and electronics and computing platforms such as Arduino and Raspberry Pi, provided some of the most visible examples of the open source community ethic which characterised the movement.

The proposition that design is an activity in which anyone can take part is not one that attracts consensus easily. Whereas writers such as Norman (2004: 224) have argued that 'We are all designers', and that deciding where to put your coffee cup and book is an act of design, practitioners such as Jonathan Ive have countered that 'It sounds egalitarian to say in future people should design their own stuff, but that's the designer's job – to solve problems' (2009, quoted in McGuirk, 2009). Mass-customisation literature commonly employs terms such as 'user-designer' (e.g. Franke and Piller, 2004) as well as assertions that 'The professional designer is replaced by the user' (Randall et al., 2003), causing designers to question the writers' understanding of the practice of design. Others have attempted simply to shut down the argument, insisting, in the words of author Andrew Keen, that 'Consumers consume; designers design. End of story' (Duffy and Keen, 2006: 116). These binary positions, which might be summarised as 'everyone is a designer' or 'only professional designers can design', have shed little light on the potential of digital fabrication technologies, or the new design processes that have emerged as a result. Fischer (2002) has previously argued against the oversimplification of these positions when suggesting that 'consumer' and 'designer' are not binary choices, and that a continuum exists between the two. Most importantly, however, such arguments have largely been ignored by those involved in the Maker Movement, who have gone ahead and designed and manufactured products whether designers and design theorists like it or not. In so doing, they have created a multitude of products: objects that function poorly and objects that function perfectly; objects that dismay and objects that delight; objects of crassness and objects of beauty; in short, they have created things that elicit a similar range of reactions to those conceived by professional designers. Thus the question 'What will designers do when everyone can be a designer?' has become ever more pertinent.

In this chapter, the author writes from the position that there is no fundamental difference between the design practised by professionals and that undertaken by amateurs. In evaluating design, we should make judgements based on the merits of the outcome, rather than the status of those involved. Nonetheless, those who have been trained and who practise design professionally will possess expertise in areas that non-professionals do not. For some advocates of user involvement in design, greater engagement is always a goal to aim for. However, one of the key differentiators of the new approaches to design discussed below is the degree to which they offer users the freedom to design their own products. For many amateur designers, the ability to utilise their own expertise (in a particular field, for a specific purpose, or simply in the understanding of what they individually require) is enabled by the expertise of professionals. Thus in many instances, it is the constraints placed on the user that provide the opportunity for involvement in design.

Consumer involvement in industrial design

The Maker Movement is a multi-faceted phenomenon, accepting of participants with interests as diverse as electronics, robotics, biology and programming, to weaving, marquetry and even performance art. However, it is the use of digital technologies, both the manufacturing hardware and the software that drives it, which encroaches most deeply into territory conventionally considered that of the designer. Further challenges come to designers from industrial manufacture, through the development of new approaches to design such as mass customisation and crowdsourcing. In order to begin answering the question posed in the title of this chapter, it is therefore necessary to understand what is meant by design, and in particular industrial design, which traditionally poses itself as the means by which industry conceives of consumer products.

The difficulty of ascertaining what industrial design actually is, was recognised by Ralph Caplan (1969: 1) in his introduction to *Design in America*, in what remains one of the most insightful and relevant essays on the practice of industrial design despite being written close to 50 years ago:

> What is industrial design? It was never an easy question to begin with, and it has not, through the years, become any easier. Essentially, industrial design determines the form of objects that are to be mass produced by machines rather than crafted by hand. But while this has long been an *essential* definition, it is no longer sufficiently comprehensive, if indeed it ever was . . . First of all, the designs are not necessarily mass produced . . . Nor is the work necessarily done for industry.

Ultimately, Caplan fails, or refuses, to define exactly what industrial design is, for reasons that appear remarkably prescient of the issues raised by digital manufacturing. Others have been less wary, typically viewing the end user as an external influence on the solutions that designers arrive at, or as part of a target market (e.g. IDSA, 2014). Some of the most widely used definitions are therefore unable to account for the possibility of consumers who design and/or manufacture their own products. In addition, definitions of industrial design that refer to 'mass manufacture' or 'volume production' (e.g. McDermott, 2007; Design Council, 2010) have increasingly proved inadequate at describing design for digital manufacture, in which low volume or even unique products are the outcome.

Definitions of industrial design based on an observation of process, rather than a description of service, overcome this problem somewhat. Fiell and Fiell (2003) for example, describe industrial design as

> the conception and planning of products for multiple reproduction – [it] is a creative and inventive process concerned with the synthesis of such instrumental factors as engineering, technology, materials and aesthetics into machine-producible solutions that balance all user needs and desires within technical and social constraints.
>
> (p. 6)

This definition is not without weaknesses: the term 'multiple reproduction' is problematic (though not to the same degree as 'mass produced'), although it could be argued that a consumer-designed product is *potentially* reproducible, even if only one is actually made. Importantly though, by listing the tasks typically carried out by the industrial designer, the definition allows for the possibility that a consumer undertaking some of the tasks (rather than all) is acting as a designer.

In a typical model of the industrial design process (Figure 5.1), the early stages of a project will involve the generation of multiple concepts for how the product might be resolved. During these stages the designer will be widening the possibilities of what the actual product might be. However, in a typical product development project, this widening might account for less than 10 per cent of the total work involved in the process of designing a manufacturable and saleable product, and rarely more than 25 per cent. The remainder will involve consolidating and filtering, rejecting unsuitable designs and refining more suitable ones, prototyping and then further refining, and repeating stages where necessary, with the ultimate goal of arriving at the smallest possible number of solutions, which can then be reproduced identically in high volume. So ingrained is this process that many industrial designers (as previous definitions illustrate), define what they do as design for mass manufacture. They believe that industrial design is about designing a single product for multiple users, and they propose that this is what distinguishes design from craft (Risatti, 2006; Walker, 1989: 38–39). Increasingly, developments in manufacturing processes are demonstrating that this belief is wrong.

The industrial design process described above is a result of the profession's service of industrial manufacturing. One of the common features of mass production is that the means of production require substantial initial investment; however, once in place, the cost of manufacturing a single part or product (relative to the initial investment) is negligible. It is therefore a basic principle of mass production that as the number of parts produced increases, the cost of production of each individual part decreases. This inevitably leads to uniformity, as even small design changes require significant reinvestment in tooling, and since products must be produced in high volume, a product's aesthetics must appeal to many, not just a few. However, without the need for significant investment in mass production tooling (Mansour and Hague, 2003), digital fabrication offers the theoretical possibility that every concept can make it through to production. As manufacturing changes, from a paradigm of mass production to one in which digital manufacturing makes unique, personalised production possible, industrial design will also be forced to change. A number of researchers have proposed that such changes represent the possibility of a future in which

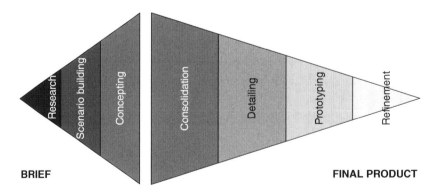

Figure 5.1 Industrial design process model.

Source: Matt Sinclair.

designer–consumer relationships more closely resemble those of pre-industrial artisanship (Campbell et al., 2003; Bonanni et al., 2008; Aldersey-Williams, 2011). This vision does not require that all consumers engage in the design and manufacture of products – 'it's not that everyone will, but that anyone can', as Nilofer Merchant (2013) puts it. Nor does it require that designers create unique designs for every individual consumer. Instead, if they are to fully exploit the potential offered by digital fabrication technologies, they must begin to become what Tonkinwise (2005) describes as 'designers capable of designing things that are not finished' (p. 99). They will be designers of products that require unique decisions and inputs from consumers, and which are deliberately designed to be incomplete without the consumers' input.

It is in this type of scenario that the question of the user acting as, or replacing, the designer starts to be resolved. When using the NIKEiD configurator for instance, a consumer choosing colours to create a personalised shoe is clearly not performing *all* of the tasks that a designer working for Nike does. But equally clearly, the consumer is performing *one* of the tasks (colour selection) that would have been the job of the designer if NIKEiD did not exist. Therefore, whilst it is not true to say that the consumer is able to replace the designer, it is undeniable that in this context the consumer possesses the expertise to do what, in other circumstances, would be described as design.

Amateur and professional expertise

The IDSA definition mentioned previously states that industrial design is 'the professional service of creating and developing concepts and specifications that optimize the function, value and appearance of products and systems for the mutual benefit of both user and manufacturer' (IDSA, 2010).

Unsurprisingly for a body whose membership consists of those who work in the industry, the emphasis on professional service implies those not *employed* as designers should not describe what they do as industrial design. The exclusive nature of such a definition points to a key differentiator between those who engage in design activities: the expertise of the professional versus that of the amateur.

Much of the literature dealing with personalisation and the involvement of the consumer in the design process has concentrated on the possibility of changing the product's appearance (e.g. Mugge et al., 2009; Bernabei and Power, 2013). The purpose of the traditional design process is not just to impose a uniform visual aesthetic however, it also refines or rejects on the basis of ergonomics, durability, safety, reliability, integration with other products and systems, cost and so on. These are all areas in which the designer's training and expertise is likely to remain the best tool to resolve the conflicting demands of a commercial product brief. However, it is in the identification of those areas where the amateur's expertise is superior to that of the professional, that we can begin to identify how the role of the designer might change in future.

In the past, one of the key advantages of the professional designer – what allowed them to engage in design to a higher level than the amateur – was their access to the means of production. This advantage no longer exists. Online services mean that anyone can access digital manufacturing technologies equal in sophistication to those that the professional designer can use. Nowadays, the main difference between professional and amateur is that the professional designer designs what someone else (the user) wants, and what someone else (the client) specifies. In contrast, and what is especially interesting about the work done within the Maker community, is the fact that so much of it is created for personal use. Obviously, many designs are shared, re-used and modified, but this represents a very different scenario to that of the professional designer's task of trying to take a 'target market' into account from the beginning of a project. That *the user and the designer are the same person* is what differentiates amateur expertise from professional.

Within the field of industrial design, strategies such as user-centred design and co-design are common-place methods for the integration of user needs into the design process (Sanders and Stappers, 2008). The implementation of such strategies has been criticised as often misguided or ineffectual (Ulwick, 2002; Goodman-Deane et al., 2010; Steen, 2011), leading to incremental improvements rather than significant new ideas. Nonetheless, it is now commonplace for brands to talk of the extent to which they are customer-driven (Binder et al., 2008). Conventional wisdom holds that products that emerge from a focus on the needs of users better address those needs and thus lead to greater consumer satisfaction and, ultimately, greater profitability (Vredenburg et al., 2002; Design Council, 2008). But, conventional wisdom rarely questions the causes of the need to be user-oriented, or why professional design expertise must spend so much effort attempting to understand the user. The reason is not that understanding the user is inherent to the nature of design, rather it is because *failing to understand* the user is inherent to mass production. As Aldersey-Williams (2011) observes, user-centred design is intended 'to ensure not the best outcome for one consumer but the least worst outcome for all consumers, and thus the best result for the manufacturing company'. It is the nature of mass production that demands designers create one single product that appeals to thousands or even millions of users, which in turn means trying to uncover the problems or characteristics that all users share. This tendency was previously alluded to by Redström (2008), who observed that the conventional need to understand the user becomes confused, if not contradictory, in situations where users themselves participate in acts of personalisation and design. Thus, in responding to the requirement of mass production to conduct user-centred design, professional designers reveal a significant flaw in their expertise – no matter how well they understand the user, they will not understand him/her as well as the amateur who is designing for themselves.

New approaches to industrial design

In an idealised user-centred design process, the brief will be written in the full understanding of what the user believes to be important. The designer will work to, or perhaps challenge, the brief based on observations and discussions with consumers, who will be invited to comment on concepts and designs (Black, 2007). Co-design extends the scope of user involvement by encompassing both 'designers and people not trained in design working together in the design development process' (Sanders and Stappers, 2008: 6). However, in both methods, the designer remains in a position of power – ultimately, the degree to which the user's expertise is followed or ignored is the decision of the designer. This is a situation that a number of new approaches to design have challenged.

Sinclair and Campbell (2014) present a classification of Consumer Involvement in New Product Development (NPD), which compares these new approaches to more conventional methods (Figure 5.2). In the model, the extent to which design processes facilitate user engagement in design is mapped according to the degree to which the designer is committed to the involvement of the user.

The designer's commitment to consumer involvement in NPD refers to the degree of autonomy enjoyed by the user in the personalisation or design of products. Within Figure 5.2, moving along the horizontal axis from left to right shows an increasing opportunity for the user to affect decisions about a product's creation. On the left of the diagram, in more conventional design processes such as user-centred design and co-design, the designer employs professional expertise in order to act as an interpreter of user needs and wishes. This 'executive approach' (Oudshoorn and Pinch, 2003: 7) 'assumes a specific type of power relations . . . in which designers are represented as powerful and users as disempowered relative to the experts'. However, as the degree of user autonomy increases, a 'tipping point' is reached where these traditionally unchallenged power relationships are inverted. Products that users customise (examples of which include cars, PCs and even coffee machines) are modified with considerable freedom with respect to the product's functionality, appearance and the tools and methods used to customise them. Nonetheless, despite their very high degree of consumer involvement, such modification takes place without the designer's permission; customised products therefore exhibit a very low degree of designer's commitment. In contrast, open design products are deliberately provided in formats that are easy to modify, and ideally with instructions or tutorials as to how modification can be carried out. The new approaches to design therefore require that the designer no longer acts as an interpreter of needs, but instead as a facilitator (Siu, 2003) of the consumer's desire to personalise products to better address his/her own requirements. Clearly, in such circumstances not only has the nature of the designer's relationship with the user changed, but also the way in which a designer's own work is conventionally understood. Designers working within processes on the right of the diagram will have thus transferred considerable responsibility for a product's final manifestation, relying instead on the expertise of the user to create a fully resolved product.

As well as user involvement in NPD as a result of the designer's commitment, Sinclair and Campbell's (2014) classification also illustrates the effectiveness of

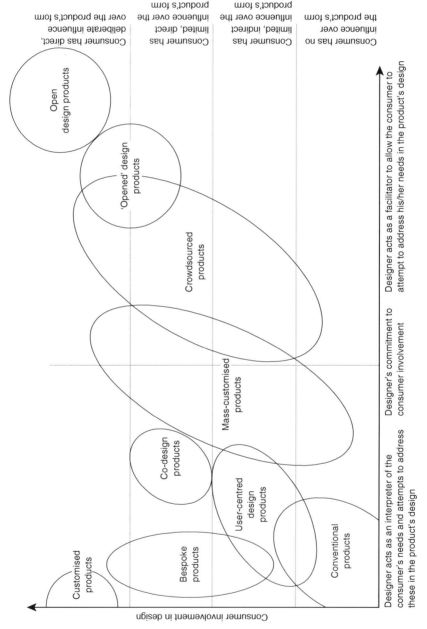

Figure 5.2 A classification of consumer involvement in New Product Development.

Source: Matt Sinclair.

user involvement with regard to the creation of unique products. Existing models of NPD (e.g. Ulrich and Eppinger, 1995; Perks et al., 2005) divide the process into phases, summarised as Conception, Specification, Design and Manufacture. Depending on the design method involved, a user may exert influence in any of these phases, thus approaches to design in which a user is involved in these phases naturally provide him/her with more effective means of influencing the final, manufactured product. The vertical axis of consumer involvement is therefore divided into four regions corresponding to an increasing influence over the product's form, whether for aesthetic, ergonomic or functional purposes. The first region represents the lowest level of consumer involvement, and corresponds to most conventional models of design within NPD. In this region consumers have no possibility of exerting direct influence over a product's design. At the second level the consumer may exercise indirect influence over product form. In a user-centred design process this influence is limited to interactions with the product's designer, who uses their professional expertise to judge the extent to which those interactions should determine the object's design. Alternatively, as part of a mass-customisation process, influence over a product's form (usually its size) will indirectly result from requirements of fit. It is at the third level of involvement that the consumer begins to directly influence product form. In the case of a co-design or bespoke design process, this will again be mediated through the designer's expertise, but in a mass-customisation process the designer will have no veto on the final outcome: instead, the user will be limited by the number and type of components available. It is only at the fourth level of user involvement that opportunities for influence over a product's three-dimensional form are manifested. At this level user influence is both deliberate and unmediated: form can be modified and defined without the approval of the designer and without the constraints imposed by predetermined modules or components. This is not to suggest that no constraints exist – a consumer-designed object must take account of materials and production realities in the same way that a professionally designed object must. In fact, the ability of the designer to provide the user with creative freedom, within pre-existing constraints, will in future be one of the criteria that distinguish professional expertise from amateur, as discussed at the conclusion of this chapter.

Mass customisation

The approaches in which designers facilitate the most effective engagement in NPD, mass customisation, crowdsourcing, opened design and open design, appear to the right of Figure 5.2. Mass-customised products are those whose design and specification are modified with direct consumer input, usually through online configuration tools (von Hippel and Katz, 2002; Piller, 2005; Franke et al., 2010). The concept was first described by Stan Davis (1987), who envisaged a future where the concept of mass production for mass markets was replaced by one in which every customer could have goods and services tailored to their individual needs and wishes. This concept was substantially

100 *Matt Sinclair*

elaborated by Pine (1993) in *Mass Customization: The New Frontier in Business Competition*, and later defined by Kaplan and Haenlein (2006: 176–177) as 'a strategy that creates value by some form of company–customer interaction at the fabrication/assembly stage of the operations level to create customized products with production cost and monetary price similar to those of mass-produced products'. Typically, this will involve the selection of features from a pre-determined menu, to create a personalised product that more accurately meets the consumer's needs than a standard offering. NIKEiD is one of the best known and most successful examples, reportedly generating more than $100 million in sales in 2009 (Wong, 2010). In recent years, however, a new class of mass customisation toolkit has begun to appear; these configurators do not rely on the choice or arrangement of modules, but instead allow the precise manipulation of a product's form. This 'fine grain' control relies on two factors: (1) a parametric design interface (Hermans and Stolterman, 2012) as part of the toolkit; and (2) the use of digital fabrication technologies, in particular 3D printing, to produce the user-customised part.

An example of this new class of toolkit is the Cell Cycle configurator by Nervous System (Figure 5.3), a design studio creating jewellery and housewares that specialises in the use of generative design – software algorithms that create forms based on both user input and the interaction of the form with itself (Rahim, 2009). Generative design typically produces naturalistic forms, a

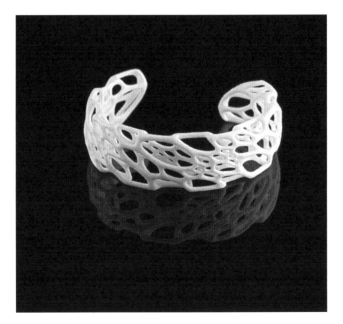

Figure 5.3 Bone Cuff in laser sintered nylon, created using the Cell Cycle configurator.

Source: Image by permission of Nervous System.

fact reflected in names given to some Nervous System products: for example, Algae, Ammonite, Dendrite and Xylem. Cell Cycle enables users to create jewellery items such as rings and bracelets via an on-screen model, which can be rotated and viewed from different angles.

On opening the configurator, the user is presented with a menu divided into three main operations. The first operation, presented in the menu to the left of the screen, allows the user to specify the type of product, the number of holes (cells), the edge style and whether the item has one or two layers. The second operation at the bottom of the screen provides fine grain control, allowing the product's profile to be twisted or 'morphed', and cells to be joined or divided. Finally, the toolkit provides a choice of materials including laser sintered nylon or precious metals, and the displayed price is continually updated according to the user's design decisions. By allowing the user control over certain parameters pre-determined by the designer, and by updating the image of the model as the user manipulates its form, a significant degree of control over the product's final design is transferred to the user. Nonetheless, the Cell Cycle configurator exhibits a very carefully considered solution space, and it is difficult to imagine a product designed within the system that would not display a strong sense of the designer's intended aesthetic. In addition, and crucial to the success of the toolkit, the limits set within it ensure that the consumer designed product is manufacturable – for example, the minimum material thickness for a piece manufactured in silver is 0.9 mm, but this specification automatically updates to 1.2 mm if nylon is selected instead. As such, Cell Cycle can be considered an early example of the potential for designers to enable user expertise in the final design of products.

Crowdsourcing

Crowdsourced products are those whose definition, specification and design occur with multiple direct consumer inputs. Kleeman et al. (2008) identify seven types of crowdsourcing, of which two – participation of consumers in product development and configuration, and product design – are relevant to this discussion. A crowdsourcing exercise will begin with an 'open call' for the submission of solutions to a problem (Howe, 2006a). Submitted solutions will then be considered by the 'crowd' with the aim of generating consensus around a popular solution that will be further developed for manufacture (Howe, 2006b). Crowdsourcing has attracted considerable attention within the field of graphic design, with many designers opposing a model that they see as devaluing their work (Howe, 2009) and organisations such as the American Institute for Graphic Arts (AIGA) taking positions that discourage members from engaging in the practice. However tangible, manufactured goods often require significantly greater interaction between designers and production engineers than graphic design projects, and so crowdsourcing within NPD is a much rarer phenomenon. Where it does occur, projects can exhibit a number of similarities to co-design, in that the user-designer will be invited

102 *Matt Sinclair*

to collaborate with an in-house team of product developers. Importantly however, in a crowdsourced project the design concept will have originated from the consumer alone, whereas in a co-design exercise it will more likely have been conceived by a designer working with the consumer.

Perhaps the best known example of crowdsourced NPD is the Rally Fighter by Local Motors (Figure 5.4). Founded in 2007, Local Motors utilises crowdsourcing as a way of generating, selecting and developing designs for low production-volume cars, which are then assembled (by their owners) in micro-factories under the supervision of Local Motors engineers.

The first commercially available vehicle, the Rally Fighter, was conceived by Sangho Kim, a student at Art Center College of Design in California, whose design was judged (by other members of the Local Motors 'crowd') to be the best entrant to a competition to design an off-road (but street-legal) vehicle. Kim's design was then developed in response to both engineering constraints and feedback from the crowd. At the same time, other members competed and submitted designs for elements of the car, for example, the interior was designed by Mihai Panaitescu, a Romanian designer; side vents were designed by Laurent Raphael from Switzerland; and new graphic treatments were developed by Derek Salgado from Mexico (Rogers, 2010). Performance and safety-critical elements such as the chassis, engine and transmission were designed and sourced by Local Motors engineers (Anderson, 2010). Thus, a collaborative model of crowdsourcing allowed the expertise of interested users

Figure 5.4 Rally Fighter.

Source: Image by permission of Local Motors Inc.

to select a design, influence the way the design was developed, and fed into the functional specification, whilst at the same time utilising the professional expertise of automotive design engineers to ensure the vehicle functioned reliably and conformed to legal and regulatory requirements. In so doing, the Rally Fighter was designed and manufactured five times faster than the industry standard (Rogers, 2010). The vehicle, as a product that resulted from a crowdsourced design process, is a single design, much like that which would result from a traditional design process. However, Local Motors also provides files for many of the car's parts, which can be freely downloaded and used to modify or improve the design: the Rally Fighter therefore also contains some of the characteristics of further new design approaches.

Open design

Open design is an approach, closely related to open source, defined as 'the free revealing of information on a new design with the intention of collaborative development of a single design or a limited number of related designs for market or nonmarket exploitation' (Raasch et al., 2009: 383). It has recently received significant attention following the publication of *Open Design Now* (van Abel et al., 2011), a collection of essays documenting the history, practice and future direction of open design. Katz (2011: 63) characterises open design as follows:

> A design is an open design if it bears four freedoms. One: The freedom to use the design, including making items based on it, for any purpose. Two: The freedom to study how the design works, and change it to make it do what you wish. Three: The freedom to redistribute copies of the design so you can help your neighbour. Four: The freedom to distribute copies of your modified versions of the design to others so the whole community can benefit from your changes. Access to the design documents is a precondition for these freedoms.

Open design products are those whose IP rights have been relaxed by the owner so that the consumer is free to modify all aspects of the product, from concept and specification through to design and manufacture. Subsequent IP rights will be determined by the terms of the licence under which the design is made available: whilst some impose no restrictions, others require that derivative works must be offered under the same terms (see, for example, the 'Attribution-Share-Alike' licence from Creative Commons). A product that has gained notoriety in recent years, as an example of the potentially far-reaching consequences of openly sharing designs, is the 3D-printed Liberator gun, manufactured by Defense Distributed, and also referred to as the 'Wikiweapon'.

The passions generated by the issue of gun control and the rights of American citizens as a result of the 2nd Amendment,[1] means that it has often been difficult to separate the arguments surrounding the Liberator project from what it demonstrates about open design and digital fabrication. Even before the gun was first manufactured, the project aroused controversy when it was taken off the crowdfunding site Indiegogo (for violating the terms of service), an act quickly followed by Stratasys (the manufacturer of the 3D printer that Defense Distributed was leasing), which repossessed its machine (Defense Distributed, 2014). Nonetheless, Cody Wilson, co-founder of Defense Distributed, denies that the company is trying to make a 2nd Amendment argument, instead insisting that, 'The basic idea is to take a technology, play futurist, and surprise people' (Dillow, 2012).

In terms of what the Liberator reveals about the future of design and its relationship to digital fabrication, the project has three lessons. First, the argument that design in the fullest sense of the word cannot be practised by non-professionals is shown to be false. Wilson is not a designer or an engineer (he studied law at the University of Texas), but in creating the Liberator he was able to act as both. The design of the Liberator is far from a simple translation of an existing design – it uses two spiral springs that cock the trigger spring into position, a removable barrel and a body capable of withstanding the forces generated by the exploding round, all made from laser-sintered plastic. Numerous prototypes were tested and part design refined before a working product was achieved (Atherton, 2013a); a product whose appearance and material structure are unlike any gun previously made. Second, the distributive power of the Internet means that a design that is sufficiently compelling to users will proliferate uncontrollably. Four days after Defense Distributed made the CAD files for the Liberator freely available, the US State Department requested the files were removed, citing possible violation of trade controls regarding the export of firearms (Preston, 2013), yet by that time the files had been downloaded more than 100,000 times (Atherton, 2013b). And finally, the four freedoms of open design mean that any design must be considered a prototype of a subsequent design that modifies it. Within open design, the notion of a 'finished' product is redundant. The original Liberator gun fired only one shot, requiring the barrel to be changed before it could be re-fired, leading critics to dismiss it as expensive and impractical. Less than two weeks later however, news emerged of a new version, produced using a 3D printing technology (fused deposition modelling) much cheaper than the original laser-sintered version, which was capable of firing eight shots (Greenberg, 2013). Furthermore, the new barrel incorporated rifling, enabling the design to comply with some regulations of the National Firearms Act, which govern improvised weapons.

Opened design

Despite the precision of Katz's definition of open design, examples of NPD which do not fully embrace the four freedoms have nonetheless been described as open design. Tooze et al. (2014: 538) note that open design is 'a catchall term for various . . . design and making activities', including those in which either contributions or solutions are not completely open. In particular, products that allow modification but that restrict distribution (for example) cannot be classed as open design under the strict conditions of Katz's definition. For this reason, Sinclair and Campbell (2014) introduce a new term, 'opened design', to describe products whose IP rights have been relaxed by the owner, but to a lesser degree than with open design. Typically, these rights provide for the modification of an existing design and distribution of the resultant product, but with subsequent IP rights accruing to the original owner.

One designer who has been experimenting with opened design strategies for a number of years is Ronen Kadushin (though confusingly, Kadushin refers to his work as open design). First published in 2005, his open design manifesto celebrates the new opportunities presented by CAD files, CNC machining, and the power of the Internet to distribute and share designs (Kadushin, 2010). The ability of interested users to modify, personalise and re-imagine the original design is also fundamental to the work. Speaking of his Hack Chair (Figure 5.5) design Kadushin (2011, quoted in Troxler 2011) explains:

> If you want to make it more comfortable, it's an open design. Go ahead, make it comfortable, add your nice round radiuses . . . I could have designed it to be straight and rounded and nice, but I chose not to . . . This is my choice; you have other choices, and you can have other points of view.

Figure 5.5 Hack Chair.

Source: Image by permission of Ronen Kadushin. Photography: Chanan Strauss.

Visitors to Kadushin's website are able to download, for free, the designs for approximately 30 products, which are supplied as DXF files. These can be opened using 2D drawing software such as Adobe Illustrator, consumer-oriented 3D modelling software such as SketchUp, or professional-level 3D CAD software such as Solidworks. Kadushin's designs therefore demand that the amateur designer possesses a certain level of expertise in the tools required for modification or re-design, in the same way that Wilson's Liberator does.

Also supplied with the DXF files are a set of instructions for how to make the product, including suggestions for material types and thicknesses (the majority of designs are intended to be laser cut, then hand-bent into shape). Kadushin thus satisfies freedoms 1 and 2 of Katz's definition above, and the ability to pass on the DXF files to others satisfies freedom 3. However, a condition of sharing any new design is that it is redistributed under a Creative Commons 'Attribution-Non Commercial-Share Alike' (By-NC-SA) licence, which prohibits commercial uses. Kadushin is up-front about the reasons for this: 'I am saying: please copy. But if you want to make a business out of it, then please call me and we'll discuss royalties. It is my intellectual property, after all' (Kadushin, 2011, cited in Troxler, 2011: 111), and it may reasonably be argued that for a designer trying to make a living from their work, this is the most sensible option to take. Nonetheless, the By-NC-SA licence is one of the more restrictive Creative Commons licences, and does not satisfy the requirements for approval as a Free Cultural Work (Creative Commons, 2014). It also fails to fully satisfy the fourth of Katz's freedoms, in that it places restrictions on the redistribution of modified designs. Kadushin's work therefore raises questions about the extent to which truly open design presents a viable option for those who wish to make a profession from design.

What will designers do when everyone can be a designer?

It is often tempting, when imagining the future, to predict that new technologies will displace and make redundant previously established ways of doing things. The reality is usually much more nuanced, with new technologies being used in different ways, many of them previously unpredicted, often alongside the old technologies they were supposed to usurp. To state that in future, digital fabrication will fundamentally change all industrial design practice, is likely to prove a reckless claim. Mass production technologies will continue to be best suited for products where identical, standardised, parts are required; this will include both 'low-value' items such as packaging, but also high-value items such as components that require extensive performance testing, which it might be unfeasible to undertake for individually designed parts. It is also likely that mass production and digital fabrication technologies will be combined to create hybrid production processes, utilising the particular advantages of each system. What may be more accurate to say, therefore, is that in future the job of *some* designers will be very different to their job today. The opportunities that digital fabrication presents for the manufacture of items in low volume, perhaps in tens or hundreds of units, means that some designers will specialise in the design of niche products, for small markets, in the manner suggested by Aldersey-Williams (2011). Others will design products requiring user inputs via toolkits enabled by 3D printing and other digital fabrication technologies, using their expertise whilst making decisions about which elements of a product's design should be changeable and which should be constrained.

Much of the discussion surrounding digital fabrication and its impact on the work that designers do has emphasised the expertise of the amateur, whether alone or as part of a crowd, and the opportunities that are presented by access to the means of production. As Anderson (2010) writes:

> The tools of factory production, from electronics assembly to 3-D printing, are now available to individuals, in batches as small as a single unit. Anybody with an idea and a little expertise . . . can become a virtual micro-factory, able to design and sell goods without any infrastructure or even inventory.
>
> (p. 63)

This ability to act as designer and manufacturer, without the need to sell an idea to a company with the financial might to buy access to mass production technology, is crucial to an understanding of the future of design, and is fundamental to what makes that future different from the past. But what Anderson pays less attention to is the nature of the expertise required to engage with this future. In the four approaches to design outlined above, all require significant expertise in order for a beautiful, functioning object to result from the process. In only one of these, open design, is that expertise the sole domain of the user. In future mass-customisation scenarios, professional expertise will continue to be required to imagine the object, to define the parameters of the solution space (Franke and Piller, 2004) such that function, safety, brand image, cost, etc. are reconciled with the user's designs. In addition, a new type of design specialism will require the expertise to direct the user's interactions with the customisation toolkit such that the experience is one that they wish to repeat. In crowdsourced NPD projects, professional expertise will be required for the same reasons, except the design of the customisation toolkit will be replaced with the design of the competition that users enter. Similarly, professional expertise will again be required in open design situations, where the design of the toolkit and the design of the competition will be replaced by the design of the instructions for modification and production. In all three situations the user will then apply their own expertise in modifying and finishing the design, ensuring the resulting product is one that best fits their requirements. Thus, the future of design using these methods is one of collaboration between the expertise of the professional and amateur.

Mass customisation, crowdsourcing and open design all, to varying extents, constrain the ability of the user to modify the original design. This allows brands and manufacturers to retain a degree of control over the manifestation of the design of products that users engage with. Yet, these constraints also offer significant advantages to the consumer, by simplifying design and manufacturing tasks whilst at the same time setting limits on what such tasks can achieve. A consumer engaging with a brand that offers the ability to personalise its products will also benefit from assurances of safety, compliance with trade standards and consumer law, compatibility with other products where required, and, in some circumstances, a manufacturer's warranty. Such assurances may be worth little to the user whose knowledge of, and interest in, a particular product is sufficient to enable him/her to engage in open design. For a user with less time or expertise, who instead wants to personalise an existing product such that it better suits their requirements, design spaces that are less open will be more appropriate. It is therefore apparent that in many, and perhaps most, situations it will be the restraints placed on the user that enable them to engage in design.

Open design is exceptional, in that it does not require the expertise of the professional designer. But this does not mean that that the expertise required of the designer is any less; rather it requires that the expertise of the amateur is equal to that of the professional. In the case of the Liberator gun, as Wilson points out, 'These aren't the only gun files on the internet . . . there's CNC gun files all over . . . There are files out there to make metal gun components or various dangerous things' (Atherton, 2013b). However, in these instances, designing and manufacturing a working gun requires expertise and skill using numerous workshop tools and machines. In contrast, the user who downloaded files of the Liberator and printed them without making modifications would not be acting as a designer; instead, they would be acting merely as a consumer of a product created as a result of an open design process. To re-design the gun in a way that made it cheaper and more reliable, as described above, required significant expertise both in the design and construction of guns, and the CAD software needed to modify the original part files.

The power of the Liberator as a means of drawing attention to the possibilities of open design undoubtedly lies in its ability – as a gun – to arouse strong passions. This, in turn, leads to interesting questions regarding the ethics of encouraging, or expecting, users to engage in design and personalisation. In *Moralizing Technology*, Verbeek (2011: 64) considers the question of whether artefacts have morality, and concludes that moral agency lies in an assembly of the user and the object: 'A gun is not a mere instrument, a medium for the free will of human beings . . . the gun and the man form a new entity, and this entity does the shooting'.

The composition of this new entity is particularly relevant to the consideration of expertise amongst those engaged in design. Many hobbyists use legally available parts to build guns, and books with titles such as *Home Workshop Prototype Firearms* (Holmes, 1994) are available in both paperback and Kindle formats from Amazon. In Verbeek's construction of the gun and the man as a new entity, there is little difference between a 3D-printed Liberator capable of firing a single shot, and a hand-crafted replica duelling pistol made by an expert amateur gunsmith. But what appears to have caused most concern amongst opponents of the

Liberator project is not that it is legal for amateurs to make their own firearms, but rather that distribution of the CAD files might allow someone with little expertise to make a gun. Arguing from such a position, it appears the morality of the gun-man entity is modified by the expertise of the person making the gun. This attitude – that workshop proficiency is a good indicator of suitability to own a gun – is somewhat peculiar. Yet, in banning the distribution of the CAD files needed to manufacture the Liberator, it is nonetheless one that US legislators appear to endorse. The pervasiveness of such an idea, when applied to less contentious products than guns, may determine the speed at which a future of consumer-designers arrives.

When everyone can be a designer, there will not just be one future for designers, but a number of different ones. Some designers will work in ways that appear very similar to designers today, working to briefs set by clients to create products that are mass produced. Others will be employed by brands to design unfinished products that users will personalise in the knowledge that the final design will be safe and reliable, or that utilise digital fabrication technologies to enable niche products in low-volume production runs. Designers employed by brands that engage in crowdsourcing will work in collaboration with users to bring products to production. And some people will practise design with a high degree of expertise, even though they may not be trained and it may not be their full-time job. Perhaps the only certainty is that when the means of design and production are placed in the hands of users, they will use them in ways we cannot currently anticipate.

Note

1 The Second Amendment of the United States Constitution (the so-called 'Right to Bear Arms') reads: 'A well regulated Militia, being necessary to the security of a free State, the right of the people to keep and bear Arms, shall not be infringed'.

References

van Abel, B., Evers, L., Klaassen, R. and Troxler, P. (eds) (2011) *Open design now*, Amsterdam, The Netherlands: BIS.

Aldersey-Williams, H. (2011) *The new tin ear: manufacturing, materials and the rise of the user–maker*, London: RSA.

Anderson, C. (2010) Atoms are the new bits, *Wired*, 18(2) (February), 63.

Atherton, K. D. (2013a) How the world's first 3-D printed gun works, *Popular Science* [online], available from: http://www.popsci.com/technology/article/2013-05/worlds-first-fully-3-d-printed-gun-here [accessed 7 December 2014].

Atherton, K. D. (2013b) Defense Distributed's Cody Wilson on being told to remove 3-D printed gun plans: 'we win', *Popular Science* [online], available from: http://www.popsci.com/technology/article/2013-05/defense-distributeds-cody-wilson-takedown-notice-we-win [accessed 7 December 2014].

Bernabei, R. and Power, J. (2013) Designing together: end-user collaboration in designing a personalised product, in *Proceedings of the 10th European Academy of Design Conference*, 17–19 April, Gothenburg, Sweden.

Binder, T., Brandt, E. and Gregory, J. (2008) Design participation(-s) – a creative commons for ongoing change, *CoDesign*, 4(2), 79–83.

Black, A. (2007) *User-centred design* [online], Design Council, available from: http://web.archive.org/web/20071021042720/http://www.design-council.org.uk/en/About-Design/Design-Techniques/User-centred-design-/ [accessed 7 December 2014].

Bonanni, L. A., Parkes, A. J. and Ishii, H. (2008) Future craft: how digital media is transforming product design, in *Proceedings of the 2008 Conference on Human Factors in Computing Systems*, CHI 2008, April 5–10, Florence, Italy.

Campbell, R. I., Hague, R., Sener, B. and Wormald, P. (2003) The potential for the bespoke industrial designer, *The Design Journal*, 6(3), 24–34.

Caplan, R. (ed.) (1969) *Design in America: selected work by members of the Industrial Designers Society of America*, New York: McGraw-Hill.

Creative Commons (2014) *Understanding free cultural works* [online], available from: http://creativecommons.org/freeworks [accessed 7 December 2014].

Davis, S. (1987) *Future perfect*, Reading, MA: Addison-Wesley.

Defense Distributed (2014) *DD history* [online], available from: https://defdist.org/dd-history/ [accessed 7 December 2014].

Design Council (2008) Ten ways you can profit from design, *Design Council Magazine*, Issue 5, Autumn 2008, 12–15.

Design Council (2010) *Introducing product design* [online], available from: http://web.archive.org/web/20130827124810/http://www.designcouncil.org.uk/about-design/Types-of-design/Product-design/Introducing-product-design/ [accessed 7 December 2014].

Dillow, C. (2012) Q+A: Cody Wilson of the Wiki weapon project on the 3-D printed future of firearms, *Popular Science* [online], available from: http://www.popsci.com/technology/article/2012-12/qa-cody-wilson-wiki-weapons-project-3-d-printed-future-firearms [accessed 7 December 2014].

Duffy, J. and Keen, A. (2006) Can anyone be a designer? *Fast Company*, Issue 109, October 2006, 116.

Fiell, C. and Fiell, P. (2003) *Industrial design A–Z*, Köln: Taschen.

Fischer, G. (2002) Beyond 'couch potatoes': from consumers to designers and active contributors, *First Monday*, 7(12), available from: http://firstmonday.org/ojs/index.php/fm/article/view/1010/931 [accessed 7 December 2014].

Franke, N. and Piller, F. (2004) Value creation by toolkits for user innovation and design: the case of the watch market, *The Journal of Product Innovation Management*, 21, 401–415.

Franke, N., Schreier, M. and Kaiser, U. (2010) The 'I designed it myself' effect in mass customization, *Management Science*, 56(1), 125–140.

Goodman-Deane, J., Langdon, P. and Clarkson, J. (2010) Key influences on the user-centred design process, *Journal of Engineering Design*, 21(2–3), 345–373.

Greenberg, A. (2013) $25 gun created with cheap 3D printer fires nine shots (video), *Forbes* [online], available from: http://www.forbes.com/sites/andygreenberg/2013/05/20/25-gun-created-with-cheap-3d-printer-fires-nine-shots-video/ [accessed 7 December 2014].

Hermans, G. and Stolterman, E. (2012) Exploring parametric design: consumer customization of an everyday object, *in Leading Innovation through Design: Proceedings of the DMI 2012 International Research Conference*, 1–4 July, Chulalongkorn University, Bangkok, Thailand.

von Hippel, E. and Katz, R. (2002) Shifting innovation to users via toolkits, *Management Science*, 48(7), 821–833.
Holmes, B. (1994) *Home workshop prototype firearms: how to design, build and sell your own small arms*, Boulder, CO: Paladin Press.
Howe, J. (2006a) *Crowdsourcing: a definition* [online], available from: http://www.crowdsourcing.com/cs/2006/06/crowdsourcing_a.html [accessed 7 December 2014].
Howe, J. (2006b) The rise of crowdsourcing, *Wired* [online], available from: http://www.wired.com/wired/archive/14.06/crowds_pr.html [accessed 7 December 2014].
Howe, J. (2009) Is crowdsourcing evil? The design community weighs in, *Wired* [online], available from: http://www.wired.com/2009/03/is-crowdsourcin/ [accessed 7 December 2014].
IDSA (2014) *What is industrial design?* [online], available from: http://www.idsa.org/what-is-industrial-design [accessed 7 December 2014].
Kadushin, R. (2010) *Open design manifesto* [online], available from: http://www.ronen-kadushin.com/files/4613/4530/1263/Open_Design_Manifesto-Ronen_Kadushin_.pdf [accessed 7 December 2014].
Kadushin, R. (2011) Quoted in Troxler, P. (2011) The beginning of a beginning of the beginning of a trend, in B. van Abel, L. Evers, R. Klaassen and P. Troxler (eds), *Open design now*, Amsterdam, The Netherlands: BIS.
Kaplan, A. and Haenlein, M. (2006) Towards a parsimonious definition of traditional and electronic mass customization, *Journal of Product Innovation Management*, 23(2), 168–182.
Katz, A. (2011) Authors and owners, in B. van Abel, L. Evers, R. Klaassen and P. Troxler (eds), *Open design now*, Amsterdam, The Netherlands: BIS, p. 63.
Kleeman, F., Voß, G. G. and Rieder, K. (2008) Un(der)paid innovators: the commercial utilization of consumer work through crowdsourcing, *Science, Technology and Innovation Studies*, 4(1), 5–26.
Mansour, S. and Hague, R. (2003) Impact of rapid manufacturing on design for manufacture for injection moulding, in *Proceedings of the Institute of Mechanical Engineers, Part B, Journal of Mechanical Engineering Science*, 217(4), 453–461.
McDermott, C. (2007) *Design: the key concepts*, London: Routledge.
Merchant, N. (2013) *Onlyness: Nilofer Merchant at TEDxHouston 2012* [online], available at https://www.youtube.com/watch?v=h-8MXo-tJoQ [accessed 8 December 2014].
McGuirk, J. (2009) Fabbers, dabblers and microstars, *Icon*, Issue 73, 14.08.2009, 48–52.
Mugge, R., Schoormans, J. P. L. and Hendrik, N. J. (2009) Emotional bonding with personalised products, *Journal of Engineering Design*, 20(5), 467–476.
Norman, D. (2004) *Emotional design*, New York: Basic Books.
Oudshoorn, N. and Pinch, T. (2003) How users and non-users matter, in N. Oudshoorn and T. Pinch (eds), *How users matter*, Cambridge, MA: MIT Press, p. 7.
Perks, H., Cooper, R. and Jones, C. (2005) Characterizing the role of design in new product development: an empirically derived taxonomy, *Journal of Product Innovation Management*, 22(2), 111–127.
Piller, F. (2005) Mass customization: reflections on the state of the concept, *International Journal of Flexible Manufacturing* Systems, 16(4), 313–334.
Pine II, B. J. (1993) *Mass customization: the new frontier in business competition*, Boston, MA: Harvard Business School Press.
Preston, J. (2013) Printable-gun instructions spread online after state dept. orders their removal, *New York Times*, 10 May 2013.

Raasch, C., Herstatt, C. and Balka, K. (2009) On the open design of tangible goods, *R&D Management*, 39(4), 382–393.

Rahim, A. (2009) Uniformity and variability in architectural practice, in L. Spuybroek (ed.), *The architecture of variation*, London: Thames and Hudson, pp. 40–47.

Randall, T., Terwiesch, C. and Ulrich, K. (2003) Principles for user design of customized products, *California Management Review*, 47(4), 68–85.

Redström, J. (2008) RE:Definitions of use, *Design Studies*, 29(4), 410–423.

Risatti, H. (2006) Craft vs. design / recognition vs. understanding, *Metalsmith*, 26(2), 14–17.

Rogers, J. (2010) Can a community design a car? *The Do Lectures* [online], available from: http://www.thedolectures.com/jay-rogers-can-a-community-design-a-car#.VIHS6zGsV8E [accessed 7 December 2014].

Sanders, E. B.-N. and Stappers, P. J. (2008) Co-creation and the new landscapes of design, *CoDesign*, 4(1), 5–18.

Sinclair, M. and Campbell, R. I. (2014) A classification of consumer involvement in new product development, in *Proceedings of DRS 2014. Design's Big Debates: Pushing the Boundaries of Design Research*, 16–19 June 2014, Umeå University, Sweden, pp. 1582–1598.

Siu, K. W. M. (2003) Users' creative responses and designers' roles, *Design Issues*, 19(2), 64–73.

Steen, M. (2011) Tensions in human-centred design, *CoDesign*, 7(1), 45–60.

Tonkinwise, C. (2005) Is design finished? Dematerialisation and changing things, *Design Philosophy Papers*, 3(2), 99–117.

Tooze, J., Baurley, S., Phillips, R., Smith, P., Foote, E. and Silve, S. (2014) Open design: contributions, solutions, processes and projects, *The Design Journal*, 17(4), 538–559.

Troxler, P. (2010) The beginning of a beginning of the beginning of a trend, in B. van Abel, L. Evers, R. Klaassen and P. Troxler (eds), *Open design now*, Amsterdam, The Netherlands: BIS.

Ulrich, K. and Eppinger, S. (1995) *Product design and development*, 5th edn. New York: McGraw-Hill.

Ulwick, A. W. (2002) Turn consumer input into innovation, *Harvard Business Review*, January, 92–97.

Verbeek, P.-P. (2011) *Moralizing technology: understanding and designing the morality of things*, Chicago, IL: The University of Chicago Press.

Vredenburg, K., Mao, J.-Y., Smith, P. W. and Carey, T. (2002) A survey of user-centered design practice, in *Proceedings of the SIGCHI Conference on Human Factors in Computing Systems* (CHI '02), ACM, New York.

Walker, J. (1989) *Design history and the history of design*, Eastbourne, UK: Pluto.

Wong, D. (2010), NIKEiD makes $100M+: co-creation isn't just a trend, *Huffington Post* [online], available from: http://www.huffingtonpost.com/danny-wong/nikeid-makes-100m-co-crea_b_652214.html [accessed 7 December 2014].

6 The history and application of additive manufacturing for design personalisation

Guy Bingham

Introduction

Public awareness of additive manufacturing (AM) technologies, more popularly known as 3D printing, has escalated dramatically during the last five years and it is now commonplace to see news and stories about it in the mainstream media. However, the public's appreciation of the technical limitations and implications of the technology is still quite limited – the popular perception of 'anything can be printed' is somewhat misguided. Nevertheless, this perception is part of the allure of AM and its almost magical realisation of 3D objects has ignited interest and captured the public's imagination. The increasing interest has been further solidified by the apparent accessibility of the technology and the affordability and capability of desktop 3D printing. A growing number of home, desktop systems can be purchase for a few hundred pounds and these are helping provide a new creative outlet for the emergent population of home-based 'hackers, makers and tinkerers' (MakerSpace 2015).

The accessibility and the apparent capability characteristic of AM is in stark contrast to traditional manufacturing techniques, especially those developed for mass production, such as injection moulding. Their costs and need for significant infrastructure make these industrial processes completely inaccessible to the general public. AM technologies are fundamentally different from such processes in practically every aspect. They are digital, flexible and, because they are now available as desktop systems, they are affordable. However, there are significant differences between AM technologies that can be 'industrialised' and the increasingly popular desktop 3D printers that have captured so much public interest.

What is not so apparent to the general public, and may never need to be, is the significant volume of research and development work that led to the current era of desktop 3D printing. Research in the area of AM is of long standing and can come as a surprise that the initial development work in the field started in the early 1980s, with the first working stereolithography system being produced in 1984 (Hull 1986). This was a very exciting period for the technology and in the decade after Hull's stereolithography process came alternatives like laser sintering (Deckard 1989), Fused Deposition Modelling (Crump 1992) and a host of different technologies that all allowed the digital, additive fabrication of 3D geometries. While the development of these new systems was quite quick, it initially lacked an application in production and led to their use as prototyping systems, which ultimately led to them being identified under the catch-all phrase 'Rapid Prototyping' (RP).

The term 'Rapid Prototyping' is somewhat misleading and anyone with first-hand experience of using the technology would struggle to describe it as anything near rapid. The term was developed in the 1980s by 3D Systems – the US-based company and the leader in consumer and industrial 3D printing and manufacturing – to capture the capability of the technology when directly comparing it to the alternative and established techniques of model making being used for the production of prototypes. Model making is a high-level craft but the timescale for realising intricate and detailed 3D prototypes using these skills can be measured in weeks and months. The development of RP systems reduces this to hours and days, establishing RP as the most effective process for efficient and accurate realisation of 3D physical prototypes.

Research surrounding RP has continued and concentrated on improving the accuracy, reliability and efficiency of the various technologies available and on developing effective build materials. During the mid-1990s, advances in computer-aided design (CAD) software and the general increase in desktop computing power allowed a new avenue of research to develop, specifically investigating the design potential or 'design freedom' of additive techniques (Campbell 1994; Burns 1995). The flexibility of RP was already appreciated by the design community but during this period it was realised that additive techniques could facilitate a new level of geometric freedom unimaginable from the perspective of conventional manufacturing techniques. While much has been reported on the design freedom of AM and its capability to create 'impossible' geometries, it is important to note that by definition, nothing that can be achieved is actually impossible and it is more meaningful to say that AM has the capability to create highly complex geometries that are simply impractical by any other means. Given enough time, patience and skill, many supposedly 'impossible' geometries could be made by hand but the true advantage of AM lies in its ability to realise *impractical* forms, more efficiently and repeatably, without needing great fabrication skill. However, skill has not been completely removed from the process of generating such complex and impractical geometries, rather it has been shifted from one stage of the fabrication process to another. Digital manufacturing techniques need digital inputs to generate physical outputs and it is here that high levels of skill are still required, in the operation of 3D CAD and the generation of complex 3D manufacturing data. The need for this high level of skill with CAD is often highlighted as one of the barriers preventing the wider-scale adoption of AM techniques which remains a significant area of research activity today (Hopkinson et al. 2005). However much hyped, the design freedom and its research surrounding AM have helped develop some of the core philosophies of the technology and provided important direction for its future research, development and application.

During the early 2000s, the dramatically improving accuracy, reliability, efficiency and build materials, in conjunction with the realised design freedom, led to the desire to elevate the technology from a prototyping platform into a manufacturing process. Originally named 'Rapid Manufacturing', denoting a natural progression from Rapid Prototyping, this description was quickly replaced with 'additive manufacturing', pioneered by Neil Hopkinson and Philip Dickens (Hopkinson and Dickens 2003). They proposed that the technology would eventually mature and directly compete with the established mass-manufacturing processes in terms of accuracy and the quality of products/components. They also highlighted that removing all tooling (moulds, jigs and fixtures) and any existing Design for Manufacture (DfM) constraints (such as draft angles, part extraction issues) that plague all established mass production techniques, would allow the economic manufacture of a single unit, or 'n = 1' as the engineers like to say. This simple but important principle had significant implications for product/engineering design because it means that there are no longer any geometric restrictions and forms can be readily achieved at almost any level of complexity. It also means that each object manufactured can be different from all the others, with little or no cost implications – the complete opposite of the constraints on conventional mass production. The effects of this shift to being able to cost-effectively produce single, bespoke products or components has prompted some significant work in the area of AM-based customisation and personalisation research.

The exact definitions or distinctions between customisation and personalisation have already received significant coverage (e.g. Sunikka and Bragge 2012) and a topic of enlightened discussion within this book. The majority of existing work using AM almost definitively falls within the sphere of personalisation and the creation of bespoke, one-off, person-specific, single user examples. However, more recent work has also explored the idea of 'mass-personalisation' and promoted the application of the technology for the production of mass-produced personalised products. Mass-personalisation raises some interesting research questions and challenges, most notably the requirement to engage masses of users who can personalise a product or an artefact. There are, however, issues surrounding the ownership of design rights and the attribution of liability (Moultrie and Bibb 2015). Design research supporting the concept (e.g. Franke et al. 2010; Bernabei and Power 2013) is tackling these concerns, investigating the opportunities for 'co-design' through direct end-user engagement within the design process.

Indeed, the ongoing research and development within this field is growing and leads to an interesting question – is AM the future enabler of mass-personalisation? In order to address that particular question, it is important to document some of the previous, pivotal developments and applications of the technology within personalisation, which this chapter attempts to achieve. The examples presented here are by no means exhaustive but have been specifically selected by the author to help highlight both the scope and capability of AM technologies to deliver customised and personalised artefacts. To date, the majority of these examples lie with the Medical and Consumer application markets and it is here the impact of the technology for the creation of bespoke, one-off, person-specific artefacts can be truly demonstrated.

Medical AM personalisation

Some of the most well-known and celebrated examples of AM-based personalisation lie within the medical healthcare sector. Medical professionals, designers and engineers were some of the first to recognise the huge potential of AM techniques for the manufacture of personalised medical devices and implants. Since the late 1990s, they used the design freedom and flexibility of the manufacturing techniques to quickly and cost-effectively produce personalised geometry bespoke to the user. Interestingly, within medical applications, personalisation is perceived as vital to the functional performance of the object in question. A personalised medical product (or component) is often unseen or covert in its application and provides no self-expression by the user. There are numerous applications of AM within the medical healthcare sector, including dental implants/aligners, personalised implants and prosthetics, which are described below. However, one of the very first personalised, bestselling AM medical products that is probably the least well known is hearing aids (Figure 6.1).

Personalised hearing aids

Hearing-aid manufacturers have been engaged in the production of personalised products for many years. Much like finger prints, everyone's ear canal is unique, thus personalisation is a necessity. Prior to the adoption of AM, the manufacturing process often required several medical consultations and impressions of the inner ear to be taken for the production of moulds. This would be followed by a prolonged fabrication process to ensure correct fitting of final hearing aids and appropriate comfort to the user. While effective, the process was very time consuming and required numerous stages of fabrication with high levels of skill. With AM coming to light, this process was revolutionised dramatically, greatly reducing the time, skill and costs involved. However, the introduction of a digital manufacturing technique also requires the introduction and adoption of commentary and necessary technologies like 3D scanning and CAD, changing what was fundamentally a physical/analogue manufacturing process into a largely digital one. The stages of production can be summarised as follows:

- The customer/patient has a medical consultation where a wax impression of the inner ear is taken.
- The wax impression is 3D scanned and converted into 3D CAD data of the hearing aid shell.
- The 3D CAD data is then used to virtually construct the complete hearing aid by checking clearance for all necessary componentry.

- The 3D CAD data of the shell is then 3D printed, cured and finished to the required level.
- The 3D-printed shell is then fitted with the necessary componentry and final assembly is completed.

Hearing aids are a relatively simple but extremely effective application of AM and it may surprise most people that 99 per cent of all hearing aids are now manufactured using some form of AM technology. It is also reported that up to 10,000,000 pairs of AM hearing aids are being worn today by people all over the world and therefore this manufacturing process represents the largest implementation of personalisation ever recorded.

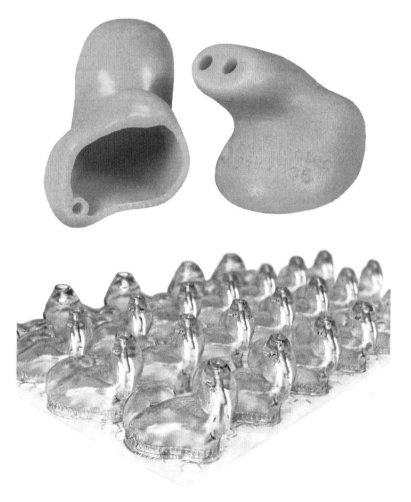

Figure 6.1 Personalised AM hearing aids.
Source: Courtesy of EnvisionTEC.

118 Guy Bingham

Personalised orthodontic aligners

Another highly successful implementation of AM-based personalisation are orthodontic aligners and specifically the work completed by Invisalign (Invisalign 2015). The system they developed involves the manufacture of a series (typically 13–52) of clear orthodontic aligners that eventually culminates in a straightened set of teeth for the patient (Figure 6.2). Usually, the process can take between six months and two years and normally requires a revised aligner to be worn every fortnight. The Invisalign system is supported by a very sophisticated 3D CAD platform that models the required movement of the teeth over the period of treatment until the final intended outcome is realised. Invisalign were very early adopters of Stereolithography (SL) technology and recognised its design freedom and flexibility that could be very successfully applied to manufacture all the subtly different aligners a patient would require over the course of their treatment. Unlike the example of hearing aids, where AM is specifically used to create the final outer shell, Invisalign use AM technology to create the intermediate tooling (mould) that allows the manufacture of the final aligners from thermo-formed clear thermoplastic. To date, Invisalign claim to have treated more than three million people, which represents another hugely successful implementation of AM-based personalisation.

Figure 6.2 Invisalign orthodontic aligner.
Source: Courtesy of Align Technology Inc.

Personalised medical implants

Other notable examples of personalisation within the medical field include those of implants and prostheses. Similar to hearing aids, the personalisation of these products existed long before the development and subsequent application of AM technologies. However, the level of personalisation was less sophisticated and the frequency of its implementation was on a much smaller scale. Prior to the introduction of AM, standardised medical implants would often be modified by the surgeons during the medical procedure itself to ensure an appropriate fit to the patient. The application of more complex or bespoke implants would often require a prolonged fabrication process prior to any surgery and then be subjected to a potentially lengthy medical validation process preceding any form of implantation. The introduction of AM techniques significantly reduced the cost and timescales involved in production of medical implants and also enabled a step-change in the achievable complexity and frequency of their use. A significant aspect of the research and development work within personalised AM implants has involved the introduction of biocompatible materials and approval by the various medical regulatory bodies such as the Medicines and Healthcare products Regulatory Agency (MHRA) within the United Kingdom and the Food and Drug Administration (FDA) within the United States of America. Titanium is a desirable build material for many applications due to its inert characteristics (such as corrosion resistance) and excellent mechanical properties. This led to its early development as a build material for metal-based AM technologies like Direct Metal Laser Sintering (DMLS) created by the EOS firm of Munich (Germany) and Selective Laser Melting (SLM) introduced at the Fraunhofer Institute ILT in Aachen in 1995. These technologies were used to manufacture direct parts for a variety of industries including aerospace, dental and medical. However, it was the biocompatibility of titanium (non-toxic and acceptance by the body) and its capacity for osseointegration (a process that occurs when bone cells attach themselves directly to the titanium surface) that really elevated the use of AM for personalised orthopaedic implants. These highly desirable characteristics coupled with the design freedom of AM meant that extremely complex and bespoke orthopaedic implants can be generated that physically bond with bone and living tissue without any forms of additional adhesives. While personalised AM implants are being successfully used for dental, hip and knee procedures, it is within the field of cranio-maxillofacial surgery that AM has made some of the most significant impacts within personalisation.

The skull and jaw are arguably some of the most complex parts of the human skeletal system and the fabrication of implants to treat cranio-maxillofacial trauma and disease has historically been difficult. Through the utilisation of Magnetic Resonance Imaging (MRI) or Computed Tomography (CT) scanning, complex, personalised digital data of the patient can be captured and translated into useable 3D CAD format to facilitate the design of bespoke fitting implants. Notable work in the field has been completed by OBL – a manufacturer of implants for maxillofacial surgery, neurosurgery and plastic

120 Guy Bingham

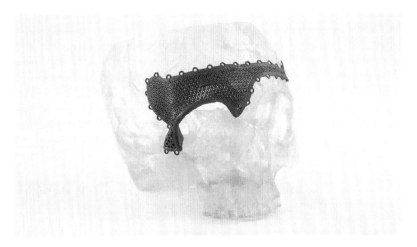

Figure 6.3 Cranio-maxillofacial titanium implant.
Source: Courtesy of © Materialise.

surgery (OBL 2015) who are part of the Materialise group (Materialise 2015) as demonstrated in Figure 6.3.

More recent innovations include the award-winning work completed by Xilloc and LayerWise (Xilloc 2015; LayerWise 2015) and their application of AM for the production of a complete lower titanium jaw implant (Figure 6.4). Developed in collaboration with the University of Hasselt BIOMED Research

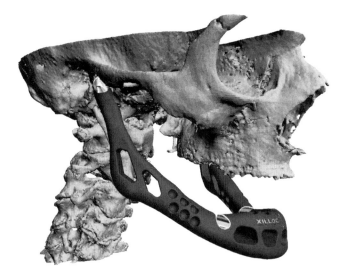

Figure 6.4 AM Titanium mandible replacement.
Source: Courtesy of Xilloc, the Netherlands.

Institute (Belgium), LayerWise printed the complex titanium mandible replacement that incorporated articulated joints and dedicated features. This was the first implementation and operation of its kind.

Personalised prosthetic fairings

Moving away from medical implants, but still within the medical/healthcare sector, AM has also been very successfully applied to manufacture of prosthetic fairings, specifically for leg amputees (Figure 6.5). Some of the most notable work to date has been completed by Bespoke Innovations, now a division of 3D Systems (3D Systems 2015).

Functional or articulated prostheses have developed significantly in recent years and have the inherent capability to dramatically improve the quality of their user's life. While biomedical engineers have done an extraordinary job in delivering the functionality, these very intermit and personal devices have not received a similar level of industrial design. The application of AM for these products is not primarily functional, or indeed covert, but in fact purely aesthetic and explicit. The personalisation aspect of the work in this field is actually two-fold. It not only utilises personalised human body data for the generation of the fairing geometry, but also allows the personalisation of form and aesthetics for individualised expression. The process employed by Bespoke

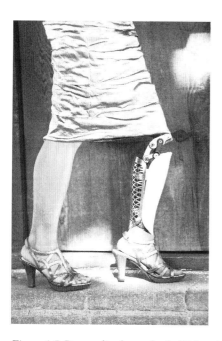 

Figure 6.5 Personalised prosthetic fairings by Bespoke Innovations (designer/inventor Scott Summit).

Source: Courtesy of 3D Systems Inc.

122 *Guy Bingham*

Innovations when working with the single leg amputees involves 3D scanning of the 'sound-side' or remaining leg, which is used as reference geometry for the generation of the personalised fairing, ensuring appropriate body symmetry of the individual. The 3D body data is then applied as a template to construct a digital 3D model of the fairings panels with appropriate fixings to the underlying mechanical prostheses. The secondary personalisation aspect then involves the user selecting the aesthetic form and the final finish of the fairing. Here, the process differentiates from all other medical-based applications of AM by encapsulating the end user's design aspirations.

The above overview of AM-enabled personalisation is not meant to be exhaustive, but merely provides key examples of its effective use within the medical and healthcare sector. But it is fair to say that personalisation of medical applications has not only been accepted as a recognised manufacturing solution, but also becomes more and more widespread as a means for individual aesthetic expression.

Consumer AM personalisation

Outside the medical and healthcare sector the existing examples of AM-based personalisation are much less numerous and many of them add little to the debate on the future of personalisation or increase the understanding of the opportunities that AM can provide. That being said, however, there are new developments of AM-based personalisation in such fields as footwear, lighting, ornaments, figurines and trinkets, which ignite a lot of interest in the current direction and applications of AM within the consumer personalisation sector. The flexibility of AM along with other forms of digital manufacturing techniques are providing new possibilities for mass-personalisation, where every single product or component could be personalised to a single user's taste and requirements. Unlike 'mass customisation' where the customisation of an object or system could be applicable to many potential users and based on a series of predetermined configurable options; mass-personalisation within the consumer sector seeks to involve the user within the design process. This could result in a potentially mass-produced, bespoke product for an individual user.

Personalised jewellery

One of the earliest examples of AM-enabled mass-personalisation was in the jewellery sector. Notably, Future Factories was amongst the first creative industries to employ AM to add value to their products through 'creative freedoms and manufacturing flexibility of digital technologies' (Future Factories 2015). The Icon pendant (2007) was a limited production of AM jewellery that utilised a 3D modelling script to continually transform the complex, organic form of the pendant over a specific time frame (Figure 6.6). Through a web-based portal, costumers could stop or freeze the transformation of the pendant and select to purchase a particular stage of this unique design metamorphosis. This approach not only used the design freedoms of AM to create a complex, organic form

Additive manufacturing and personalisation 123

that would be highly impractical to reproduce with any other manufacturing techniques, it also embraced the flexibility of AM to provide a personalised product to every single consumer. Furthermore, due to the 3D modelling script being used, every single design created within the limited production-run was instantly recognisable as being part of the Icon range, maintaining the product unique identity.

This very early example of mass-personalisation using AM demonstrated the potential of the technology for consumer applications and also brought to light several key concepts that have been developed further within more recent examples of this growing trend. The main concept introduced was the generation of a 'seed object' or 'seed design'. This acts as the starting point for all subsequent transformations and is specifically created to allow some form of personalisation by the intended end-user/customer. The second concept was the application of 'co-design' or 'co-creation' within the personalisation process, enabled through some form of web-based portal. The distinction between

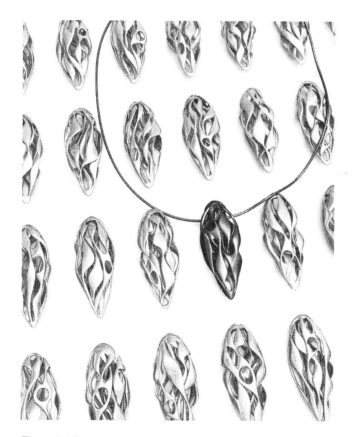

Figure 6.6 Future Factories Icon pendant range.

Source: www.futurefactories.com.

the activity of 'co-design' or 'co-creation' is quite narrow, but Sanders and Stappers (2008) define the difference between the two as: co-design is a process that explicitly involves the end-user throughout the whole design process, whereas co-creation is a broader term that involves the end-user somewhere within the design process, irrespective of where it may occur.

The growing trend for consumer-based, mass-personalisation using AM certainly seems to favour co-creation as the mechanism by which to involve the end-user. Every available example to date uses some form of seed object/design that has been initially created by a designer without any prior connection or communication with the end-user. The end-user is only presented with the opportunity to personalise the form or function of the seed object/design through a web-based portal prior to fabricating it and completing the co-creation process.

Several companies are now taking advantage of the flexibility that AM and other digital manufacturing techniques offer in order to provide opportunities for mass-personalisation through co-creation. Some of the current examples are extremely specific and concentrate solely on one product type, whereas others are more flexible and can accommodate a range of product variations.

Personalised sex toys

Possibly the most humorous example of mass-personalisation through co-creation is the web-based portal 'Dildo Generator' (Dildo 2015) offering personalised sex toys. While somewhat whimsical, the system is actually quite well conceived and quickly allows anyone with almost no previous design skill or experience to design a personalised sex toy to suit their individual preferences. It is important to note that while AM is not directly used for the manufacture of the sex toy, it is used to create the mould tool for subsequent silicone moulding of bio-compatible materials. The dedicated system takes the end-user through a five-stage creation process that not only allows the complete design, but also the final purchasing of their personalised product.

Customers are first invited to select the type of sex toy they require from a predetermined list of product types (seed objects) before specifying certain size dimensions. The personalisation of the actual form is controlled by a simple and intuitive spline-based manipulation of the 2D profile by adding/subtracting spline points and simply dragging these around on the screen with a mouse. A 3D rendering of the design is updated in real time so the customers can instantly see the impact of their personalisation work (Figure 6.7). Once completed, the colour and surface texture can be specified before finally purchasing their unique personalised design.

While this example might be unusual and certainly has the potential to offend, it has been cited because it demonstrates a very important aspect within the growing trend of AM-enabled mass-personalisation activities – the almost complete removal of any required design skill or expertise by the end-user/customer. As previously discussed within the introduction of this chapter, AM technologies offer unrivalled design freedom and any complexity of geometry

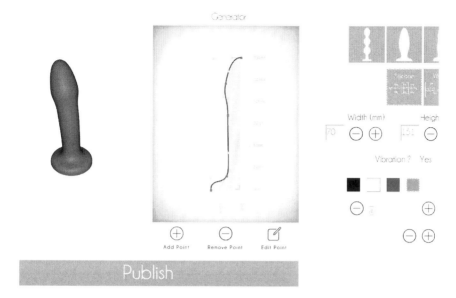

Figure 6.7 Dildo generator software.
Source: Courtesy of www.dildo-generator.com.

can be created efficiently, repeatedly and economically. However, in order to achieve such complexity, a 3D modelling of a form in a CAD system is necessary. CAD is a fundamentally expert system requiring extensive skill and knowledge to operate. This fundamental prerequisite of the AM technology significantly limits the number of people that can effectively interact with and utilise its extraordinary capabilities to create personalised products. The development of simplified web-based portals that allow the real-time transformation of seed objects suddenly removes this barrier and enables a significantly larger population to interact with the technology – the scale consumer-based mass-personalisation has never experienced previously. However, not all of the current examples of web-based personalisation portals are quite so simple. With an increase in the product sophistication comes an obvious increase in the portal intricacy and complexity as described in the following section.

Web-based portals for personalised consumer products

Nervous System (Nervous 2015) is a design studio that pioneered the use of generative design and AM techniques to provide a range of personalised products. Since 2007 they have developed a series of 'web-based generative design apps' that allow users to generate unique and affordable art, jewellery, and housewares manufactured using AM. Their web-based portal provides access to a range of dedicated software, including Cell Cycle (Figure 6.8), which offers a fairly

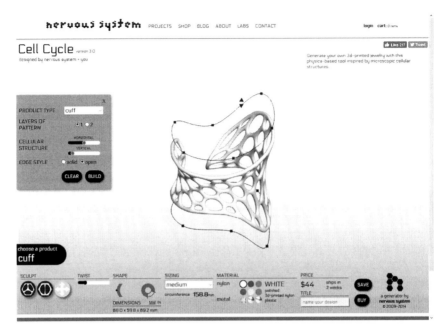

Figure 6.8 Nervous System – Cell Cycle software.
Source: Courtesy of Nervous System.

extensive array of transformation options to modify and personalise a bespoke piece of AM jewellery featuring their distinct cellular architecture. Once again, the transformations are updated in real-time and the system allows the user to instantly see the results of their personalisation work on a rendering of the actual 3D data that will be used for manufacture. The user can specify the finish and material for their products, and is instantly informed about both the cost and delivery time of their design if purchased.

Possibly the most notable aspect of Nervous System's work involves the Kinematics Cloth software, which allows users to design a personalised 3D-printed garment in real-time (Kinematics 2015). The software is again accessible through their web-based portal and allows a variety of clothing items to be generated including dresses, skirts and shirts. Through a series of staged options, users can design the silhouette and hemline of their garment and determine the pattern of the garment's unique tessellated AM fabric structure. What makes this a particularly interesting example of personalisation is the ability for users to import their own 3D body scan data upon which to generate their personalised garments – allowing not only the form to be fully personalised but the garment to be custom-fitted to the user.

The examples above demonstrate the incredible potential for the personalisation of consumer products when using AM as the manufacturing solution.

Additive manufacturing and personalisation 127

However, a distinct limitation of the portals developed so far is that of product variation. The vast majority tend to be dedicated to a single product type or product family (variations on a base product) and currently lack the versatility to allow the personalisation of a diverse range of merchandise. This is mainly linked to the complexity of developing a bespoke 3D modelling system that not only allows transformation of the 3D form but also accessibility through a web-based portal. These fundamental restrictions severely limit the wider opportunity for the personalisation of consumer products using co-creation and therefore the number of examples currently available on the market. In order to achieve a greater opportunity for the personalisation of consumer products, a fundamental change in how product designs are created and made accessible through web-based portals is needed. One of the most developed and versatile mass-personalisation portals to date is the platform developed by Digital Forming (a UK-based software company) and their proprietary ODO software (Digital Forming 2015). The rationale behind Digital Forming's work is to provide designers and businesses with a software solution and publishing platform to allow the generation of 'open' product designs personalised by the user. The platform developed by Digital Forming aims to connect designers, retailers and online marketplaces with a network of digital manufacturers by offering a series of intuitive tools to exploit AM for mass-personalisation and on-demand production (Figure 6.9).

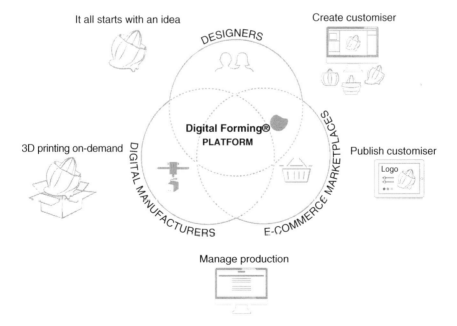

Figure 6.9 Digital Forming's platform.
Source: Courtesy of Digital Forming.

While the number of example consumer products currently available through Digital Forming's platform is somewhat limited, the variation in product types is significant and presents the largest collection of personalised AM consumer products to date. However, what is more noteworthy is the potential of their platform and the likely impact it could have on the personalised consumer product market. The platform represents the first universal system to allow the wholesale creation of personalised consumer products and provides all the necessary tools for designers and businesses to fully engage within this developing market sector. This marks a distinct shift in the evolution of consumer product manufacturing, through embedding the opportunity for personalisation in almost any product design. As adoption increases, so will the number of personalised consumer products and it is anticipated to become far more commonplace in the next few years.

Conclusion

The examples discussed in this chapter are by no means complete and there are other instances where AM has been successfully utilised to provide opportunities for personalisation. Those cited, however, do demonstrate where AM is making a significant contribution to both the opportunity and application of personalisation. Within the medical healthcare sector AM has become an established and key manufacturing solution for the physical realisation of personalised products. It has not only allowed a step-change in the availability and suitability of products intimately personalised to the human form (implants), but also facilitated personalisation for individual expression (prosthetic fairings). The examples of hearing aids and orthodontic aligners reinforce its value as a manufacturing solution and demonstrate where AM has been vital in providing success for the mass-personalisation of commercial products.

Outside of the medical healthcare sector the examples of AM-based personalisation are less numerous and potentially more trivial in comparison. While there appears to be a real desire for the personalisation of consumer products, effective interaction with the technology and the generation of personalised 3D manufacturing data remains a significant barrier to further exploitation of the technology. The field of mass-personalisation requires continuous research and development work in order to provide the methodology and conceptual framework for the effective interaction with the technology. The ongoing development of web-based portals means that the ability to personalise a consumer product will soon become no more difficult than navigating a website. This apparent simplicity and availability will without doubts facilitate a steady increase in the future number of personalised consumer products available on the market.

So, returning to the original question – is AM the future enabler of mass-personalisation? AM is an incredible technology and provides extraordinary possibilities for design and personalisation. Within the medical healthcare sector it has already established itself as the key manufacturing solution for the mass-personalisation of commercial products. However, within the consumer products sector it is currently being utilised 'on-demand' for low-volume production while the means of engaging the consumer are fully developed. AM is slowly maturing as a manufacturing solution and continues to improve in terms of accuracy, speed and build materials. Will it become the future enabler of mass-personalisation of consumer products? You decide.

References

Bernabei, R. and Power, J. (2013) Designing together: end-user collaboration in designing a personalised product, *10th European Academy of Design Conference*, 17–19 April 2013, Gothenburg, Sweden, pp. 1–12.

Burns, M. (1995) The freedom to create. *Technology Management*, 1(4), 157–163.

Campbell, I. (1994) Design for rapid prototyping: developing a methodology. In Case, K. and Newman, S. E. (eds) *10th National Conference on Manufacturing Research, Proceedings of the 10th National Conference on Manufacturing Research*, Loughborough, UK, pp. 521–525.

Crump, S. S. (1992) Apparatus and method for creating three-dimensional objects, US Patent 5121329 A.

Deckard, C. R. (1989) Method and apparatus for producing parts by selective sintering, US Patent 4863538 A.

Franke, N., Kaiser, U. and Schreier, M. (2010) The 'I designed it myself' effect in mass customization. *Management Science*, 56(1), 125–140.

Hopkinson, N. and Dickens, P. M. (2003) Analysis of rapid manufacturing – using layer manufacturing processes for production. *Proceedings of the Institute of Mechanical Engineers, Part C: Journal of Mechanical Engineering Science*, 217(C1), 31–39.

Hopkinson, N., Hague, R. J. M. and Dickens, P. M. (eds) (2005) *Rapid manufacturing – an industrial revolution for the digital age*, New York: John Wiley.

Hull, C. W. (1986) Apparatus for production of three-dimensional objects by Stereolithography, US Patent 4575330 A.

Makerspace (2015) http://www.makerspaceuk.com/, accessed April 2015.

Moultrie, J. and Bibb, R. (2015) Design for Additive Manufacturing (D4AM). EPSRC Grant reference EP/N005953/1.

Sanders, E. and Stappers, P. J. (2008) Co-creation and the new landscapes of design. *CoDesign*, 4(1), 5–18.

Sunikka, A. and Bragge, J. (2012) Applying text-mining to personalization and customization research literature – who, what and where? *Expert Systems With Applications*, 39(11), 10049–10058.

Websites

3D Systems (2015), www.3dsystems.com.

Digital Forming (2015), www.digitalforming.com

Dildo (2015), www.dildo-generator.com

Future Factories (2015), www.futurefactories.com

Invisalign (2015), http://www.invisalign.co.uk

Kinematics (2015), www.n-e-r-v-o-u-s.com/kinematicsCloth

LayerWise (2015), http://www.layerwise.com

Materialise (2015), http://cranio-maxillofacial.materialise.com

Nervous (2015), www.n-e-r-v-o-u-s.com

OBL (2015), http://www.oblparis.com/?lang=en

Xilloc (2015), http://www.xilloc.com/patients/stories/total-mandibular-implant.

Part III
Personalising health

7 The 4 Ps

Problems in personalising a public service (a personal view of personalisation in the NHS)

Kath Checkland

Introduction

> In the late 1980s, I was a graduate student in the US, and was taught by Charles Sabel, co-author with Michael Piore of *The Second Industrial Divide*. Its argument was simple: the era of mass production would be superseded in the advanced economies by the age of flexible specialisation, products previously produced for a mass market now to be tuned to personal need. That revolution in business, fuelled by rising affluence and expectations, has not been confined to the world of business. It has found its way into social norms through the end of deference; **its manifestation in public services is the demand for high standards suited to individual need**.
>
> (extract from speech by David Miliband, 2006, p. 23)

In this speech, given at a conference organised by the Department for Education 'innovation unit', David Miliband expressly links the 'personalisation' of public services to the revolution in design upon which this volume has its focus. The argument is relatively simple: 'the public' have become accustomed to products 'tuned' to their personal need; by extension, they now expect public services designed in the same way. Leaving aside issues of evidence (how does he know?), this rhetorical claim has found its way into every aspect of public policy in the UK, from social care to criminal justice, and from education to employment. The NHS has not been neglected: whilst it is difficult to date this exactly, the first explicit policy commitment to 'personalising' the NHS probably occurred in the 2000 'NHS Plan' (Secretary of State for Health, 2000). This document had the illuminating subtitle: 'A Plan for Investment, A Plan for Reform', and it marked the end of a period of austerity in the NHS spanning the 1990s. The document contained the following commitment: 'Step by step over the next ten years the NHS must be redesigned to be patient centred – to offer a personalised service' (Secretary of State for Health, 2000, p. 17). In total there were 5 mentions of personalisation in 150 pages of text. By 2006, the pace had increased, with the so-called 'Darzi Report' (Department of Health, 2008a; NHS England, 2013) giving 52 mentions in 90 pages, promising:

That is why it is right that we should seek to renew the NHS for the 21st century. To meet the rising aspirations of the public, the changing burdens of disease and to ensure that the very latest, personalised healthcare is available to all of us, not just those able to pay.

(Darzi Report, preface by Gordon Brown, p. 2)

The practical manifestations of this discourse have included an increased focus on providing choice, particularly choice of service or choice of hospital, and, most recently, the rolling out of 'personal health budgets'. These give patients suffering from long-term conditions a budget that they can spend on anything that they believe will improve their health.

At one level, such aspirations and policies are unobjectionable. Of course those providing NHS care should seek to be as patient centred as possible, and it is hard to argue that the service should be 'depersonalised'. However, a focus on the needs and aspirations of individuals in this way carries within it a number of assumptions and dangers, and tends to ignore the needs of wider society. This chapter highlights some of the potential pitfalls that I believe are consequent upon the personalisation agenda. An initial section traces in more detail the development of personalisation as a guiding principle for public services in the UK. I then explore in turn each of the '4 Ps' that I have identified, including: **p**rivileging the pushy; res**p**onsibilisation; **p**olicy by **p**ersonal anecdote; and bracketing out the **p**olitical. A final section offers some reflections on the concept of personalisation and its use in public services, seeking to delineate more clearly the boundaries within which it might offer something valuable for those responsible for service design and provision in the NHS.

Personalisation in public services in the UK[1]

There is general agreement that the current focus on personalisation and the related concept of 'choice' in public services in England started in the early 2000s under the Blair government (Cutler et al., 2007; Needham, 2009). Cutler et al. (2007) describe the rise of what they term 'epochal' arguments, in which 'bad, old' approaches are contrasted with 'good, new', with Tony Blair, for example, highlighting 'a personalised service' as essential in 'a re-casting of the 1945 welfare state to end entirely the era of "one size fits all"' (Blair, 2004). This linguistic trend pervaded UK government in the early 2000s, with 'modernisation' elevated to a guiding principle across the public services (Department of Health, 2001; Harrison, 2002; Secretary of State for Health, 1997). Rhetorical calls to be 'modern' served to implicitly denigrate what had gone before, which came, by extension, to be identified as 'old-fashioned' and out of date. Needham (2011a, 2011b) suggests that personalisation has become a potent 'storyline' in UK public services, dominating debate and, in its very imprecision, providing legitimacy for a wide variety of policy decisions and programmes. Needham (2011a, p. 30) itemises the policies that she sees as sheltering under this broad and expansive umbrella (Figure 7.1).

- **Adult social care:**
  - Self-directed support, with greater choice of services
  - Personal budgets for social care
- **Children and families:**
  - Individual budgets for disabled children
  - The naming of a 'lead professional' for families requiring support
  - The 'problem families' programme, focusing intensive support on high users of services
- **National Health Service:**
  - Person-centred approach to behaviour change and health education
  - Greater choice of service provider, including 'choose and book' technological solution for booking of hospital appointments
  - Personal health budgets
- **Housing:**
  - Personalised support for vulnerable people in need of housing
  - Inclusion of a housing element in some personal care budgets
  - Increased choice for those in receipt of social housing
- **Employment:**
  - Personal advisors for the long-term unemployed
  - Move towards a 'welfare to work' model, with multiple different providers bidding to provide targeted support for clients, paid for on the basis of the percentage success rate achieved
- **Education**
  - Focus on the 'personalisation' of teaching and learning
  - Diversity in the provision of school places, with a range of new providers including academies and free schools
  - A 'pupil premium', providing additional funding for schools for their disadvantaged pupils
  - The introduction of tuition fees for higher education
- **Criminal justice**
  - Increased diversity of provision of offender management services, with payment based upon outcomes

Figure 7.1 UK Government policies focusing upon 'personalisation'.

Source: Adapted from Needham (2011a, p. 30) with author's permission.

The two things that stand out from these examples are a focus on increasing choice and diversity in provision, and interest in new models of payment, including personal budgets and payment according to the achievement of predetermined 'outcomes'. The benefits claimed for such changes are legion, with Needham identifying what she calls five 'recurrent themes' arising across the public service arena (Needham, 2011a, p. 49). These include:

- Personalisation 'works' and can 'transform lives'.
- Personalisation saves money.
- Person-focused approaches match the ways that people live their lives.
- Personalisation can be applied to everyone.
- People are the experts in their own lives, and therefore know best what they need.

Such 'storylines' (Needham, 2011b) are given different weight by different commentators, and are buttressed by a mixture of formal evidence, highly emotive personal stories and appeals to common sense. Such 'evidence' is hard to refute, making critics appear to be defending a notion of services both unresponsive and unlikely to meet the needs of individuals.

Within the social care arena, personalisation soon became inextricably linked with the notion of direct payments, allowing those with social care needs to purchase their own package of support (Dickinson and Glasby, 2010). In the NHS, the personalisation agenda initially focused upon choice, with a number of reforms introduced to enable patients to exercise greater choice over their care. Greener (2009) analysed the use of 'choice' in UK NHS policy documents, finding that rhetorical commitment to increased choice is often linked to notions of responsiveness. Furthermore, such policy documents suggest that patient choice is a powerful tool to drive service providers to better focus their services on the needs of individual patients:

> The NHS Confederation believe that giving patients greater choice is a key priority for the health service. It holds out the prospect of a more responsive NHS, where services are tailored around the individual and patients are genuine partners in decisions about their care.
> (Department of Health, 2003, p. 15)

Since 2003, there have been a number of practical initiatives in the NHS designed to make such choice real. These have included: the development of an IT system known as 'Choose and Book', which allows GPs to book hospital appointments for their patients from a menu of service providers (Greenhalgh et al., 2014); forcing commissioners to contract with a variety of providers (including private providers) for at least two service areas (a policy known as 'any qualified provider' (Department of Health, 2011)); and the application of the principles of competition law to NHS services (Department of Health, 2010).

More recently, the focus in the NHS has shifted towards direct payments. Drawing analogies from the experience of direct payments for social care services, a pilot programme was initiated in which selected patients were provided with a personal budget with which to purchase services to address their health needs (Alakeson and Rumbold, 2013). Following an evaluation (Forder et al., 2012), it was announced that the policy will be rolled out across the NHS, initially focusing on those patients with the most complex health needs (Department of Health, 2012). Finally, it was announced in 2014 that GPs must ensure that all patients over the age of 75 have a named GP responsible for their care (Soteriou, 2013). It was argued that this would restore the link between a GP and his or her patients, with older patients guaranteed a doctor who would know them personally.

Taken together, these initiatives represent a clear policy shift in the English NHS towards the development of a more personalised service, focused upon the needs and wants of what are assumed to be engaged patients, actively choosing between rival service offers. The benefits claimed for this shift include better services, value for money and better outcomes.

The first P: privileging the pushy

As we have seen, advocates of increasing choice in the NHS make bold claims about its potential to improve services. A widely cited study by Cooper et al. (2011) argues that increasing choice and competition improved the quality of care received in hospitals, and this study has been picked up and widely quoted by politicians who favour this agenda, including David Cameron. Others, however, have disagreed, arguing that Cooper et al.'s study was flawed (Pollock et al., 2011). Whatever the rights and wrongs of these somewhat esoteric arguments about econometric analysis, it remains a fact that critiques rarely attract the same attention as the more positive claims.

Whatever the macro-level arguments about the value of choice, making a personal choice requires agency, with psychologists using the term 'self-efficacy' (Strecher et al., 1986) to describe a state of being in which individuals feel themselves to be able to direct their lives and make meaningful choices. Inequalities in income and social disadvantage have an impact on this, with studies showing that those who experience social deprivation are less likely to feel in control of their lives, and to have lower rates of self-efficacy (Gecas, 1989). Health promotion experts have identified a related concept, 'health literacy', which refers to individuals' ability to understand and act upon knowledge about their health and healthcare (Nutbeam, 2000). Low levels of health literacy are also correlated with social deprivation (Brown et al., 2004). Taken together, it is clear that the ability to take advantage of proffered choices is unequally distributed within the population, with those suffering deprivation least likely to choose. This has obvious implications for equity within a system based upon personal choice, with Fotaki arguing:

> If choice is not to exacerbate the inequalities that already exist, wider strategies addressing the causes of inequality will be needed over and above purposefully designed measures to support the choice policy, with a focus on specific requirements of various underprivileged and less vocal groups.
> (Fotaki, 2010, p. 909)

In practice, commissioners found it necessary to erect a bureaucratic framework around the choice policy by, for example, employing advisors to support patients using the 'Choose and Book' system. Even those who are strongly in favour of increasing choice recognise these challenges, with, for example, Dixon and Le Grand (2006) arguing for the appointment of choice advisors and payment of transport costs for poorer citizens in order to allow them to avail themselves of the available menu of choices. However, such costly systems can only provide support to a small number of people, leaving the majority to navigate the system as best they can, and 'choice advisors' provide an easy target for those desperate to make savings without cutting frontline services. Advocates of choice argue that it can be a powerful motivator for improvement, with providers responding to patient flows in order to maximise the appeal of their service over and above their rivals (Le Grand, 2007). What might services in such an ideal choice-based system look like? It seems at least possible that services designed to maximise their appeal will be biased towards the needs of those best equipped to choose: privileging the pushy and providing services for the articulate middle classes, whilst those who find making choices difficult will be further disadvantaged.

The second 'P': responsibilisation

A second danger arises from the pressures imposed by the process of choosing. Responsibilisation is defined as 'the self-management of risk by an autonomous individual' (Liebenberg et al., 2013). The 'responsibilised' individual is responsible for making the right choices, pushing for the right care and for disciplining their behaviour to fit a defined norm. Leadbeater (who is acknowledged to be one of the most influential voices behind the personalisation agenda in public services (Needham, 2009)) puts it thus:

> Public policy increasingly needs to shape the choices people make about their lives, to reduce the risk that they will make a costly call on public services by encouraging them to take responsibility for their actions . . . That means people have to shoulder more responsibility for assessing and managing the risk of their own behaviour.
> (Leadbeater and Lownsbrough, 2005, p. 27)

'Responsible' citizens will thus make 'the right' choices, disciplining their behaviour and ensuring that they avoid becoming a burden on the state. However, advocates of personalisation in public services rarely talk explicitly about responsibility in this way. In what could be called a linguistic sleight of hand, consumers and users are to be 'empowered'. Leadbeater et al. (2008) argue that self-directed services transform public service. They can 'be good for equity because they empower those people who are the least confident and able to get what they want from the current system' and 'give people a real voice in shaping the service they want and the money to back it up'.

McDonald (2004) explored the rhetoric of 'empowerment' in a Primary Care Trust in England. Middle-grade managers in the Trust were selected to attend a series of training events, designed to 'empower' them to contribute more fully to the work of the organisation. In practice, McDonald found that the programme focussed upon increasing organisational control by shaping employee identities and encouraging them to 'self-discipline' in order to curb attitudes and behaviour that did not contribute to organisational goals. The quote above from Leadbeater and Lownsborough implies a similar underlying agenda in the empowerment of engaged citizens, whose identity as responsible consumers will prevent them becoming a 'costly' burden on the state. Ferguson (2011) highlights the ethical and philosophical issues associated with this discourse, in particular the potential stigmatisation of the need for publicly funded care and support. Peacock et al. (2014) go further, arguing that the neoliberal discourse of responsibilisation forces individuals in receipt of benefits to internalise a negative image of themselves, and that this partially explains the negative impact of societal inequality on health and wellbeing.

McDonald (2004) explores the ethical issues surrounding the development of a responsibilised and self-governing populace. Perhaps of more practical concern is the potential impact on the responsibilised individuals themselves. In many situations, empowering individuals to make choices is unproblematic. We make choices about which supermarket to use, and we bear the risk of getting it wrong – the only consequence will be paying too much for our vegetables. We choose a queue in which to stand at the checkout, and watch in frustration as it inevitably moves more slowly than the one next door. In health, by contrast, making the 'wrong' choice can be catastrophic. If you actively choose your hospital, and your operation goes wrong, you may carry a load of regret. If you choose your breast cancer treatment and your cancer returns, you might feel that you are responsible for your own demise. People vary in the extent to which they are comfortable with this; the danger is that a policy context that elevates personal choice to a guiding principle risks forcing those reluctant to bear the personal responsibility for their health choices to do so. Sensitive management by someone who knows the patient well can mitigate this risk, but, in an increasingly fragmented NHS (in part due to the choice policy), such protective personal relationships are, paradoxically, less common.

Peckham et al. (2011) studied the implementation of choice policies in the NHS across all four constituent administrations (England, Scotland, Wales and Northern Ireland). They explored the stories told about choice at three levels: the macro level, asking policy makers to explain their intentions; at the meso level, undertaking case studies to explore how choice was being operationalised by those responsible; and at the micro level, exploring how patients and GPs used the choices available to them. They found that policy in England was dominated by an ideological commitment to 'choice' as a public good, whereas in the other UK territories choice was more often framed in the context of reducing waiting times and ensuring that the 'public voice' was heard in the commissioning process. In spite of these differences, patient's *experience* of choice was very similar in all contexts. Peckham et al. suggest that, in part, the failure to translate headline policy commitments into concrete patient experience is the product of the complexity inherent in designing a publicly funded system that enables choice without further disadvantaging those least able to choose. Moreover, and perhaps most interestingly, they found that patients identified a *personally responsive* system not as one that offered them a wide range of choices, but as one in which they were in contact with caring professionals who listened to them and supported them in navigating the system.

In summary, therefore, I am arguing two points here. Advocates of personalisation in public services in general and in healthcare in particular emphasise the potential for empowerment, but the downside of empowerment is responsibilisation, with associated risk of regret and the implicit denigration of dependence. Moreover, the evidence that the public want to bear such responsibility is lacking, at least in the healthcare field. Personalisation and responsiveness for many patients and service users is more about personal relationships with their care givers than it is about choice.

The third P: policy by personal anecdote

As the rhetoric of personalisation has taken hold across UK policy, there has been a parallel rise in the use of personal stories to justify policy decisions. Historically, health White Papers were rather dry affairs, carefully and judiciously setting out evidence and arguments in densely written prose. Since the 1980s, however, the tone and substance of these documents have changed. For example, the 1972 White Paper, NHS Reorganisation: England (Secretary of State for Social Services, 1972) contains a Foreword from the Secretary of State. It begins: 'The National Health Service should be a single service. Its separate parts are intended to complement one another, not function as self-sufficient entities' (p. 1). The 2006 White paper 'Our Health, Our Care, Our Say' (Department of Health, 2006) also starts with a Foreword, this time provided by the then Prime Minister, Tony Blair. It starts with a much bolder statement, evoking a heroic and far-reaching vision: 'This White Paper is an important new stage in building a world-class health and social care system' (p. 1). The former document is measured in tone, printed on rough paper and contains some approving references to the work of the previous government; the latter contains glossy photographs, 'case studies' illustrating the value of what is proposed, supportive quotes from those consulted, and castigates the previous administration for 'decades of underinvestment'. Modern White Papers are thus pieces of rhetoric, designed to persuade rather than appraise evidence using rhetorical devices such as so-called 'pull quotes' and illustrative anecdotes. These illustrative anecdotes put a face upon the claims made, often literally. At best, such stories can highlight important arguments and provide a human face to render complex problems comprehensible. Journalists have long known the value of providing a personal story to illustrate a more general issue, and it is unsurprising that policy makers and those responsible for persuading local actors to change the way they do things should adopt the same approach.

The policy decision to roll out personal health budgets in England provides an interesting example of this tendency in practice. Personal health budgets were first mooted by the Labour Government in 2009. The argument made was essentially an extrapolation from the experience of councils implementing personal budgets for social care:

> Learning from experience in social care and other health systems, personal health budgets will be piloted, giving individuals and families greater control over their own care, with clear safeguards.
> (Department of Health, 2008b, p. 10)

The rhetorical justification for the policy brings to bear many of the 'storylines' identified by Needham, emphasising the potential of personal health budgets to reduce inequalities, match services to the way people live their lives and improve health and wellbeing (Department of Health, 2008b). Following the general election in 2010, a series of pilots were established across the country, in which selected patients with long-term conditions were provided with budgets to purchase additional services. The underlying premise was that empowering patients in this way would improve their general health, and that this in turn would reduce their need for other services (Gadsby et al., 2013). This latter point is important, as the policy was introduced at a time of shrinking budgets, with no additional money attached. The scheme must thus be self-funding if it is to be sustained. The pilots were subject to an exhaustive evaluation, covering both the processes by which the policy was implemented and the outcomes experienced by the patients involved (Forder et al., 2012). The evaluation report is long, covering 215 pages and examining carefully and in depth the different programmes, their implementation and their impacts. Careful economic analysis calculated value for money, whilst valiant attempts were made to quantify changes in service use. The findings are nuanced. Personal health budgets were found to be of value for some people in improving their quality of life. However, there was no impact on their health status, and no clear evidence that those in receipt of the budgets would use fewer services in the future or that overall costs would reduce. The Department of Health press release announcing the roll out of the policy stated:

> Care and Support Minister Norman Lamb said:
>
> 'Independent analysis has now shown that personal health budgets can put people back in control of their care and make a significant difference to their quality of life. It's inspiring to hear the human stories of success that these budgets have brought to people'.
> (https://www.gov.uk/government/news/personal-health-budgets-to-be-rolled-out)

Caveats and nuanced findings were lost, with the press release going on to offer us 'Nikki's story', a personal story that highlights the extent to which a personal health budget has transformed Nikki's life. In essence, a long, complicated and nuanced evaluative report is reduced to a personal story of transformation. This could be seen as no more than good public relations, but I remain concerned. The authors of the personal health budgets evaluation conclude that their roll out could be justified IF society agreed that the cost associated with the small quality of life gain was justified. The report does not, however, discuss how such a roll out should be funded; in a cash-limited system the funding for a new service must inevitably come at the cost of some other intervention. The press release and associated NHS England website (http://www.personal healthbudgets.england.nhs.uk/) do not, however, discuss these trade-offs; both simply provide a number of inspirational stories. This approach puts the sceptic in the position of denying individuals something that has power to transform their lives; if I argue that limited NHS resources might be better spent in some other way, I am arguing that Nikki (a specific person) should be denied something she values. The widespread use of these anecdotes in government documents, on websites and in official presentations seems designed as much to silence opposition as to inform.

The final P: bracketing out the political

In many ways, all of my 'Ps' so far are examples of this final category: focusing on the personal, and offering an NHS that will respond to everyone's individual needs is a sleight of hand that allows politicians and policy makers to duck the hard question: how can the service be paid for? The 2008 Darzi Report is perhaps the most egregious example of this sleight of hand; funding is not mentioned, and the 'personal' is elevated to a moral guiding principle:

> We are also beginning to see the impact, and opportunities, that face us from recent generations – the children of the last three decades of the 20th century. These generations are influenced by new technologies that provide unprecedented levels of control, personalisation and connection. They expect not just services that are there when they need them, and treat them how they want them to, but that they can influence and shape for themselves. Better still, they will want services that instinctively respond to them using the sophisticated marketing techniques used by other sectors. This is more than just a challenge for healthcare, but for our whole model of how we think about health.
>
> (Department of Health, 2008a, p. 26)

Just as David Milliband, in the quote opening this chapter, links personalisation in public services to personalisation in design, Lord Darzi here links it to consumerism, situating users of health services as sophisticated consumers. The footnote accompanying this section of the report makes this linkage explicit, highlighting approvingly the way in which Amazon provides browsers with suggestions linked to their previous purchases. Nowhere in this vision is there room for trade-offs and political decisions, no apparent recognition that meeting all of your personal needs (and even desires) might mean that there is no money left to meet mine.

One of the important roles that politics plays in the life of a country is in determining the distribution of limited resources. In discussing the need to redistribute healthcare resources towards primary healthcare services, Segall argues thus:

> Equity is a political concept. To the extent that the preferential allocation of resources to the needy implies fewer resources for the beneficiaries of the present situation, we have entered the political arena. The social distribution of resources is the stuff of politics.
>
> (Segall, 1983, p. 1947)

The Conservative government in power in the 1980s and 1990s in the UK was, in many ways, an ideological one (Crewe and Searing, 1988). New Labour, by contrast, coming to power in 1997 after nearly 20 years in the political wilderness, identified themselves in a more technocratic way, coining the term 'the third way' (Rose, 2000) to describe an approach in which 'what works' is elevated to a guiding principle. The health White Paper published in 1997 (Secretary of State for Health, 1997) highlighted aspects of 'what works' and 'what doesn't work' within the NHS, going on to firmly state:

> The internal market was a misconceived attempt to tackle the pressures facing the NHS. It has been an obstacle to the necessary modernisation of the health service. It created more problems than it solved. That is why the Government is abolishing it.
>
> (Secretary of State for Health, 1997, para. 2.9)

In practice, no such abolition occurred, and subsequent policy extended market principles much more widely throughout the NHS. This was done without any political argument ever being made as to why this was necessary: policy documents focused upon the *utility* of choice and competition, not their ideological roots (Department of Health, 2006). Policy relating to personalisation was articulated in a similar way, with the focus upon personalisation as a practical means to improve services, alongside a moral/ethical justification based around the idea of citizen empowerment; the glaring hole here is the failure to address the question of resources.

Against this background, I would argue that the focus that I have demonstrated on providing individuals with a *personalised* service represents a loss of nerve on behalf of politicians. The pretence that all can have what they 'need' ducks hard questions about trade-offs and the messy business of redistributing limited resources between competing needs; it brackets out the difficult political questions, in favour of a populist message.

Discussion and conclusion

In this chapter, I have shown how widely the rhetoric of personalisation has been embedded within the English NHS, and highlighted my concerns. On one level, I have some sympathy with politicians who are scared to articulate in public the hard reality that NHS services are finite. In the 1990s academics and others started to debate the idea of rationing in the NHS (Harrison and Hunter, 1994; Harrison and Moran, 2000; Heginbotham, 1997; Lenaghan, 1996; New, 1997). However, during the New Labour government in the 2000s there was a significant injection of money into the NHS, and rationing disappeared from the policy agenda. In the late 2000s, as the economy began to fail, the NHS again began to feel the pressure of resource constraint. The focus on personalisation provided a policy narrative that chimed with wider societal norms, and which avoided the need to pre-specify who should have what; if a service is to be *personal*, its content can only be specified once your unique characteristics are taken into account. Rationing focuses upon the needs of groups and equitable distribution of resources between those groups; the narrative of personalisation finesses this by pretending that tailoring to the individual will be so efficient that resource use need not be considered.

Ferguson (2011) provides a possible explanation for the rather puzzling observation that personalisation finds champions from across the political spectrum. He describes the 'two discourses' that underpin the concept. The first, coming from the left, emphasises a democratic model, in which personalisation empowers citizens to take a full role in society. Cutler et al. (2007a) and Needham (2011b) both identify the Demos think tank as an important influence in this agenda, building upon the work of the disability rights movement. Charles Leadbeater published a number of pamphlets (Leadbeater, 2004; Leadbeater et al., 2008), highlighting the benefits of personalisation in public services, arguing that:

> putting users at the heart of services, enabling them to become participants in the design and delivery, services will be more effective by mobilising millions of people to co-produce the goods they value.
> (Leadbeater, 2004)

Duffy (2010) goes further, arguing that social justice *demands* the provision of personalised support for the disabled, enabling them to fully contribute as citizens. The second discourse identified by Ferguson comes from the right of the political spectrum. This discourse arises from the neoliberal emphasis on the individual, and focuses upon choice and control. This ideological approach sees competition between providers as an important driver for improvement, and links personal choice of how to spend a budget with individual autonomy. Ferguson goes on to conclude:

> The construction of personalisation . . . as both 'modern' (in the sense of being in tune with the globalised world) and also politically and ethically

progressive (in addressing the legitimate demands of service users for greater freedom and control) has proved to be a heady brew.

(Ferguson, 2011, p. 61)

The rise of policy by personal anecdote that I have identified contributes to this discourse, rendering opposition mute.

It is clear that one of the motivating factors underlying official enthusiasm for personalisation and, by extension, the provision of personal budgets for services, is the argument that services organised and distributed in this way will be cheaper – especially if the neoliberal aspiration that recipients will be 'responsibilised' to minimise the 'burden' they put on the state is realised (Needham, 2011b). Glendinning (2012) offers a cautionary message: whilst personal budgets in social care have provided users with choice and have improved some people's lives, chronic underfunding of social care has brought with it significant dangers, which personal budgets alone cannot overcome. As the NHS budget is squeezed, it is unlikely that 'personalising' health services will deliver anything like the savings needed to maintain the service free at the point of need.

As a GP, I am deeply committed to the idea of healthcare that takes account of the characteristics, needs and desires of the person receiving the care. However, I remain profoundly suspicious of the argument put forward by the Darzi Report (Department of Health, 2008a) that the public want – and can have – an NHS that is designed to 'instinctively' respond to all their needs. The NHS is a cash-limited service, and we spend less of our GDP on health than almost any other developed country (Davis et al., 2014). Deciding how the money is spent is a political decision, and one that should not be finessed by pretending that the service can be all things to all people. The study by Peckham et al. (2011) exploring the operation of 'choice' in the NHS may suggest a sensible way forward: respondents across the countries of the UK identified a good, warm relationship with a care-provider who knows them as an individual as the most important aspect of a 'responsive' system. This highlights perhaps the most important issue that policy documents and discourses ignore: the difference between a *personalised system*, in which services are designed around the needs and desires of increasingly atomised individuals, and *personalised care*, by which, within an equitable system characterised by open debates about the necessary trade-offs between the needs of different groups, individuals receive a service that takes account of their personal circumstances. In my view, the 'personalisation' of public services should focus upon this, rather than upon the chimera of choice and the individualisation of budgets.

Acknowledgements

I am grateful to Tom Fisher, with whom I discussed and refined these ideas, and to participants in the Workshop at Nottingham Trent University in January

2014, whose questions and comments helped me to clarify my concerns. I would also like to thank my colleagues: Erica Gadsby, whose work on the personal health budget programme provided the stimulus for this work; and Stephen Peckham, Pauline Allen, Anna Coleman, Julia Segar and Imelda McDermott with whom these issues and ideas were discussed. Anna Coleman and Julia Segar also read and commented upon earlier versions of this manuscript.

Note

1 In the UK, devolution of responsibility for some areas of public policy to Scotland, Wales and Northern Ireland has resulted in a complicated picture of public services for some of the policy areas discussed here (e.g. housing), responsibility for UK policy lies in Westminster. For others, such as health and education, responsibility lies with the devolved administrations. The NHS in England has gone further than in the other devolved nations in the direction of personalisation and choice.

References

Alakeson, V. and Rumbold, B. (2013) *Personal health budgets: challenges for commissioners and policy-makers*. Research summary, London: The Nuffield Trust.

Blair, T. (2004) Speech on public services. Available at: http://news.bbc.co.uk/1/hi/uk_politics/3833345.stm.

Brown, A. F., Ettner, S. L., Piette, J., Weinberger, M., Gregg, E., Shapiro, M. F., Karter, A. J., Safford, M., Waitzfelder, B., Prata, P. A. and Beckles, G. L. (2004) Socioeconomic position and health among persons with diabetes mellitus: a conceptual framework and review of the literature, *Epidemiologic Reviews*, 26(1), 63–77.

Cooper, Z., Gibbons, S., Jones, S. and McGuire, A. (2011) Does hospital competition save lives? Evidence from the English NHS patient choice reforms, *Economic Journal*, 121(554), 228–260.

Crewe, I. and Searing, D. D. (1988) Ideological change in the British Conservative party, *American Political Science Review*, 82(02), 361–384.

Cutler, T., Waine, B. and Brehony, K. (2007) A new epoch of individualization? Problems with the 'personalization' of public sector services, *Public Administration*, 85(3), 847–855.

Davis, K., Stremikis, K., Squires, D. and Schoen, C. (2014) Mirror, mirror on the wall: how the performance of the U.S. health care system compares internationally: the Commonwealth fund. Available at: www.commonwealthfund.org/publications/fund-reports/2014/jun/mirror-mirror.

Department of Health (2001) *Local modernisation reviews: background information*. London: The Stationary Office.

Department of Health (2003) Building on the best; choice, responsiveness and equity in the NHS. London: The Stationary Office. Available at: http://webarchive.nationalarchives.gov.uk/+/dh.gov.uk/en/consultations/responsestoconsultations/dh_4068391.

Department of Health (2006) *Our health, our care, our say: a new direction for community services*. London: The Stationary Office. Available at: https://www.gov.uk/government/uploads/system/uploads/attachment_data/file/272238/6737.pdf.

Department of Health (2008a) High quality care for all: the NHS next steps review final report. London: The Stationary Office. Available at: https://www.gov.uk/government/uploads/system/uploads/attachment_data/file/228836/7432.pdf.

Department of Health (2008b) *Our NHS, our future: NHS next stage review*. London: The Stationary Office. Available at: http://webarchive.nationalarchives.gov.uk/+/dh.gov.uk/en/publicationsandstatistics/publications/publicationspolicyandguidance/dh_079077.

Department of Health (2010) *Equity and excellence: liberating the NHS*. London: The Stationary Office. Available at: https://www.gov.uk/government/uploads/system/uploads/attachment_data/file/213823/dh_117794.pdf.

Department of Health (2011) Operational guidance to the NHS: extending patient choice of provider. *Gateway ref 16242*. Available at: https://www.gov.uk/government/uploads/system/uploads/attachment_data/file/216137/dh_128462.pdf.

Department of Health (2012) *Press release: personal health budgets to be rolled out*. London: The Stationary Office. Available at: https://www.gov.uk/government/news/personal-health-budgets-to-be-rolled-out.

Dickinson, H. and Glasby, J. (2010) *The personalisation agenda: implications for the third sector*. Birmingham, UK: Third Sector Research Centre. Available at: http://www.birmingham.ac.uk/generic/tsrc/documents/tsrc/working-papers/working-paper-30.pdf.

Dixon, A. and Le Grand, J. (2006) Is greater patient choice consistent with equity? The case of the English NHS, *Journal of Health Services Research and Policy*, 11(3), 162–166.

Duffy, S. (2010) The citizenship theory of social justice: exploring the meaning of personalisation for social workers, *Journal of Social Work Practice*, 24(3), 253–267.

Ferguson, I. (2011) Personalisation, social justice and social work: a reply to Simon Duffy, *Journal of Social Work Practice*, 26(1), 55–73.

Forder, J., Jones, K., Glendinning, C., Caiels, J., Welch, E., Baxter, K., Davidson, J., Windle, K., Irvine, A., King, D. and Dolan, P. (2012) *Evaluation of the personal health budget pilot program*. Canterbury: PSSRU.

Fotaki, M. (2010) Patient choice and equity in the British National Health Service: towards developing an alternative framework, *Sociology of Health & Illness*, 32(6), 898–913.

Gadsby, E., Allen, P., Segar, J., Checkland, K., Coleman, A., McDermott, I. and Peckham, S. (2013) Personal budgets, choice and health – a review of international evidence from 11 OECD countries, *International Journal of Public and Private Health Care Management and Economics*, 3(3–4), 28.

Gecas, V. (1989) The social psychology of self-efficacy, *Annual Review of Sociology*, 15, 291–316.

Glendinning, C. (2012) Home care in England: markets in the context of underfunding, *Health and Social Care in the Community*, 20(3), 292–299.

Greener, I. (2009) Towards a history of choice in UK health policy, *Sociology of Health & Illness*, 31(3), 309–324.

Greenhalgh, T., Stones, R. and Swinglehurst, D. (2014) Choose and book: a sociological analysis of 'resistance' to an expert system, *Social Science & Medicine*, 104(0), 210–219.

Harrison, S. (2002) New Labour, modernisation and the medical labour process, *Journal of Social Policy*, 31(3), 465–485.

Harrison, S. and Hunter, D. (1994) *Rationing health care*. London: Institute of Public Policy Research.

Harrison, S. and Moran, M. (2000) Resources and rationing: managing supply and demand in health care. In Albrecht, G. R., Fitzpatrick, R. and Scrimshaw, S. (eds) *The handbook of social studies in health and medicine*. London: Sage, p. 493.

Heginbotham, C. (1997) Why rationing is inevitable in the NHS. In New, B. (ed.) *Rationing: talk and action in healthcare*. London: BMJ Publishing Group, pp. 43–57.

Le Grand, J. (2007) *The other invisible hand: delivering public servcies through choice and competition*. Princeton, NJ: Princeton University Press.

Leadbeater, C. (2004) *Personalisation through participation: a new script for public services*. London: Demos. Available at: http://www.demos.co.uk/files/Personalisation ThroughParticipation.pdf.

Leadbeater, C., Bartlett, J. and Gallagher, N. (2008) *Making it personal*. London: Demos. Available at: http://www.partnerships.org.au/Making%20It%20Personal.pdf.

Leadbeater, C. and Lownsbrough, H. (2005) Personalisation and participation: the future of social care in scotland. *Final Report Commissioned by Care 21 for the Social Work Review*. London: Demos.

Lenaghan, J. (1996) *Rationing and rights in healthcare*. London: Institute of Public Policy Research.

Liebenberg, L., Ungar, M. and Ikeda, J. (2013) Neo-liberalism and responsibilisation in the discourse of social service workers, *British Journal of Social Work*, 45, 1006–1021.

McDonald, R. (2004) Individual identity and organisational control: empowerment and modernisation in a primary care trust, *Sociology of Health & Illness*, 26(7), 925–950.

Miliband, D. (2006) Choice and voice in personalised learning, in *Personalising Education Conference*, OECD Publishing, Paris, DOI: http://dx.doi.org/10.1787/9789264 036604-2-en.

Needham, C. (2009) Interpreting personalization in England's National Health Service: a textual analysis, *Critical Policy Studies*, 3(2), 204–220.

Needham, C. (2011a) *Personalising public services*. Bristol, UK: Policy Press.

Needham, C. (2011b) Personalization: from story-line to practice, *Social Policy & Administration*, 45(1), 54–68.

New, B. (1997) The rationing agenda in the NHS. In New, B. (ed.) *Rationing: talk and action in healthcare*, London: BMJ Publishing Group, pp. 8–30.

NHS England (2013) Draft framework of excellence in clinical commissioning Nov 2013. Available at: https://www.england.nhs.uk/wp-content/uploads/2013/11/frmwrk-exc-cc1.pdf.

Nutbeam, D. (2000) Health literacy as a public health goal: a challenge for contemporary health education and communication strategies into the 21st century, *Health Promotion International*, 15(3), 259–267.

Peacock, M., Bissell, P. and Owen, J. (2014) Dependency denied: health inequalities in the neo-liberal era, *Social Science & Medicine*, 118(0), 173–180.

Peckham, S., Sanderson, M., Entwistle, V., Thompson, A., Hughes, D., Prior, L., Allen, P., Mays, N., Brown, M., Kelly, G., Powell, A., Baldie, D., Linyard, A., Duguid, A., Davies, H. (2011) A comparative study of the construction and implementation of patient choice policies in the UK. Final report. NIHR Service Delivery and Organisation programme. Available at: http://www.netscc.ac.uk/hsdr/files/project/SDO_FR_08-1718-147_V01.pdf.

Pollock, A., Macfarlane, A., Kirkwood, G., Majeed, F. A., Greener, I., Morelli, C., Boyle, S., Mellett, H., Godden, S., Price, D. and Brhlikova, P. (2011) No evidence that patient choice in the NHS saves lives, *The Lancet*, 378(9809), 2057–2060.

Rose, N. (2000) Community, citizenship, and the third way, *American Behavioral Scientist*, 43(9), 1395–1411.

Secretary of State for Health (1997) *The new NHS: modern, dependable*. London: The Stationary Office.

Secretary of State for Health (2000) *The NHS plan: a plan for investment, a plan for reform*. London: The Stationary Office.

Secretary of State for Social Services (1972) *NHS reorganisation: England*. London: HMSO.

Segall, M. (1983) Planning and politics of resource allocation for primary health care: promotion of meaningful national policy, *Social Science & Medicine*, 17(24), 1947–1960.

Soteriou, M. (2013) GP contract 2014/15: GPs to be named accountable clinician for 4m patients, *GP magazine*. Available at: http://www.gponline.com/gp-contract-2014-15-gps-named-accountable-clinician-4m-patients/article/1221144.

Strecher, V. J., McEvoy DeVellis, B., Becker, M. H. and Rosenstock, I. M. (1986) The role of self-efficacy in achieving health behavior change, *Health Education & Behavior*, 13(1), 73–92.

8 Designing for personalisation in predictive and preventive medicine

Olga Golubnitschaja, Heinz Lemke, Marko Kapalla and Tony Kent

Introduction

In spite of the scientific and technological progress seen in the twentieth century, it is evident that our health is under relentless attack from both external and internal factors. These extend from our lived environments to personal lifestyles and could have been eliminated by existing technologies: advances in diagnostic devices and biometric databases have been notably successful in this context. Although life expectancy is increasing, the quality of life in older age is questionable even in developed countries and, as a result, people spend many years of their lives visiting physicians and hospitals instead of enjoying life with their families and friends.

In meeting these needs, healthcare systems absorb enormous amounts of money in the treatment of preventable diseases. Typically, between 7 and 12 per cent of GDP worldwide is spent on healthcare, amounting to 10.2 per cent in 2012, to the value of $7.5 trillion in 2013 (World Bank, 2015a; World Bank, 2015b). Over the past ten years, the National Institutes of Health have argued that to reduce costs while improving health and healthcare, medicine must move away from its Industrial Age roots in providing 'one size fits all' therapies to become more predictive, pre-emptive, personalised, and participative over time (www.nih.gov/strategicvision.htm). Costs could be reduced by changing from an unsustainable and imbalanced disease-oriented healthcare philosophy, 'diseasecare', to a health-oriented healthcare: an economically viable, systematic, and progressive alternative. Vital scientific and technological support for such a change can be delivered from a novel type of healthcare facility, *predictive, preventive and personalised medicine (PPPM) centres* (Kapalla et al., 2014).

Personalised medicine can be defined as 'the use of genomic and other biotechnologies to derive information about an individual that could be used to inform types of health interventions that would best suit that individual' (Savard, 2013: 197). PPPM is intended to provide a system for healthcare that is patient centred and also cost effective. The predictive element of PPPM determines an individual's predisposition to a disease before its onset to integrate targeted preventive measures in a personalised treatment and lifestyle regime. PPPM will involve effective population screening, disease prevention early in childhood, the identification of at-risk people, and the stratification of patients for optimal therapy. The approach will enable planned treatments that can predict and reduce adverse drug–drug or drug–disease interactions by adopting emerging technologies, such as imaging, disease modelling and individual patient profiles. This level of integration of treatment elements has significant implications for the conceptualisation, facilitation and communication of PPPM through design. PPPM requires that responsibility for 'personal' health be distributed between the individual person, medical practitioners and the material elements of the PPPM system that store and mediate information. Its effectiveness in cost-effectively bringing about good health outcomes is dependent on the effectiveness of the relationships between these elements.

This chapter approaches these relationships from two perspectives, reflecting the authors' backgrounds. From a medical perspective, the chapter discusses some consequences for life-time health of two moments in the human life span – birth and puberty/adolescence, setting out the system by which PPPM can model disease and treatment over the life-span. From a design perspective, the chapter builds on the patient participation that is key to PPPM in order to outline a 'human-centred' approach to the modelling. This approach is informed by work that acknowledges the culturally inflected mediation necessary in effective engagement with complex information systems.

EPMA and the vision of the PPPM centre

PPPM centres are the vision of the European Association for Predictive, Preventive and Personalised Medicine (EPMA).[1] These networked entities will combine the physical environment of medical units, clinical and analytical laboratories, with nutrition and other health-related synergy divisions and knowledge-based imaging techniques, bioinformatics and specific computer models. These components are essential for the evidence-based early prediction of health problems to enable preventive action and promote an attitude in apparently healthy individuals, which means they care enough about their own health to avoid ever being called 'a patient' (Kapalla and Matušková, 2009; Kapalla, 2010; Kapalla et al., 2014). The envisioned PPPM centre will facilitate both transdisciplinary co-operation, a range of health-related science and its application in healthcare.

In 2013, EPMA identified the main issues concerning the implementation and integration of scientific and technological innovation in medicine and healthcare. Long-term international partnerships and multidisciplinary projects will be necessary. Therefore, successful implementation will require an unprecedented level of collaboration amongst stakeholders formed from professional partnerships of public and private entities, including universities, state-funded research institutes, hospitals and physicians, and also drug companies, diagnostics and information providers. In addition, it is evident that PPPM will have to engage with legal and regulatory bodies, to establish a robust platform to ensure acceptance and compliance.

Personalisation and the essential role of design in PPPM

Personalisation of healthcare is relevant to policymakers for its alleged ability to reduce healthcare costs, and to individuals regardless of age, gender, religion and nationality for its promise to improve their personal health. This will require innovative design approaches to PPPM-related medical services and new products resulting from research, as well as from education and learning materials. The focus will be on the communication of predictive diagnostics, for targeted prevention and engagement with patients to provide treatments tailored to individual needs.

Personalisation in this field concerns both diagnosis and medication, with priority given to early and predictive diagnostics as the pivotal stage prior to the cost-effective preventive measures and treatments tailored to the person: their personalised medication. For optimal treatments it is essential to include information at all levels, from personality type to tissue, cellular, sub-cellular and molecular characterisation. Personalisation as the personal story of a patient and the creation of their personal profile is currently less well understood. An individual profile establishes more complex and detailed knowledge of the person through their family health history, the illnesses and conditions that have been evident in the past in other family members, and typified by descriptive elements going back to birth. Profiles are concerned with hereditary/genetic as well as the epigenetic (environment-regulated modifiable risk factors) make-up of the individual.

The profile leads to the modelling of predictive health elements for each person and the implementation of a predictive database. Although routine health checks currently include health questionnaires that cover some of this ground (disorders), a more advanced personal profile will include other contributory factors. For example, employment and career options determine physical and mental wellbeing and the profiling of the external environment will indicate the impact of pollution, living and work conditions. Furthermore, resource and utility availability will also have an effect on general health. At present, an assessment of general risk is missing, and its definition alone is problematic. Nevertheless, an interactive model of these elements will ultimately lead to high-quality personalised treatment and higher degree of prevention of serious illnesses. From the information processing, knowledge structuring and health status result reporting point of view, it is obvious that smart design in all these PPPM-IT-related services and products is of great importance. It is crucial for effective communication between the particular person/patient and all other healthcare professionals.

Design should be recognised at the centre of personalisation as the essential attribute of any 'trans-domain' action in the effective interplay of the stakeholders. In addition to the design of products, design should be recognised as a strategic tool in the redesign of processes and services capable of bringing innovative solutions to complex issues. There is a need for a broader approach to design that can bring added-value in the public sector, driving innovative and economically sustainable solutions. As Koskinen and Thomson (2012: 58) observe:

We need to put people at the centre of future user-centred approaches, service re-design and improvement... Demands from the public for greater personalisation of services will require public sector managers to understand their users' needs much better and provide flexible, agile and in some cases co-produced services.

This raises the important issue of engagement and communication between medical professionals and all users of PPPM, for example doctors and their patients, and between researchers and hospitals. The development of a communications system should include the appropriate design of multi-disciplinary education about PPPM between professional groups and the selection of appropriate media. Moreover, designers have to recognise that changes in patient lifestyles and their environmental contexts require effective targeted communication, which will be identified through patient profiling. A second aspect is the optimisation of didactic and learning materials primarily to engage with different professional groups, but also across the whole spectrum of stakeholders.

All these characteristics inform a multidisciplinary approach to preventative medicine, and it is this approach that is groundbreaking: the concepts, professional initiatives and potential solutions. The specific design challenges for PPPM are discussed in the following sections, with a focus on EPMA's mission to promote a new culture in healthcare by facilitating communication between the professional actors involved.

Multidisciplinary communication: interactome design

The specific challenge for multidisciplinary communication is the design of media to facilitate effective interaction amongst professional groups in PPPM. These groups currently use different disciplinary languages that reinforce their professional perspective and frequently underestimate the added value of the transfer of products and services between disciplines. The specific output of this designing activity is the 'professional interactome'. The concept of interactome was introduced in 1999 by Bernard Jacq and colleagues to describe molecular interaction networks in cells, to acknowledge their high degree of interrelation and interconnection and simplifying these complex systems into components (nodes) and interactions (edges) between them. Although such simplification risks downplaying the functional richness of each node, the concept of interactome is used here as an analogy for the system of relationships between human and mechanical agents that PPPM implies.

Figure 8.1 represents a model of healthcare organisation designed to implement effective interaction amongst the professional groups in PPPM. The circle represents the 'health information space' with interrelated clinical databases (DB) available to all the interacting professionals and other participants at different levels with different access rights. The flow, exchange and sharing of information are highlighted as light grey and dark grey arrows.

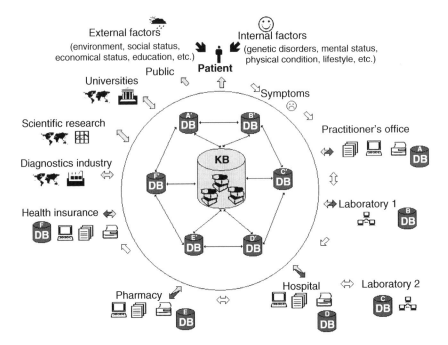

Figure 8.1 Professional interactome design.

Source: Adapted from Kapalla and Matušková (2009).

The white arrows highlight the possible physical route of the patient. The clinical databases (DB) contribute to a continually updated knowledge base (KB) along with current scientific research and existing data.

The distinctive feature of this approach to medical care is the integration of research from industry and academia into the knowledge base, with data from health insurers concerning incidence of medical conditions and above all, risk. In this model, universities provide not only medical research but also related research in social sciences, and medical training at all levels. Thus, practitioners working in the patient's micro-environment, doctors and health providers in hospitals, but also pharmacists in the community, are networked into an informed and dynamic system.

The PPPM system develops the patient's individual health profile from factors both internal and external to the patient. The internal factors concern personal aspects of the patient's health, including their lifestyle, while external factors concern the patient in their environment. From the presentation of initial symptoms, treatment is dependent upon a sequence of interactions with institutions and organisations, some having a direct relationship with the patient, and others more distantly informing and mediating the treatment.

With the increasingly complex relationship between basic research and clinical application, there is a pressing need to bridge the translational gap from laboratory to clinic using integrative methods. The mission of 'translational bioinformatics'[2] is, therefore, to provide infrastructure and techniques that enable integrative modelling of the whole biological system across multiple scales. Design can contribute to this part of the project through conceptualisation, mapping and visualisation of the complex sets of requirements, to realise the integrative objective of PPPM. Since PPPM aims to enable a multitude of purposes in the frame of individualised healthcare, a significant amount of personalised data and information should be managed for proper individualised diagnosis and prognosis. As mentioned above, integrative modelling approaches of bioinformatics provide a suitable medium for fusion of such data and interpretation of the information derived from specific predictive and preventative models. Consequently, integrative modelling approaches become the major building block of future PPPM efforts as their potential in bridging the translational gap is increasingly appreciated and will lead to the first examples of model-driven, personalised treatment optimisation.

Personalisation in PPPM and human-centred design

The design challenges in defining and building the professional interactome are grounded in bioinformatics. However, PPPM, with its focus on personalisation and a detailed understanding of individuals and their needs, can achieve other objectives through a human-centred design (HCD) approach. In HCD, researchers and designers attempt to cooperate with and learn from potential users, in professional groups and other stakeholders, and ensure that their needs and demands are taken into account in all phases of design (Beyer and Holtzblatt, 1998).

The aim of HCD is to develop products or services, and in PPPM to consider the integration of the two, that match users' practices, needs and preferences. These can be combined in two dimensions: first, as a balance of users' and designers' knowledge and ideas, and, second, as a balance between an understanding of current or past practices with the envisioning of alternative or future practices (Harder et al., 2013). Steen (2012) proposes six different approaches to achieve these balances: participatory design, ethnography, the lead-user approach, contextual design, co-design and empathic design. Moreover, they advocate that HCD practitioners critically reflect on their practices, their methods and their own involvement, so that they can more consciously follow specific HCD approaches and more mindfully cope with the two tensions.

World-leading design consultancy IDEO, conceptualises HCD as a process and set of techniques used to create new solutions that can include products, services, environments, organisations, and modes of interaction. The HCD process begins by examining the visions, needs and behaviours of the people, in this case the professionals and other participants in the interactome, to be affected by the designer's solutions. This requires the designer to listen to and understand what they want, in IDEO's definition using the 'desirability lens' throughout the design process. Once what is desirable has been established, the designers view solutions through the lenses of 'feasibility' and 'viability' in the later phases of the process (IDEO, 2010).

This perspective has informed 'design thinking', an approach that emerged in the 2000s in response to corporate and national attention on the strategic importance of creativity and innovation and their advantages in complex and competitive environments. Design thinking is described as a methodology that imbues the full spectrum of innovation activities with a HCD ethos (Brown, 2008). This allows designers' sensibility and methods to be applied to managerial problem solving, regardless of the problem, in the way that designers approach design problems (Lockwood, 2010; Dunne and Martin, 2006). While Martin (2009) proposes that managers learn how to apply this methodology more widely to such processes as strategy development and business model innovation, design thinking can also be employed successfully by public sector organisations (Terrey, 2013).

The methodological approaches that could be used to model the flows of information and knowledge and the networks they create in PPPM, are in part located in the toolkits of design thinking. Simonse (2014) demonstrates their application to modelling solutions:

- An actor map depicts the transactions between actors in a network. The aim is to visually capture connections, through interviews and to monitor and evaluate situations with many stakeholders who 'influence'.
- A role perspective tool supports the identification of stakeholders in a network or community as key holders of insights and clues for system solutions. For example, the HCD toolkit of IDEO (2010) which holds desirability lenses, such as the 'community driven discovery' lens, and encourages design by empathy through intentional adoption of different viewpoints on the situation.
- An activity map makes use of infographics or photos to illustrate the activities. For example, in a business context, the tool of a 'customer journey' to generate user insight and to design a service. In the PPPM context, different journeys could be mapped from the activities and interactions of professionals from different organisations.

Creating value in network contexts is not so much an activity of an individual designer as it is a cooperative effort because it requires a broader skill set (Bitner et al., 2008). As experienced in many cases, experts on a certain topic and with the most insight for the design challenge are the people in the wider PPPM community, not only in the professional groups but also the patients themselves. This aspect should not be overlooked in the multidisciplinary design of the interactome.

Creating new didactic and educational measures

The specific challenge facing the educational dimension of PPPM is to design new didactic approaches for successful educational measures among professional participants. These will introduce the innovative concepts of PPPM that shift from a delayed reactive medical care, to a predictive and preventive one. The ultimate goal of this designing activity is to support the formation of a new generation of professionals in medicine who will be able to implement a holistic approach to patient care. It will recognise the complexity and individuality of any organism instead of treating the patient as a disaggregated 'pool of organs'.

The unique PPPM concepts are reflected in a series of publications designed to provide learning materials for specialised educational measures to create optimal multidisciplinary interaction and a new generation of professionals in innovative medical fields (Golubnitschaja, 2012). The design issues in this context relate to the mapping of complexity and subsequent creation of interdisciplinary educational courses and materials. The main challenge is the creation of a robust educational platform for holders among whom there are a wide spectrum of complementary activities arising from the multifunctional professional groups working in this field. In response, EPMA promotes an integrative approach to related educational measures amongst healthcare stakeholders, governmental institutions, educators themselves, funding bodies, patient organisations and other bodies in the public domain. In keeping with an HCD approach, patients as 'end-users' should be considered in this process.

The expected impacts for healthcare education and communication can be categorised by their predictive objective and target population. Some will focus on effective population screening, prevention early in childhood, and identification of persons at-risk. Others will determine the stratification of patients for optimal therapy planning. A third group involves the prediction and reduction of adverse drug–drug or drug–disease interactions relying on emerging technologies, such as pharmacogenetics[3] and pathology-specific molecular patterns.[4]

The broader educational design implications can be assessed within the context of the concepts and methodologies discussed in the preceding section, but also service design. Stegall (2006) emphasises the designer's role and responsibility for influencing individuals and societies to adopt sustainable behaviour. Moreover, he maintains that products should, through their design, increase the 'literacy' of individuals by demonstrating the superiority of systems, raising awareness and developing a kinship with the topic to hand. The ultimate aim is for the worldview of individuals to be affected by their reflection on products, to effectively 'interact' with the 'learning' of the designer when they come into contact with the product and at that point to be raised to a deep level of 'learning alongside' the designer (Stegall, 2006; Harder et al., 2013). Specifically, the design contribution will be to map, organise and create accessible and motivational learning materials for interdisciplinary professional groups.

This will require an understanding of the different disciplinary languages and professional approaches to healthcare, primarily scientific and technical, but to some extent organisational and social. Second, there will be a design need to consider the objectives of informing the wider PPPM community about the changes between reactive and predictive healthcare.

Innovative technologies, approaches and services in PPPM

Personalised medicine presents specific challenges in the design of new technologies, approaches and services aiming at the practical realisation of the holistic concepts of PPPM. As discussed above, the most important ones are individualised patient profiling, early and predictive diagnostics, cost-effective targeted prevention, and treatments tailored to the person. The design innovation is summarised in Figure 8.2, in which data are defined as patient-oriented inputs to create knowledge outputs. 'Model-guided medicine' describes the computational technologies for holistic PPPM approaches and the requirement for the design of new technologies, devices, tactics and services in the healthcare of the twenty-first century. Patient data follow well-established procedures, but these are only partial, depending on the condition and treatment of the patient. Also, the focus is on the specific health problems that are already manifested as chronic pathologies, e.g. different cancer types, neurological and cardiovascular diseases, diabetes mellitus and/or its individual complications.

PPPM envisages a more comprehensive approach, gathering complex data from specialised functions from the micro level of the body's biochemistry (internal factors) to lifestyle elements concerning nutrition, environment, hygiene, social interactions and other (external) factors. These levels and types of complex data must be systemically analysed to create a personalised profile for the patient. Individual patient data serves as an input for the general model in which it is analysed, and offers expert assistance for clinical decisions. Feedback is an essential part of the entire system for reliable predictions because, on the base of new information and knowledge, it allows actors within the networked system to correct, refine or even change previous predictions. In the future, a unique personal model might be available for each patient (Kapalla and Matušková, 2009; Kapalla, 2010). Knowledge of the patient is thus extended beyond specific problems with a limited range of solutions to one that can provide a diversity of medical interventions, treatments and therapies. Hence, the *individual patient profile* as a tool, evaluates relevant health and disease aspects of a patient and may lead to a more accurate methodology for a new personalised, patient-specific diagnosis, prognosis and treatment system. Information and communication technology (ICT) tools, such as intelligent agents, may assist in the decision-making processes for a PPPM system through their ability to perceive and react, or pro-actively respond, to changes in the environment. These features relate to earlier discussion about the engagement of designers with the system's users to define problems and create solutions, and the role of design in the visualisation, simplification and communication of complex data.

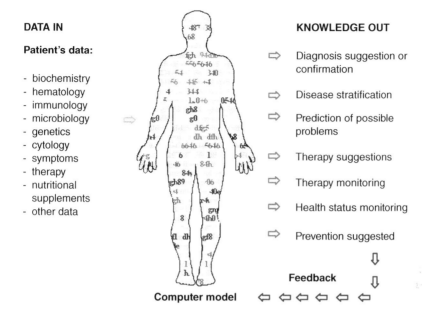

Figure 8.2 Interactive computer model of human metabolism and other biological interactions.

Source: Adapted from Kapalla and Matušková (2009).

Individual patient data (patient profile, 'data in') serve as an input for the general model that offers an expert assistance with clinical decisions ('knowledge out'). It is important to stress the inevitable role of feedback in order to further develop and refine the model as well as the important role of HCD in PPPM information technology-based services. When all particular experts in PPPM contribute with their knowledge and experience, a unique personal model (Figure 8.2) shall, hopefully, be available for each patient. In years to come, such models will be engaged in the envisioned PPPM centres.

The optimal interrelationship between 'medical unit/doctor and patient'

The challenge facing the interrelation between the medical unit/doctor and the patient is to design the optimal model of this relationship. The model should address issues of professional qualification, education of both parties, quality of individual outcomes, economy (cost effectiveness) of the interaction (micro and macro level) and ethical aspects such as satisfaction of both providers and patients. A number of studies have demonstrated that the most effective cooperation takes place when both parties are well motivated to achieve the best possible results (Costigliola, 2011). Therefore, both doctors and patients need to play an active role in the effective implementation of PPPM. The concept of participatory medicine sees patients as responsible drivers of their health, in which providers encourage and value them as full partners. Consequently, participatory medicine advances knowledge of a patient about, and their active involvement in, the treatment's multimodality choice and successful performance, as well as the most optimal behavioural adaptation in the post-treatment periods of life (see also the section 'Self-management of health, disease prevention and optimal care for chronically diseased persons' below).

The doctor–patient interrelationship should be considered within the overall context of the current evolution of demographic profile of societies with a multi-ethnic population, increasing mobility of patients and increasing number of people suffering from the age-related chronic pathologies. The diagnostic and treatment approaches should be correspondingly adapted to the needs of the changing society. To be well informed about all steps in the medical treatment as well as to refuse it is considered to be a fundamental and legitimate human right. It is in this context that HCD takes a central place in participative and relational model building: between the providers of medical treatment and their patients. The humanisation of healthcare relationships can be understood as the sum of 'all the actions, the measures and behaviours that concur to guarantee the safeguarding and the dignity of every human being as a user of health care facilities' (del Nord, 1997: 14). The user is at the centre of every design decision, not only as a producer of functional requirements but principally to give expression to human values that must be considered of ever-increasing importance. In the case of hospital facilities, the perception of their tangible and non-tangible aspects by every user

> stimulates a direct relationship between a personalised mental image and a specific meaning assigned to the image's objects . . . in order to design the physical environment, the organisational system and the behavioural models properly one must proceed on the user's physical and cultural context.
>
> (del Nord, p. 15)

This leads to a second perspective of design and the concept of user experience. Designing for user experience moves beyond products and services providing for pragmatic needs: they must also support users' hedonic needs, such as stimulation and self-expression (Nuutinen and Keinonen, 2011). For PPPM, the implications are to design interactions *with* patients that take a broader account of users' emotional, contextual and dynamically evolving needs, and the impact of users' previous experiences on new experiences. The goal should be to create something that attracts and creates new meanings for the patient, but also other users in the system. New design methodologies in this field explain experience design as moments of engagement or interaction with the aim of creating positive memories (Ardill, 2008) and worth-centred design as a consideration of digital design and the need for interaction and connectivity with users (Cockton, 2008).

A significant element in this broadly conceptualised doctor–patient relationship is the media, which has the capacity to affect the image and performance of medical care. Many printed and online media sources identify information deficits for patients; consequently, the type and quality of available information should be highly valued. However, information available on the Internet can trigger serious consequences by providing misleading medical statements, descriptions, advertising of medication, and approaches to treatment. In future, information circulating through social media may amplify these problems. Therefore, considerable attention should be paid to the implementation of a professional information service that provides both patients and medical doctors with approved issue-related information. This provision should be integrated into the design of PPPM's communication and educational programmes, so that all 'touchpoints' with users provide seamless and consistent advice.

Self-management of health, disease prevention and optimal care for chronically diseased persons

Current demographic changes have led to an increase in ageing subpopulations in the developed world. To meet the health provision challenges that accompany this increase requires innovative thinking and processes to promote health and enable the management and stabilisation of chronic diseases cost effectively. To meet these requirements the *design of distanced and self-monitoring technologies and devices* is being given extensive consideration. These are designed to advance medical services and stimulate a more patient-centric health management process in order to meet a number of objectives:

- the daily control of individually relevant health parameters;
- the empowerment of patients increasing their self-care management capabilities and personal responsibility over their health;
- an increase in preventive care action;
- maintaining the stability of chronic diseases and the avoidance of unnecessary visits to a medical unit/doctor;
- control over potential disease progression;
- reduction in severe exacerbations, acute and/or long-term hospitalisation.

Self-management offers advantages to both patient and medical service providers, whether doctors, hospitals or other agencies. By 2014, the UK National Health Service had embraced wearable medical devices, such as the Apple watch, which enables patients to monitor their medical condition. However, a number of issues arise from the distanced and patient-centred use of technological devices, demonstrated in issues surrounding ownership, privacy and usability. In a broad context, the 'sensor society' is concerned with the social, legal and policy implications of the growing network of sensors that provide streams of data about personal lives and movements throughout the course of the day. Continuous information accumulation, its complexity and ubiquity have implications for privacy, power and surveillance in the world of interactive devices. Control over the sensing infrastructure, the databases, and the response platforms will play a crucial role in how information is used and who benefits. At a processing level, the wealth of data is problematic too, in terms of capacity and storage for data mining and pattern identification, qualified personnel resources, the skills and time implications for those who have access to such data and where they are located or distributed.

These perspectives should inform the design of personal medical devices. In the context of an ageing society, particular attention should be paid to their practicality for older people, their aesthetics and ability to convey meaning. Motivation to use and keep using the device is critical, otherwise doctors or other care providers will have to intervene, and interventions are neither cost effective nor efficient.

PPPM and its application to life stages

Birth

PPPM is appropriate at every life stage with each one demonstrating specific characteristics. Of immediate interest are the earliest stages of life, and the opportunities of the PPPM approach to inform the care of newborn babies and adolescents. These are considered in more detail in this section.

Perinatal morbidity accounts for more than a half of all child deaths, which indicates the impact of perinatal complications in newborns on adult health. This impact is accompanied by a lack of knowledge about and/or practical application of targeted prevention and effective treatment of neonatal, perinatal and postnatal pathologies. The lack of integrated knowledge about these conditions presents particular problems in the design of an appropriate PPPM system that can take account of their effect on adult health.

An oxygen deficit at delivery, which can be fatal or lead to mild or severe hypoxic ischaemic organ damage, is the most frequent complication in newborns, potentially resulting in neurodegenerative pathologies, diabetes type 2 and cancer. The task of design for PPPM is therefore to facilitate the use of individual prediction, targeted prevention and personalised treatments before the manifestation of the life-long pathologies usually developed by newborns with asphyxic deficits. This would allow robust diagnostic approaches targeted at the molecular pathways affected by perinatal asphyxia, biomarker-candidates and potential drug-targets for tailored treatments in neonatology and paediatrics (Golubnitschaja et al., 2011; Yeghiazaryan et al., 2009).

Puberty/adolescence

Puberty/adolescence is considered a particularly sensitive phase of physical and mental development. Optimal healthcare for teenagers may play a crucial role in maintaining good physical and mental health through adulthood. Current studies convincingly demonstrate that exposure to stress in this life stage may lead to syndromes that range in severity from anxiety states to more severe psychopathologies later in life.

The role of design in PPPM for this life stage encompasses both the design of personalised healthcare communications and its mediation: attracting, motivating and maintaining interest and engagement is important. Moreover, definitions of teenagers, beyond a literal description, are complex; the age range is as wide as from 8 to over 24. Driven by information, for example through smart devices and social media, this is the most socially connected age-group and they can be characterised by unstable, small-scale, affectual groups held together by shared lifestyles. These complexities suggest there is a pivotal role for an integrated design solution for communications and media targeted at specific sub-groups of teenagers. Communication design can accommodate external factors of socio-economic status, educational level, sport/physical activities and gender differences and the issues of hormonal status and genetic and epigenetic predispositions – for example, hereditary genetic/metabolic alterations – that may be the consequences of perinatal complications.

One significant task considering this spectrum of young people's needs is to design motivational messages targeted at specific subgroups drawing insights from marketing. One example that could be adapted from branded marketing communications (Grant, 2004) is the ways in which PPPM can be positioned in the eyes of teenagers as a brand that is a 'navigator', 'weaver', 'host', or as 'owned by' adolescent patients. The aim is to use design insights to help PPPM support the development of individuality and well-justified personal choices and responsibility, as an alternative to conforming to standard roles and models. This can promote the teenager's understanding of their personal significance and value in society on the one hand, and on the other, to create an understanding of personal responsibility in society. Healthy lifestyles including sport, diet and appearance are very individual during the teenager years and their lifestyle choices have a corresponding impact on health conditions in the long term.

Model-guided medicine: cost-effective modernisation of healthcare

This section turns to the problem of costs in healthcare and presents an integrated information system, as the foundation of model-guided medicine resulting in cost-effective, focused healthcare. Designers can make valuable contributions to the model, particularly in the visualisation of the problems, modelling techniques and their solutions. Design-thinking allows new insights and the creative exploration of possibilities and the principles of HCD enable systems designers to understand the users' perspective and to consider real-life settings.

Currently, the diagnosis and treatment of individual health problems requires a combination of information from medical records and other sources, including the patient themselves. These are integrated by the physician to create an abstract 'mental model' of the patient. It must be as close as possible to reality to serve as a basis for decision-making with respect to the medical procedure to be followed. The limitations of clinical judgement are inherent in limitations in the information available to the physician and the physician's ability to appropriately apply it to treat the patient. It is traditionally centred on medical records; that is, based on information component listing and summary reporting of the patient as a person. PPPM proposes a strategy to transcend these limitations of clinical judgement with the data-base 'interactome' outlined above; an ICT-based holistic presentation of the individual patient and corresponding medical process/procedure *redesigned* within a given medical domain, such as common cardiovascular, neurological, diabetic or oncologic disorders. EPMA argues that a prerequisite for effective PPPM is a Medical Information and Model Management System (MIMMS), with an architecture and core functionalities indicated in Figure 8.3.

The practice of medicine will be substantially transformed with a holistic presentation of a specific patient based on appropriate mathematical modelling methods, such as probabilistic relational models, process models and advanced ICT-enabling tools. The result will be model-based medical evidence (MBME) providing transparency of clinical situations, processes and decisions for both patient and physician.

The Medical Information and Model Management System (MIMMS) will assist physicians in dealing with the overwhelming amount of information that is available to them. It will provide appropriate clinical support tools that form part of the advanced ICT, and allow the physician to prioritise and integrate all relevant individual patient data into a formal ICT-based patient specific model (PSM) to assist in the decision-making processes. Such a model would represent all of the health and disease aspects of a patient, and when linked to medical process models, will lead to a more accurate methodology for a new personalised, patient-specific diagnosis, prognosis and treatment paradigm: model-guided medicine (MGM).

In the future, once the ICT information and communication technology is developed, MIMMS can be disseminated throughout the world, wherever IT and communication interfaces are available. The consequence will be a profound and cost-effective change to the organisation of healthcare. ICT is applied here in a synergistic spirit with disciplines such as biology, medicine, engineering, informatics and mathematical modelling. It is, in effect, a comprehensive presentation of patient-specific situations and medical processes, combined with information from industry and other stakeholders. It will be accomplished through close cooperation with expert partners of excellence in healthcare, medicine, education and ICT. After successful realisation of the ICT MIMMS concept, the reproducibility, effectiveness, economics and patient outcome of medical procedures should experience a dramatic improvement. In the long term, this model-guided medicine, vision and system, if designed, implemented and employed as suggested, will be disruptive to current medical practice and has the potential to transform it. The beneficiaries of

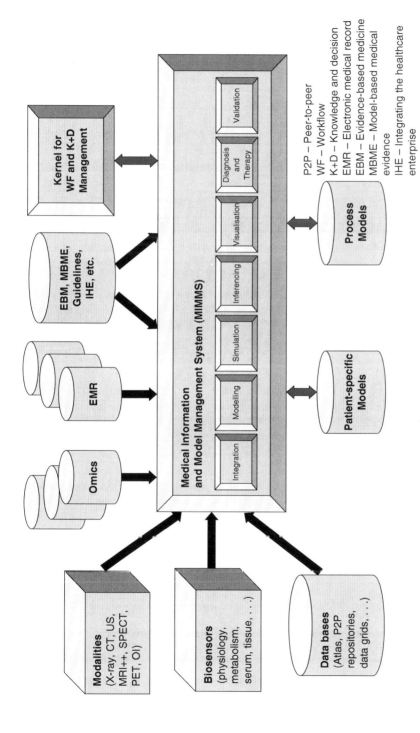

Figure 8.3 ICT component architecture for integrated (model-based) patient care with MIMMS.

Source: Lemke and Golubnitschaja (2014).

these transforming methods and technologies will include patients, healthcare providers, and society at large.

In particular, both physicians and patients will be able to use and leverage the vast amounts of medical information and knowledge from medical disciplines. HCD can contribute to the methodology in creating the MIMMS and tools to provide cost-effective and improved healthcare. Further, it can assist with new methods of organising and visualising the collection of – statistically valid – medical data as model-based medical evidence. It is proposed that once the ICT is developed, employed and assessed, it will substantially transform medical education and training. With this essential educational component, the dissemination of model-guided medicine and associated technologies throughout all parts of the world, wherever IT and communication interfaces are available, will result in profound and cost-effective modernisation of healthcare.

Designing ethical counselling services in PPPM

Recent advances in understanding the molecular bases of diseases, their systemic correlations to genetic predisposition, and their interactions with individual lifestyles and environments, are drastically changing perceptions of diagnosis and therapy. Given this scenario, innovative ethical analyses and ethical interventions are demanded, especially in order to put the individual patient and his/her needs at the centre of this new way of thinking and practising medicine. PPPM aims at addressing the investigation, construction and implementation of an ethical counselling service (ECS) as a tool both for patients and for clinicians. One issue is that the *judgements* as to what constitutes a 'condition' means PPPM medicalises conditions (as pre-dispositions) that have hitherto not been considered significant, therefore raising ethical questions about what are appropriate actions for the 'person' to take.

Therein the main task for PPPM is to break through decisional paralysis that can occur in difficult clinical cases. It is designed to help:

- the patient and/or his/her relatives to undergo clinical decisions involving ethical perspectives and values. The patient could benefit from the counsellor's help in clarifying the ethical values involved, his/her personal value hierarchy, and in engaging a rational deliberation that results into an empowered decision making;
- the clinician (i) to have a complete as possible picture of the ethical issues involved in the cases in question, so that his/her interaction with patients/relatives could be ethically aware, non-directive, non-paternalistic and autonomously respectful; and (ii) to develop an ethical sensitivity in order to make him/her able to analyse, also from an ethical standpoint, all those cases he/she might cross with.

ECS could be realised whenever 'epidemiology/statistics vs. personalisation' is the issue in question. The gap between 'epidemiological vs. personalised' i.e. 'statistically justified vs. real for the individual' risk increases patient's confusion and uncertainty, thus inducing stress, anxiety and fear. By explaining the significance of the probability analyses, this service is able to provide the patient with a complete and always updated framework concerning his/her individual effective risk and thus offering him/her better tools for his/her decision (Bruni et al., 2012).

Conclusion

This chapter has demonstrated how optimal design is essential for the successful implementation of PPPM as the future of medicine. Design in this context is specifically applied to comprehensive professional activities and products, at any level of successful PPPM implementation. Taken as a whole, PPPM would benefit from holistic problem-solving approaches used by designers, and throughout this chapter, engagement with stakeholders has been a central issue. One strategy that can be adopted is design thinking, as an approach and technique to integrate every process and stage of development of the system. Transferring Liedtka's (2013) organisational perspective of design in strategic planning to the integration of PPPM, it can involve more people

> in two-way strategic conversations . . . [to] view the process as one of iteration and experimentation, and pay sequential attention to idea generation and evaluation in a way that attends first to *possibilities* before moving onto *constraints*.
>
> (p. 25)

In this mode, design thinking can be applied to planning at the highest levels, as well as operationally and in project management, and is considered to be widely participative and accessible to non-designers. It is seen as a transferable skill to be acquired and added to the repertoire of thinking tools, and designers themselves have proposed initiatives in the development of healthcare infrastructures (Collins and Linscott, 2013).

Specifically, there are a number of PPPM objectives that will benefit from engagement with service and user experience design, but also product and communication design. The objectives include the optimisation of the professional set-up in healthcare to satisfy patient needs, creation of optimal, individualised medical services, and implementation of cost-effective healthcare systems, with multi-level communication, focused education and learning materials, better visibility and marketing of high-quality products, and effective promotion of predictive and preventive medicine. Some concrete examples of the needs and corresponding solutions were provided in the preceding discussion. The potential beneficiaries of optimal design in PPPM may include patients, healthcare providers and society as a whole. In the context of PPPM, design should be recognised as a strategic tool in the redesign of processes and services capable of bringing innovative solutions to these complex issues.

Notes

1 http://www.epmanet.eu.
2 Translational informatics are 'the development of storage, analytic, and interpretive methods to optimise the transformation of increasingly voluminous biomedical data into proactive, predictive, preventative, and participatory health' (AMIA, see https://www.amia.org/applications-informatics/translational-bioinformatics).
3 Pharmacogenetics is the study of how the actions of and reactions to drugs vary with the patient's genes.
4 Pathology-specific molecular patterns are found in the origin, nature and course of diseases.

References

Ardill, R. (2008) *Experience design*. London: Design Council.
Beyer, H. and Holtzblatt, K. (1998) *Contextual design: defining customer-centered systems*. San Francisco, CA: Morgan Kaufmann.
Bitner, M., Ostrom, A. L. and Morgan, F. N. (2008) 'Service blueprinting: a practical technique for service innovation', *California Management Review*, 50(3), 66–94.
Brown, T. (2008) 'Design thinking', *Harvard Business Review*, 86(6), 84–95.
Bruni, T., Mameli, M., Pravettoni, G. and Boniolo, G. (2012) 'Cystic fibrosis carrier screening in Veneto (Italy): an ethical analysis', *Med Health Care Philos.*, 15(3), 321–328.
Cockton, G. (2008) 'Designing worth – connecting preferred means to desired ends', *Interactions*, 15(4), July/August, 54–57.
Collins, H. and Linscott, G. (2013) 'Can design and design thinking STILL add value to business innovation?' In *Proceedings of the British Academy of Management Conference*. Liverpool, UK: University of Liverpool.
Costigliola, V. (2011) 'Mobility of medical doctors in cross-border healthcare', *EPMA J.*, 2(4), 333–9.
del Nord, R. (1997) 'Dimensions in hospital design'. In *Proceedings of the Human-Centred Design for Health Buildings International Conference and Workshop*, 28–30 August. Trondheim, Norway: University of Trondheim, pp. 11–22.
Dunne, D. and Martin, R. (2006) 'Design thinking and how it will change management education: an interview and discussion', *Academy of Management Learning and Education*, 5(4), 512–523.
Golubnitschaja, O. (2012) *Advances in predictive, preventive and personalised medicine*, http://www.springer.com/series/10051. Accessed: 10 January 2015.
Golubnitschaja, O., Yeghiazaryan, K., Cebioglu, M., Morelli, M. and Herrera-Marschitz, M. (2011) 'Birth asphyxia as the major complication in newborns: moving towards improved individual outcomes by prediction, targeted prevention and tailored medical care', *EPMA J.*, 22(2), 197–210.
Grant, I. C. (2004) 'Communicating with young people through the eyes of practitioners', *Journal of Marketing Management*, 20(5–6), 591–606.
Harder, M. K., Burford, G. and Hoover, E. (2013) 'What is participation? Design leads the way to a cross-disciplinary framework', *Design Issues*, 29(4), 41–58.
IDEO (2010) 'Human centred design toolkit' (Stanford: IDEO, 2010). Accessed: 13 January 2015.
Kapalla, M. (2010) 'Healthcare information complexity and the role of informatics in predictive, preventive and personalized medicine'. In W. Niederlag, H. U. Lemke and O. Rienhoff (eds) *Personalisierte Medizin und Informationstechnologie*. Health Academy, Band 15: Dresden, pp. 83–108.

Kapalla, M., Kubáň, J., Costigliola, V. and Golubnitschaja, O. (2014) 'Vision of the first EPMA center for predictive, preventive and personalized medicine in Europe', *EPMAJ*, 5. Available at: http://www.epmajournal.com/content/5/S1/A153. Accessed: 10 January 2015.

Kapalla, M. and Matušková, D. (2009) 'Information systems as an essential component of prediction in laboratory diagnostics'. In O. Golubnitschaja (ed.) *Predictive diagnostics and personalized treatment*, New York: Nova Science Publishers, pp. 529–548.

Koskinen, T. and Thomson, M. (2012) *Design for growth and prosperity*. Brussels: DG Enterprise and Leadership Board European Commission.

Lemke, H. U. and Golubnitschaja, O. (2014) 'Towards personal health care with model-guided medicine: long-term PPPM-related strategies and realisation opportunities within "Horizon 2020"', *EPMAJ*, 5(8), 5–8.

Liedtka, J. (2013) 'Strategy as design'. In R. Martin and K. Christensen (eds) *Rotman on design: the best on design thinking from Rotman magazine*. Toronto, ON: University of Toronto Press.

Lockwood, T. (2010) *Design thinking: integrating Innovation, customer experience, and brand value*. New York: Allworth Press.

Martin, R. L. (2009) *Design of business: why design thinking is the next competitive advantage*. Boston, MA: Harvard Business School Publishing.

Nuutinen, M. and Keinonen, T. (2011) 'User experience in complex systems: crafting a conceptual framework', *Cambridge Academic Design Management Conference*, University of Cambridge.

Savard, J. (2013) 'Personalised medicine: a critique on the future of health care', *Bioethical Inquiry*, 10, 197–203.

Simonse, L. (2014) 'Modelling business models', *Design Issues*, 30(4), 67–82.

Steen, M. (2012) 'Human-centered design as a fragile encounter', *Design Issues*, 28(1), 72–80.

Stegall, M. (2006) 'Designing for sustainability: a philosophy for ecologically intentional design', *Design Issues*, 22(2), 57.

Terrey, N. (2013) 'New personas for design management: public management roles redefined for design'. In the *Proceedings of the Cambridge Academic Design Management Conference*, University of Cambridge.

World Bank (2015a) 'Health expenditure total, (% of GDP)'. Available at: http://data.worldbank.org/indicator/SH.XPD.TOTL.ZS/countries?display=graph. Accessed: 10 January 2015.

World Bank (2015b) 'GDP, Current US$'. Available at: http://data.worldbank.org/indicator/NY.GDP.MKTP.CD?display=graph. Accessed: 10 January 2015.

Yeghiazaryan, K., Peeva, V., Morelli, M., Herrera-Marschitz, M. and Golubnitschaja, O. (2009) 'Potential targets for early diagnosis and neuroprotection in asphyxiated newborns'. In O. Golubnitschaja (ed.) *Predictive diagnostics and personalized treatment: dream or reality*. New York: Nova Science Publishers, pp. 509–525.

9 Towards a Person-Centred Approach to design for personalisation

Sarah Kettley, Richard Kettley and Rachel Lucas

Introduction

This chapter reflects on the political and ethical dimensions of personalisation through an analysis of the Person-Centred Approach (PCA) as found in psychotherapy practice and research, political conciliation and education. We propose that the PCA has the potential to inform ethical frameworks in participatory design, and can help facilitate critical reflection on approaches to personalisation in healthcare and technologically connected services.

A context is provided by ubiquitous computing visions of an Internet of Things, contrasted with the needs of mental health service users, and by recent calls for explicit reflection by design researchers on the ethical and political implications of their processes. The chapter discusses models of the person found in the mindsets of design research, and in the different modes of psychotherapy practice, and positions the PCA as a generative framework (after Sanders' map of design practice and research), and as holistic, rather than behavioural, cognitive or systemic. The Person-Centred Approach of Carl Rogers is then introduced through the six necessary and sufficient conditions for therapeutic change, and a discussion on the importance of non-directivity to the approach; this is followed by a short analysis of three participatory design research projects, in which some aspects of the PCA are evident. We then develop our proposal for a Person-Centred Approach to design, following the four dimensions of *timescale, power relations, levels of participation,* and *reflection on practice* (after Vines et al. 2012). Finally, we discuss issues with the use of similar terminology by other practices, and reiterate the critical differences between the Person-Centred Approach and most approaches to designing personalisation. We hope that the chapter will allow design researchers to recognise that there are different modes of practice within the healthcare professions, and within psychology, and that these can have a significant impact on research methodology, including the configuration of participants within projects.

Context of the methodological development

At a recent conference dedicated to the development of ubiquitous computing systems, including many for healthcare applications, it became clear that personal accounts of users were seen as untrustworthy. Far preferable were the data that could be produced through environmental or on-body monitoring, which would reveal the user to themselves. Personalisation has become algorithmic, depending on the recognition of existing patterns to predict future behaviour. Such emphasis on past behaviour however, precludes change, and embodies directivity, whether through recommendation systems in retail (presented by the marketing profession as consumer 'choice'), or through interventions to match desired standards of health or other social behaviours (often referred to as 'nudge' psychology, for example in healthcare management) (Voyer 2015). Even when the individual desires the same outcomes (and signs up to them), directivity needs to be carefully considered lest it become instrumental, rather than principled (Grant 1990/2002).[1] While the personalisation of healthcare and financial systems, among others, is made possible by learning algorithms collecting biological and behavioural data, there are concerns regarding the erosion of both autonomous informed action (Lanier 2010; Thaler and Sunstein 2008). This gap between popular representations of personalisation, and what people might really need, can be seen in the contrast between visions of products personalised to people's 'needs and preferences' without their requesting them (Brand Genetics 2015), and the sentiment of the anonymous poem, 'Listen', which is often cited in the helping professions to illustrate the fine line between care for, and enablement of individuals:

> When you do something for me that
> I can and need to do for myself,
> You contribute to my fear and weakness.
>
> (Anonymous n.d.[2])

In answer to these concerns, we propose that the behavioural model is not the only option for personalisation, and that an alternative approach to designing for personalisation offers an ethical and reflective alternative. This chapter describes this Person-Centred Approach, its relationship with emerging design practices, and the confusions in terminology that may occur, particularly in personalised healthcare, through the use of terminology that draws on the person-centred tradition but is not connected to its foundations in Rogers' Person-Centred Approach (PCA). Rogers' PCA is distinct in many respects from other psychological modalities. It is humanistic in outlook and has its roots in phenomenological and existential philosophy and practice. He developed the approach from Non-Directive Therapy through Client-Centred Therapy to Person-Centred Therapy through the 1940s to 1960s, and then to the broader Person-Centred Approach, which influenced educational, sociological and political theory and practice from the 1970s onwards (Embleton-Tudor et al. 2004). It emphasises trust in the individual to grow and develop given the right environment (Joseph and Worsley 2005), and stands in contrast to deficit approaches, which focus on need rather than human potential (Freeth 2007).

This chapter's proposition, that the PCA may provide an attitude-, rather than technique-led framework for ethically sound design for personalisation, is based on work the authors are doing as part of a multidisciplinary team at Nottingham Trent University, funded by the UK's Engineering and Physical Sciences Research Council. They are developing a person-centred methodology for design research in an Internet of Things enabled by emerging e-textile technologies (An Internet of Soft Things 2015). The project offers generative design techniques to participants from the Nottinghamshire Mind Network community, including mental health service users, volunteers, staff, and managers. In the workshops, participants are seen as 'co-researchers' and through collaborative making and designing, reflect on the potential of interactive textiles to impact on their wellbeing.

The multidisciplinary research team includes different mindsets towards expertise, and different expectations regarding the role of making within the research process. For some team members, making is usually the outcome of a user-centred research process, while for others, making is a process of skills acquisition. In both these approaches to research, making is configured through expertise, either in the delivery of the prototype as solution, or in the teaching of new skills. In this project, however, we are developing a participatory methodology that gives expertise back to the participants. In this model, making offers an opportunity to experience autonomy, provided basic skills are supported as part of a non-judgemental environment (Glazzard et al. 2015). We hope that through making, participants may experience first-hand the building blocks of future technologies, which otherwise have the potential to remove personal agency.

The project shares guidelines for a Person-Centred Approach (PCA) to participatory design with mental health communities. Reflecting on our experience as a multi-disciplinary team seeking to become more inter-disciplinary, it is clear that such guidelines concern not only the participants or users, but also ourselves as researchers from diverse academic cultures, and with different experiences and training in working with people. We can only evolve as a team through reflection on our own experiences on the project, so we run de-briefing discussions as soon as possible after the participatory workshops. From these we produce audio recordings or written notes that can become material for further analysis of our approach. We find this reflective approach to research responds to recent calls for a reassessment of the user/individual in the design process, as well as the configuration of the role of designer, for example in the work of Fuad-Luke (2009) and Bezaitis and Robinson (2011). It also echoes Light and Akama's (2014) call for attention to the ethical and political dimensions of power relations in the context of users. They ask: 'What if we go further in looking at the relational aspects of designing participatively?' (2014, p. 152). A CHI special interest group report (Vines et al. 2012) called explicitly for reflection on the efficacy and the ethics of participatory work in HCI, and pointed to a need for researchers and designers to fully acknowledge the epistemological and ethical roots of their methods around four key themes:

timescale; power relations; levels of participation; and *reflecting on practice.* We propose that these are themes the Person-Centred Approach can help to address through taking a holistic view of the person, and we explore these later in this chapter.

Understanding the person in design research through the PCA

Design and healthcare both draw on a range of philosophical models of the person. In Figure 9.1, from Sanders' review of the variety of approaches to design research involving people as 'users' or 'participants', these are called 'mindsets'. In mental health services, they are referred to as 'modes' and include psychodynamic, behavioural, and person-centred practices (McLeod 2013). At the heart of each of these lies a model of the human being that has a significant impact on methodology and evaluation of outcomes: a cognitive psychologist's view of methodological rigour in research will differ fundamentally from that of a person-centred psychotherapist because of these different underlying models of the person.

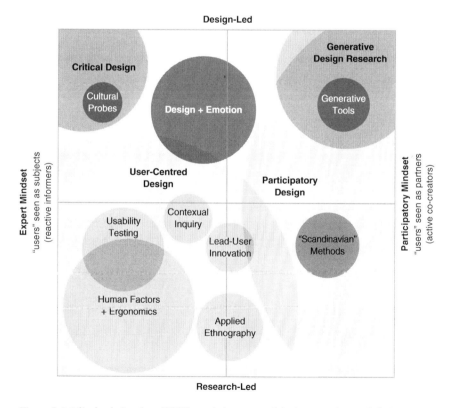

Figure 9.1 Elizabeth Sanders (2008) evolving map of design practice and design research.

Models of the person in mental health practice include the deficit model, the social (or systems) model, and the holistic model (Ladd and Churchill 2012; Tyrer and Steinberg 2009). The Person-Centred Approach (PCA) works according to the holistic model, while a behavioural psychologist would work according to either the deficit or social model. Applied crudely, design methods have tended to operate according to a deficit model, in which problem solving is understood to be at the root of 'design thinking', although this approach has recently been subject to critique (Brandt et al. 2012; Kimbell 2011).[3] The process of problem identification and solution development in design nonetheless has parallels with the diagnosis–treatment–cure model. The starting point of the deficit model is the assumption that something is wrong or broken, and needs to be fixed – and it is clear what that 'something' is. In health practice this model seeks biological or behavioural remedies and is driven by the expert role, leaving the individual patient with no responsibility beyond following a programme of treatment and, by analogy, the consumer none beyond following the product instructions. In contrast, some design aligns with the PCA in its awareness of the wicked nature of its problems and the ways they may be organically intertwined with solutions (Poldma 2015).

The social or systems model starts from the premise that the person is part of a wider ecology, and that our environment has an impact on our experiences and behaviour. Service design can be seen as operating on a social model. This approach may be more or less person-centred, in that it involves power relationships and levels of instrumentality. For example, a service design project could be carried out with the aim of improving user experience for no reason other than that users deserve to have a voice. However, if the same piece of service design is commissioned by a stakeholder with a specific agenda, such as increasing sales, or changing behaviour for more desirable health outcomes, then the approach becomes instrumental, as the stakeholder with power decides what is best for the persons involved. The presentation of toolkits from the point of view of the time-constrained organisation, which provide techniques for 'persuading' participants to take part, can be guilty of this. For example, the Social Design Methods Menu (Kimbell and Julier 2012), is informed by design management and social sciences, and while it recognises that 'tools have the potential to change who we are' (p. 7), the being of the researcher or professional designer is absent; the holistic view of the user (or 'customer', p. 2) is material to be understood by the researcher in the course of achieving the organisation's aims.

Sanders' map of design research in Figure 9.1 is organised around two dimensions: the horizontal describes mindset, while the vertical differentiates between design-led and research-led practices. The research-led approach is well established, and includes applied psychology, anthropology, and sociology (2008, p. 14). Design-led approaches involve making and prototyping, whether by the designer (critical design, on the left), or by participants (generative design, on the right); research-led approaches roughly equate to the research *for* design paradigm, while design-led approaches align more with research *through* design (Frayling 1993). The horizontal dimension of mindset is relevant to our discussion because it deals with aspects of expertise and power relationships. It is along the mindset axis that we can reflexively place the evolving terminology of the user that we propose here; the Person-Centred Approach constitutes a mindset positioned on the far right of this scheme, no matter whether methods are design- or research-led, and as such it may provide a framework for other researchers who have identified the importance of a grounded, reflexive sensitivity when using participatory tools and techniques (Brandt et al. 2012; Munteanu et al. 2015; Vines et al. 2012; Vines et al. 2013; Wallace et al. 2013).

This chapter unpacks what 'the person' means according to the Person-Centred Approach, and how this might differ from the model of the person that informs some other approaches to design for personalisation. Readers from design disciplines may recognise in the PCA an approach to relational complexity that could be further explored through the lifeworlds of Hallnäs and Redström (2002), Latour's Actor Network Theory (2005), or emergent and performative perspectives (Wallis 2009), among others. Needless to say, this chapter cannot deal with all of these, and we hope that others will take up challenge to critique and develop the term 'person-centred' in relation to the people involved in design.

To fully explore the relationship between a Person-Centred Approach and more conventional approaches to 'persons' in design processes, it is appropriate now to consider in more detail the features of the Person-Centred Approach by sketching out its roots in psychotherapeutic practice.

A holistic model for participatory design: the Person-Centred Approach

Here, we introduce some details of Rogers' development of a Person-Centred Approach to psychotherapy, to indicate how its principles have been generalised into the PCA and to identify how it underpins our development of a Person-Centred Approach to design. Carl Rogers (1902–1987) was an influential American psychologist, and one of the founders of the humanistic approach to psychology. In 1951, he presented his theory of personality and behaviour as the final chapter of *Client-Centred Therapy* (1951), marking a radical departure from prevalent medicalised thinking and the traditional power dynamics of psychotherapy. This shift from diagnosis and interpretation, to listening, and a willingness to be fully present without the apparent safety of expert status and a directive attitude, offered a focus no longer intent on problem solving, but on the development of a trusting relationship, facilitating the growth and development of the individual (Casemore 2006). Consequently, the focus of the process became the person rather than the pathology, or problem. Rogers hypothesised that the individual has within him- or herself vast resources for self-understanding and self-directed behaviour, accessible through the provision of a climate of facilitative psychological attitudes (Rogers 1974, p. 116).

Rogers (1957) stated that there are six conditions for therapeutic personality change. It is important to note that Rogers emphasised that each is necessary and that together, they are sufficient for change to occur. While these have been recognised and absorbed into the work of practitioners beyond the PCA, they are often reduced to three 'core' conditions (empathy, congruence and unconditional positive regard), both in wider therapeutic training and design research (cf. Slovák et al. 2015). It is, however, the 'necessary and sufficient' nature of the six conditions that constitute the PCA, and that we are working to embed in our participatory design research. The six conditions are summarised below. As far as possible, we leave the original language of PCA as applied in therapeutic practice intact to show their origins in Rogers' decades of research and reflexive practice, out of which we build our development of an ethical approach to personalisation in design:[4]

1. Psychological Contact: there is at least a minimal relationship in which two people are aware of each other and each makes some perceived difference in the experiential field of the other.
2. Client Incongruence: one person – the client – is feeling vulnerable or anxious; this arises from a discrepancy between the actual 'felt' experience and the self-concept the individual holds of her/himself.
3. Therapist Congruence: the other – the therapist – is integrated in the relationship; s/he is able to be genuine as her/his actual experience is accurately represented by her/his awareness of her/himself.
4. Therapist Unconditional Positive Regard (UPR) for the client: there are no conditions for acceptance; there is a prizing of the person (Rogers acknowledges Dewey here); it is the opposite of a selective, evaluating attitude; it is a caring for the client as a separate person with her/his own feelings and experiences.
5. Therapist Empathic Understanding of the client's internal frame of reference and communication of this back to the client: accurate empathy might provide clarity or disentanglement from distress, leading to a sense of movement or relaxation.
6. Client Perception of the therapist's empathic understanding and UPR: the client feels accepted and understood.

Working therapeutically from a person-centred perspective requires the therapist to be highly attuned and responsive to the client's feelings (Brodley 1996), sensing 'accurately the feelings and personal meanings that the client is experiencing' (Rogers 1980, p. 116). As part of his practice-led theory, Rogers (1961) developed a concept of a continuum of process, using recorded therapy sessions to inform a scale that might be identifiable by an investigator. At one end of the scale was a:

> fixity and remoteness of experiencing . . . [in which] the individual has little or no recognition of the ebb and flow of the feeling life within him.

The ways in which he construes experience have been set by his past, and are rigidly unaffected by the actualities of the present.

(Rogers 1961, pp. 132–3)

At the other end of the scale, 'New feelings are experienced with immediacy and richness of detail . . . there is a growing and continuing sense of acceptant ownership of these changing feelings, a basic trust in his own process' (Rogers 1961, p. 151). To relate this back to the conditions described above, this process tracks the movement from incongruence to congruence.

The Person-Centred Approach was a further development, which took the theory beyond therapeutic practice, and described 'a point of view, a philosophy, an approach to life, a way of being' (Rogers 1980, p. xvii), which subsequently informed holistic approaches to groupwork in education (Rogers and Freiberg 1993) and mediation and conciliation (Ladd 2005). Embleton-Tudor et al. proposed that 'the Person-Centred Approach offers a comprehensive, coherent and holistic approach to human life and concerns' (2004, p. 3) including 'citizenship and the personal, local and global issues of justice, peace and conflict; the wider social systems of couples, groups, communities and organisations; and the environment' (Embleton-Tudor et al. 2004, p. 3).

Within the therapeutic relationship, the Person-Centred Approach is holistic in its valuing and appreciation of the whole person; in contrast with the medical model, the PCA is not deficit-based but works with what is available to us in the here and now. If Person-Centred Therapy seeks to empower the individual to change by creating an empathic, non-judgemental and genuine relationship with the therapist in which it is OK for the individual to be truly themselves, then the Person-Centred Approach reconfigures that relationship in the context of society. A person-centred design approach to personalisation would therefore seek to critically examine the ways in which the user is empowered or disempowered; this would include a frank appraisal of any organisational agendas (or 'directivity') embodied within design systems and products, much as in practice theory, where objects are understood to partially constitute practices (Kimbell 2009).

Non-directivity

Levitt asserts that 'Non-directivity is the distinguishing feature' of the Person-Centred Approach, arising from adherence to the six conditions, and it is the non-directive attitude that defines the approach as 'revolutionary and anti-authoritarian' (2005, p. i). Any person-centred practice would understand the relationship to be an end in itself, in which the therapist has 'no pre-determined and specific outcomes or intentions for the service user to achieve' (Murphy et al. 2013, p. 708). However, non-directivity is difficult as it asks the expert to put aside their own goals for the client; if we are trained to habitually diagnose and intervene, non-directivity can be the hardest aspect of the PCA to achieve (Brodley 2006). In many cases, work can be at once empathic and *instrumentally* non-directive. Instrumental non-directivity can be seen in the application of types of behaviour by the therapist to achieve a specific goal, 'such as building rapport or frustrating the client' (Grant 1990/2002; Murphy et al. 2013, p. 708). *Principled* non-directivity, in contrast, describes the ethical attitude of the therapist towards the client's ability and willingness to self-actualisation (Sanders 2006), which does not aim to solve the client's problems, but focuses solely on developing a 'trusting relationship with the client, demonstrating an inherent faith in their capacity to self-direct and acknowledging the individual's right to autonomy' (Casemore 2006, p. 6). It is principled non-directivity that we propose facilitates ethical personalisation in design research and practice, as opposed to instrumental non-directivity, which more easily fits into organisational agendas and can work to design out individuals' creativity and improvisation (Bezaitis and Robinson 2011; Wallis 2009).

Aspects of the Person–Centred Approach in design research

We propose that design, especially 'user-centred', 'human-centred' and participatory approaches, can use the six conditions of the PCA to reflect on its efforts to act ethically towards its beneficiaries. This may be most obviously applied where the designer or design researcher is in contact with users in a co-design situation, and there is a clear relationship to be defined, and managed with a duty of care to the participant. It can also find application in explicit reflexivity around 'personalisation', where some technical or political parameters must be set, in the end, by the designers of complex dynamic systems. Further, we see potential for its development in the area of designing for everyday agency, as found in Non-Intentional Design (Brandes 2008), and some definitions of Open (Kettley et al. 2011) or Relational Design (Hollingsworth 2011), which draw on Bourriaud's theory of relational aesthetics (Bourriaud 1998) and which recognise the potential for designed systems and objects to empower or disempower people (Kimbell 2009).

It is possible to point to aspects of the PCA in many design projects, particularly those that have a participatory mindset, and we briefly discuss three examples below, in which we highlight how some of the conditions are met. The provocation of this chapter is that to be truly person-centred, a design process would have to reflexively embody all six necessary and sufficient conditions, but this is open to further work and feedback.[5] These projects are cited as contemporary examples of best practice, and yet we know from *An Internet of Soft Things* that explicitly striving to enact all the conditions poses significant challenges (2015).

Democratising Technology. This project (Light 2011) aimed to inspire confident participation through design, in what Light and Akama call the 'discourses and practices of shaping techno-science' (2014, p. 153). It dealt with the invisible networks of information and communication enabled by technology that impact significantly on people's lives. In this work, Light and Akama are concerned with themes of politics, power structures, relational experience, ecologies and timescales of commitment. They reflect on the influence that design processes have, not only on the imagined user experience with an object, but on the lifeworlds of all participants. The fact that they shift the focus of attention from the object that is being designed to the relations and infrastructures that inform lived experience, especially of care, align this work with the Person-Centred Approach. The presence of this 'matter of concern' (after Latour 2005), and their focus on the ethics of care resonates particularly with the PCA's requirement for unconditional positive regard (UPR). For Light and Akama, care is not something 'done to' the person, but is rather an 'a priori and primordial condition' (2014, p. 158). Further, their stress on treating care as non-instrumental reflects the principled non-directivity that is an outcome of the six conditions for PCA:

> care is manifested as and in support of 'sustainable and flourishing relations' (after Puig de la Bellacasa 2012, p. 198), distinct from caring for or being cared for, conditions which describe a directional, instrumental relation, suggestive of a premeditated agenda and even the promotion of inadvertent learned dependencies.
>
> (Light and Akama 2014, p. 158)

Light and Akama also point to the political and ethical issues of participatory design when distributed and mobile networks of designed things may not be available to participant experience, or accessible to researcher analysis; this leads them to discuss as yet non-existent forms of ICT, as well as the timescale implications for responsible researchers. They point to approaches such as Transformation Design and HCI for Development projects,[6] which seek to create capacity for autonomous change and improvement in communities. This is described as an 'awakening' of reflective process (after Sangiorgi), and as an ongoing, living transformation rather than an end in itself (2014, p. 152). While this describes a community rather than an individual, such 'awakening' can be seen in terms of the client (community) moving from incongruence towards congruence (Rogers 1961).

Personhood and person-focused design

Jayne Wallace has developed design-led techniques for empathy with participants. Her work using design probes with dementia sufferers takes an embodied, relational approach, which is contrasted with 'conventional understandings of loss of self' (Wallace et al. 2013). Wallace's accounts of her participatory practice communicate a sense of her personal connection with her participants, achieved through an empathic listening approach (Marshall et al. 2014). The Personhood Project was based on a 'deep engagement' between Wallace as design researcher, a woman with mild dementia, and her husband. This emphasis on engagement echoes the first of the six conditions for the PCA, Psychological Contact, which must be in place before any other therapeutic activity can take place.

Wallace also responded to the sense that her role as a researcher might be more important than the experience of the couple:

> the researcher had a sense that the couple felt that there was a pressure on the researcher's time and that they should be as productive during their time together as possible. The researcher could sense that a little more reflective time and space could enable Gillian to articulate what she wanted to say more easily.
>
> (Marshall et al. 2014, p. 761)

Wallace brought different materials (wet clay) into the space for the next session, allowing the pace of conversation and activity to shift, and facilitated a more holistic experience, rather than focusing solely on the cognitive. This meant silence became acceptable, and the couple were able to contemplate and simply be, rather than produce and do. This sensitivity to the needs of the couple echoes the listening attitude of the person-centred therapist, and their empathic understanding of the client's internal frame of reference. By facilitating change in the sessions, Wallace communicated this understanding back to the couple, and there was a resulting sense of relaxation.

TAC-TILE Sounds

Researchers on the TAC-TILE Sounds project were concerned with facilitating an empathic connection with the participating children, rather than relying on the experts in the stakeholder group (Chamberlain 2010). Because the children had complex special needs, new forms of engagement, other than the more usual questionnaires and surveys, had to be developed. Instead of pursuing a research-for-design agenda, the approach was to realise a selection of vibro-acoustic furniture design concepts and then work from the children's direct experience: 'Only when the designers produced working physical prototypes could the research team interact with the users and develop any meaningful sense of understanding'. They found that, 'the working prototypes acted as a bridge between themselves, the therapists and the children' (Chamberlain 2010, p. 168). As a result of these communication difficulties, the project found itself embracing non-directivity, meaning 'tasks' became replaced with the children's own emergent means of communication with prototype artefacts; the children became accepted as the experts of their own experience, challenging the team to experience Unconditional Positive Regard for the 'user'. This example highlights the different forms that listening (and therefore UPR) can take; more used to verbal and linguistic forms of communication, the researchers used prototyping to support communication of design concepts with the children (as in Jones and Wallis' experiential approaches to ethical informed consent 2005). Further, in such situations, listening has to be enacted through the whole body rather than be a solely auditory experience (Caldwell 2005), which relies enormously on the first of the six conditions – Psychological Contact.[7] It might seem that this project differs fundamentally from the others in this respect, but it serves to demonstrate the non-medical approach of the PCA, which does not begin with a defined medical condition or lack. While research approaches in personalisation might more commonly talk about demographics, target markets and populations, the PCA challenges shared conditions or behaviours as a starting point, being more concerned with relationships and capabilities.

The examples above suggest that a Person-Centred Approach to participatory design would emphasise the reflexivity of the designer and the exploration of their relationship with the participant. It would demand critical thinking about the design process and the roles within it. Consequently, the process of designing itself becomes ethical, being based on valuing the other as opposed to 'values' which can sometimes be perceived as a static characteristic of a person; and while outcomes must remain uncertain, risk is embraced together. A side-effect of this is that a Person-Centred Approach to design means learning and self-discovery arise for both designer and participant.

In professional counselling practice, the person-centred practitioner is supported by a formalised structure of supervision. A more experienced counsellor facilitates explicit reflection sessions, in which the counsellor checks recent therapeutic encounters against the six conditions; this is a requirement for membership of professional accreditation by the UKCP (UK Council for Psychotherapy) and BACP (British Association for Counselling and Psychotherapy), and is an integral part of professional development, ethical assurance, and care for the wellbeing of the practitioner as well as the client. Arguably, a person-centred design approach would build in a similar structure for explicit reflection; without this, design projects may be experiential (in the psychotherapy terminology), but not person-centred in the classic sense.

Towards a Person-Centred Approach to design research

Returning to the four key themes that organise the epistemological and ethical roots of design methods according to Vines et al. (2012), *timescale*, *power relations*, *levels of participation* and *reflecting on practice*, this section briefly outlines how a Person-Centred Approach to participatory design might provide an ethical yet flexible framework for working with diverse communities.

Timescale

The approach to timescale in a Person-Centred Approach to design is concerned to achieve the conditions for constructive change outlined above, rather than to arrive at the correct interpretation of needs and context. As we saw in the section above on power relations, interpretation is treated somewhat differently in the PCA compared with other research milieux. As became evident in Wallace's work, a concern for timescale is a function of the phenomenological character of the Person-Centred Approach that is essential for empathic understanding to emerge. In a therapeutic setting, because the participant is in control of what is discussed and disclosed, this cannot be constrained, and so the PCA does not tend to sit well with solution-focused therapies (Iveson 2002). Consequently, it is hard to manage within a culture focused on efficiency (Murphy et al. 2013). In addition, evaluation is related to timescale, as it is enacted moment-by-moment, during participation, rather than being left until after the event (Marshall et al. 2014). Jones and Wallis (2005) developed a framework of moment-by-moment evaluation in which it is the responsibility of the facilitator to be present to the experience of the other throughout the encounter. Other ethical methods for phenomenological reflection include Interpersonal Process Recall, in which the power of interpretation rests with the participant (Kagan 1980; Kettley et al. 2015b). The timescale of analysis is also stretched, as Grounded Theory techniques are often used as part of the phenomenological approach to interpersonal meaning making (Rennie 2006).

Power relations

Respect for the autonomy of the individual is central to the Person-Centred Approach, which emphasises the personal power of the individual in the therapeutic relationship. Wilkins refutes the notion of *em*powering another, citing Rogers (1978, p. 289): 'it is not that this approach gives power to the person; it never takes it away' (Wilkins 2010, p. 18). A Person-Centred Approach to design offers a phenomenological process in which the participant owns the meaning of their experience, while researchers reflect on their own contribution to the process and respect the participant's individuality. Therefore, just as in a therapeutic context there is no expert other than the patient, in a design context a Person-Centred Approach requires that the expertise of participants is recognised as equal to that of the researchers/designers.

The BACP Ethical Framework includes a section on autonomy, defined as respect for the client's right to be self-governing, which requires counsellors to 'engage in explicit contracting in advance of any commitment by the client' (BACP 2010, p. 7). In the context of Design Research, this contracting process requires that the researcher makes clear that they are taking a Person-Centred Approach, what the implications of this are for the roles of researchers and participants and for their relationship with each other. For example, the researcher would not position themselves as an expert, but make a commitment to offering the participants an empathic, valuing environment. The participants will understand that it is their role to engage in a process aimed at capturing their experience, and that the research is not primarily goal or outcome oriented. As a pragmatic extension of this, informed consent should be seen as part of an ongoing process, which participants can review against their experience of the research as it develops, rather than as a yes/no checklist to be completed at the start of the process (Bond 2004). Good practice would therefore be to check informed consent at regular intervals and to be open to dialogue about it, with the possibility of making adjustments for individuals in response to their concerns or preferences.

Levels of participation and control

Co-design has shown interest in the ladder typology of participation first suggested by Arnstein in 1969, and developed by Hart in working with children (Arnstein 1969; Bates et al. 2011). For both Arnstein and Bates, the typology is made up of eight levels or rungs, from non-participation through tokenism, to citizen control at the top, the assumption being that 'participation without redistribution of power is an empty and frustrating process for the powerless' (Arnstein 1969, p. 216). Carroll called for a 'policing of participation', through just such a taxonomy of levels and types of participation and recognition of the different meanings of the word in different practices (cited in Vines et al. 2013, p. 429). However, the PCA differs from existing co-design and participatory design approaches in its attitude to directivity. Openness and a willingness to revise research questions and design goals with participants are increasingly evident in participatory approaches, giving more autonomy to the participant in defining the matters of concern, but the goal often remains a single technological outcome to a given problem. A Person-Centred Approach to design can also see multiple technological artefacts as a positive outcome, acknowledging the validity of practice-based evidence (as opposed to evidence-based practice). In formalising the stages of personal growth the PCA recognises that people may not be able to engage in the way researchers might implicitly value, especially at the start of a relational process (Rogers 1961). In this way, the PCA answers concerns about 'tokenism' (Arnstein 1969) and apparent lack of engagement in its listening attitude, which facilitates confidence and personal growth. Listening is in itself a giving of power, and is experienced as therapeutic when the necessary conditions continue over a period of time (Rogers 1957), whether in a participatory design group, or in a therapeutic encounter.

Reflecting on practice

One of the challenges of a commitment to the PCA is engagement with individuals and institutions who do not share the values and beliefs of the person-centred values, for example those who prioritise expertise and authority or whose primary objective is administrative and/or organisational. Mearns and Thorne (2000) used the term 'articulation' to describe a process of genuine dialogue, with others who do not share the values of the PCA. Mearns described articulation in these terms:

> I am concerned to be as clear as possible about what I want and my limits, but I am equally concerned to find out as much detail about the needs and limits of the other. Most important is that I want to learn from the articulation process. There are many possibilities for learning: I may learn from the expertise of the other; I may learn about some of my own inadequacies; I may learn how better to communicate within the articulation

process ... The opposite of articulation would be to stick rigidly and defensively to what we want, with no learning resulting and achieve a result that will probably not be the most creative.

(2006, pp. 134–5)

This suggests that the role of a person-centred designer working as part of a team or within an organisation that doesn't share the values of PCA is to maintain an open and flexible attitude, to be self-aware and self-reflexive, and to be transparent with others about experience, assumptions and aspirations.

However, the authors' current work shows that where participatory design is being undertaken with mental health service users, designers may find that such individuals are more accustomed to self-reflection than other target groups. Service users are frequently asked to co-monitor their therapeutic process and sometimes their recovery, depending on the philosophical orientation or 'modality' of therapy. Some tools such as the Recovery Star are widespread and not particular to one modality; they can be applied in a number of different ways. Further, if the relationship is an equal one, in which all participants are co-researchers in a shared process, it follows that all should reflect explicitly on that process, including the academic design researchers, as roles become blurred. External to the therapy session, trainee counsellors are supported by a system of supervision at a ratio of one hour of supervised reflection to four hours of client contact,[8] and we suggest this system is considered in the participatory design community, as the new relationships involved in a Person-Centred Approach imply at least self-reflection and possibly personal growth for the researchers.

In the authors' current research project, this is emerging as an important finding (Glazzard et al. 2015; Kettley et al. 2015a). A design research methodology is emerging in which debriefing sessions between workshop facilitators serve to support the team's shared development of the research themes, supporting individuals for whom difficult personal issues are brought to the surface and providing insight into the growth of the research team as a context for the growth of the participants.

The problem with language: when is 'person-centred' not person-centred?

Working in the person-centred mode is not necessarily straightforward. The PCA often faces political resistance[9] because it challenges embedded power relations and the status held as a result of perceived expertise, and champions subjective experience and evidence found in practice (as opposed to evidence-based practice as required by risk-averse audit cultures). It also faces issues as a result of the misappropriation of 'person-centred' as terminology, which is found conflated with 'patient-centred', 'positive psychology', and even 'personalisation'. The latter is particularly germane here as one function of this chapter is to indicate the ways in which the conception of personhood found in some of the instances of personalisation described in other chapters in this volume is at odds with that found in the PCA.

The misappropriation of the person-centred terminology to describe other practices is common. Freeth asserts that training for mental health professionals prioritises cognitive behavioural and other approaches that 'lend themselves more easily to measurement, structured working and evidence-based practice' (2007, p. 14). The personalisation of health services is often referred to as 'person-centred', despite not meeting the conditions of the PCA (Freeth 2007; Freeth 2015). As an example, the annual NICE[10] Conference includes an ongoing debate about how to put people at the centre of decision-making and planning in health and social care, but the terminology ('personalisation', 'person-centred', 'patient-led') is used interchangeably (cf. Bennett 2014; NICE 2015). Murphy et al. (2013) have challenged the ability of contemporary healthcare to be person-centred at all, given the context of managerialism in contemporary social work and Checkland (this volume) has demonstrated the degree to which 'personalised' health provision serves ideological purposes that privilege particular social groups and serves particular managerial imperatives. Misappropriation of the PCA terminology is also found in design communities. Here we see the rise of related terminology, such as: 'human-centred design' (HCD), which seeks to tackle 'grand challenges' to humanity, including poverty, famine, ecological disasters and global financial meltdown; 'people-centred design', used to describe usability analysis at the Open University (2015), and described as 'cost-effective and scalable' at Hugh Graham Creative (2013) and 'person-centred technologies' as a democratic approach to technology development as part a European project (Vanhove 2011).

Chamberlain (2010) explains that HCD is differentiated from user-centred design, as it is holistic; that is, it includes enquiry into the relationship between all stakeholders, the researchers, designers and processes of production and consumption. In addition, it works with what is now, rather than asking participants to make a leap of imagination, and focuses on the creation of products, services and environments that allow participants to live with 'dignity, independence and fulfillment' (2010, p. 168). However, design practices adhering to the ISO (international standards) for human-centred design[11] are not demonstrating a holistic mindset or mode of working, but are rather following guidance on usability, productivity and accessibility; the guidelines are written within the frame of human factors and ergonomics, in which wellbeing is understood to be an outcome of optimal system performance. Similarly, the human-centred strand at the 2014 Design Research Society conference primarily focused on ergonomics, although more holistic approaches could be found scattered throughout the rest of the event. In many cases, HCD has replaced UCD (user-centred design) as a collection of methods in which co-design, co-production and co-research practices are later analysed by the 'real' researchers – because conclusions still need to be drawn, and results delivered. In addition, user *needs* have to a large extent been augmented, if not replaced, by users *in need*, and this raises a question about the power relations in philanthropic ventures, in which the co-production of needs and ownership needs to be reflexively managed.

The ImPaCT project was co-ordinated by the European Association of Service providers for People with Disabilities (EASPD); ImPaCT in Europe was a networking project about personalised technology, financed by the European Commission Executive Agency for Education, Audiovisual and Culture in the framework of the Lifelong Learning Programme. The project ran between 2009 and 2012, and sought to develop effective person-centred technologies for health and social care services in Europe (Vanhove 2011). The project recognised the paradigm shift that had taken place in the way persons with disabilities were seen by society, and took an explicitly democratic approach to its engagement with disabled participants. However, despite attention to ethical issues and the democratic model, and the promotion of universal design, 'person-centred' and 'personalised' were used as interchangeable terms, and the project did not refer back to the Person-Centred Theory or Approach in its methodology or evaluation strategy.

Conclusion

The chapter outlined recent calls for reflection on participatory approaches in design research, and described the growing interest in a more holistic model with respect to the 'user'. We provided an introduction to the Person-Centred Approach of Carl Rogers and hope that this will help others reflect on their philosophical working models. In providing an example of a holistic mode of therapeutic practice, we also aimed to demonstrate the need for design researchers to be aware of the spectrum of approaches in the caring professions, so that they may be prepared for conflicting mindsets in interdisciplinary practice, and may be in a position to make informed decisions about the alignment of modes of practice when pursuing holistic participatory projects. We have recognised that aspects of the PCA already exist in some areas of excellent design practice, but that there is a risk of fragmentation and a current lack of a theoretical framework. This might be exacerbated if teams include psychologists working from a deficit model, which would conflict with project aims to engage with people holistically. The PCA offers such a framework for empathy and valuing, providing an underpinning theory, philosophy and a rigorously ethical methodology. It is distinct from current usages of 'HCD', 'UCD', 'patient-centred', 'people-centred', and indeed 'personalisation'. We believe it is only a matter of time before the term 'person-centred' is applied to design and we hope to critically inform its use before it becomes compromised.

Notes

1 Grant distinguished between instrumental and principled non-directivity (1990/2002).
2 These lines are taken from an anonymously authored poem commonly used in counselling training.

3 The design thinking agenda allows the process, and its artefacts and resulting products to be democratically contested by all involved (Binder et al. 2011); the normative organisational models, whether business or national health service, that instigate such design activity, however, also need to be recognised in relation to the democratic agency of each participant.
4 The 'therapist/client' terminology is therefore preserved, underlying our extension of it by analogy to the relationship between design actions and clients/users/participants/stakeholders.
5 In fact, this is also contested in counselling and psychotherapy; the PCA can be found used in integrative practice as just one tool, as a way of ensuring psychological contact, rather than as a complete framework.
6 HCI4D is a growing field of activity at the intersections of Human–Computer Interaction and socioeconomic development, based on the recognition that technology is neither culturally neutral, static nor deterministic.
7 There is a substantial literature on Contact Skills and Pre-Therapy, which seek to put this in place, as none of the other conditions can be met without it – see, for example, Prouty (2008).
8 Guidelines from the British Association for Counselling and Psychotherapy stipulate 1.5-hour supervision per month for qualified therapists.
9 This is the current situation in the UK's National Health Service provision, but can also be experienced in the cultural hierarchies of, for example, academic research communities.
10 The National Institute for Health and Care Excellence.
11 These are communicated by ISO standard 9241-210:2010 Human-Centred Design for Interactive Systems (BSI Standards 2010).

References

An Internet of Soft Things (2015) http://aninternetofsoftthings.com. Accessed 23 February 2015.

Anonymous (n.d.) Just listen. http://www.susyrudkincounselling.co.uk/listen-poem. Accessed 28 September 2015.

Arnstein, S. R. (1969) A ladder of citizen participation. *Journal of the American Institute of Planners*, 35(4), 216–224.

BACP (2010) *The Ethical Framework for Good Practice in Counselling*. http://www.bacp.co.uk/ethical_framework. Accessed 23 February 2015.

Bates, M., Brown, D., Cranton, W. and Lewis, J. (2011) The optimal level of student participation in the design of games-based learning. *Proc. 5th European Conference on Games-Based Learning (ECGBL)*, Athens, Greece, October 2011, pp. 667–674.

Bennett, S. (2014) Integration and personalisation: Two sides of one coin? NICE Conference, Birmingham, 14 May 2014.

Bezaitis, M. and Robinson, R. E. (2011) Valuable to values: How 'user research' ought to change. In A. Clarke (ed.), *Design Anthropology: Object Culture in the 21st Century*. Vienna: Springer, pp. 184–201.

Binder, T., Ehn, P., De Michelis, G., Jacucci, G. and Linde, G. (2011) *Design Things*. Cambridge, MA: MIT Press.

Bond, T. (2004) *Ethical Guidelines for Researching Counselling and Psychotherapy*. Rugby, UK: British Association for Counselling and Psychotherapy.

Bourriaud, N. (1998) *Relational Aesthetics*. Dijon: Les Presse Du Reel.

Brandes, U. (2008) *Design by Use: The Everyday Metamorphosis of Things (Board of International Research in Design)*. Basel: Birkhäuser GmbH.

Brandt, E., Binder, T. and Sanders, E. B. (2012) Tools and techniques: Ways to engage telling, making and enacting. In J. Simonsen and T. Robertson (eds), *Routledge International Handbook of Participatory Design*. Routledge International Handbooks, pp. 145–181.

Brodley, B. T. (1996) Empathic understandings and feelings in client-centred therapy. *The Person-Centred Journal*, 3(1), 22–30.

Brodley, B. T. (2006) Non-directivity in client-centered therapy. *Person-Centered & Experiential Psychotherapies*, 5(1), 36–52.

BSI Standards (2010) *Ergonomics of human-system interaction – Part 210: Human centred design for interactive systems* (ISO 9241-210:2010). London: BSI.

Caldwell, P. (2005) *Finding You Finding Me: Using Intensive Interaction to Get in Touch with People Whose Severe Learning Disabilities Are Combined with Autistic Spectrum Disorder.* London: Jessica Kingsley.

Casemore, R. (2006) *Person-Centred Counselling in a Nutshell.* London: SAGE.

Chamberlain, P. (2010) Horses, elephants and camels: Challenges and barriers to interdisciplinary user-centred design research. *Proc. DESIGN 2010, the 11th International Design Conference, Dubrovnik, Croatia.* Design Society, pp. 163–172.

Brand Genetics (2015) The future is personalised. 10 June 2015. http://brandgenetics.com/the-future-is-personalised.

Embleton-Tudor, L., Keemar K., Tudor, K., Valentine, J. and Worrall, M. (2004) *The Person-Centred Approach: A Contemporary Introduction.* Basingstoke, UK: Palgrave Macmillan.

Frayling, C. (1993) Research in art and design. *Royal College of Art Research Papers* series, 1(1).

Freeth, R. (2007) *Humanising Psychiatry and Mental Health Care: The Challenge of the Person-Centred Approach.* Oxford: Radcliffe.

Freeth, R. (2015) Psychiatric diagnosis and understanding more about psychiatric medication. Praxis CPD, Nottingham, 6–7 December 2014.

Fuad-Luke, A. (2009) *Design Activism: Beautiful Strangeness for a Sustainable World.* London: Earthscan.

Glazzard, M., Kettley, R., Lucas, R., Bates, M., Walker, S. and Kettley, S. (2015) Facilitating a non-judgmental skills-based co-design environment. *Proc. 3rd International Design4Health Conference*, Sheffield Hallam University, 13–16 July 2015.

Grant, B. (1990/2002) Principled and instrumental nondirectiveness in person-centred and client-centred therapy. *Person-Centred Review*, 5(1), 77–88. Reprinted in D. Cain (ed.) (2002) *Classics in the Person-Centred Approach.* Ross-on-Wye, UK: PCCS Books, pp. 371–376.

Hallnäs, L. and Redström, J. (2002) From use to presence: On the expressions and aesthetics of everyday computational things. In *Transactions on Computer–Human Interaction*, 9(2), June 2002, 106–124.

Hollingsworth, S. (2011) Strange sounds and other worlds: Art link sensory workshops, an evolving work. *Ideas Team, Artlink workshop.* Queen Margaret University, Edinburgh, 23–24 February 2011.

Hugh Graham Creative (2013) People-centred design. http://hughgrahamcreative.com/people-centered-design. Accessed 14 May 2015.

Iveson, C. (2002) Solution-focused brief therapy. *Advances in Psychiatric Treatment*, 8(2), 149–156.

Jones, I. and Wallis, M. (2005) Securing informed choice and adequate evaluation strategies for people with learning disabilities accessing the arts in the east midlands.

Arts Work with People Project (AWP) for Arts Council East Midlands. https://salamandatandem.files.wordpress.com/2015/03/salamanda-tandem-informed-choice-pdf-march-2005.pdf. Accessed 25 February 2015.

Joseph, S. and Worsley, R. (2005) A positive psychology of mental health: The person-centred perspective. In S. Joseph and R. Worsley (eds), *Person-Centred Psychopathology: A Positive Psychology of Mental Health*. Ross-on-Wye, UK: PCCS Books, pp. 348–357.

Kagan, N. (1980) *Interpersonal Process Recall: A Method for Influencing Human Interaction*. Unpublished manuscript. Houston, TX: Mason Media.

Kettley, S., Jones, I. and Downes, T. (2011) Embodied textiles for expression and well-being. *Proc. First European Conference on Design 4 Health*, 13–15 July 2011, Sheffield, pp. 189–205.

Kettley, S., Kettley, R. and Bates, M. (2015a) An introduction to the person-centred approach as an attitude for participatory design. *Adjunct Proc. 2015 ACM International Joint Conference on Pervasive and Ubiquitous Computing (UbiComp 2015)*, 7–11 Sep., Osaka, Japan.

Kettley, S., Kettley, R. and Bates, M. (2015b) An introduction to IPR as a participatory design research method. *Adjunct Proc. 2015 ACM International Joint Conference on Pervasive and Ubiquitous Computing (UbiComp 2015)*, 7–11 Sep., Osaka, Japan.

Kimbell, L. (2009) Beyond design thinking: Design-as-practice and designs-in-practice. *Proc. CRESC Conference*, Manchester, September 2009.

Kimbell, L. (2011) Re-thinking Design Thinking Part 1, *Design and Culture*, 3(3), 285–306.

Kimbell, L. and Julier, J. (2012) *The Social Design Methods Menu*. London: Fieldstudio Ltd.

Ladd, P. (2005) *Mediation, Conciliation, and Emotions: A Practitioner's Guide for Understanding Emotions in Dispute Resolution*. New York: University Press of America.

Ladd, P. and Churchill, A-M. (2012) *Person-Centered Diagnosis and Treatment in Mental Health*. London: Jessica Kingsley.

Lanier, J. (2010) *You Are Not a Gadget*. London: Penguin Books.

Latour, B. (2005) *Reassembling the Social*. Oxford: Oxford University Press.

Levitt, B. E. (2005) *Embracing Non-directivity: Reassessing Person-Centred Theory and Practice in the 21st Century*. Ross-on-Wye, UK: PCCS Books.

Light, A. (2011) Democratising technology: Making transformation using designing, performance and props. *CHI '11 Proceedings of the SIGCHI Conference on Human Factors in Computing Systems*, ACM Press, pp. 2239–2242.

Light, A. and Akama, Y. (2014) Structuring future social relations: The politics of care in participatory practice. *Proc. 13th Participatory Design Conference 2014 (PDC '14)*, 6–10 October 2014, Windhoek, Namibia, pp. 151–160.

Marshall, K., Thieme, A., Wallace, J., Vines, J., Wood, G. and Balaam, M. (2014) Making wellbeing. A process of user-centred design. *ACM Conference on Designing Interactive Systems (DIS 2014)*, pp. 755–764.

McLeod, J. (2013) *An Introduction to Counselling*. Maidenhead, UK: Open University Press.

Mearns, D. and Thorne, B. (2000) *Person-Centred Therapy Today*. Sage: London.

Mearns, D. (2006) Psychotherapy: The politics of liberation or collaboration? A career critically reviewed. In G. Proctor, M. Cooper, P. Sanders and B. Malcolm (eds), *Politicizing the Person-Centred Approach: An Agenda for Social Change*. Ross-on-Wye, UK: PCCS Books, pp. 127–142.

Munteanu, C., Molyneux, H., Moncur, W., Romero, M., O'Donnell, S. and Vines, J. (2015) Situational ethics: Re-thinking approaches to formal ethics requirements for human–computer interaction. *CHI '15 Proceedings of the 33rd Annual ACM Conference on Human Factors in Computing Systems*, ACM Press, pp. 105–114.

Murphy, D., Duggan, M. and Joseph, S. (2013) Relationship-based social work and its compatibility with the person-centred approach: Principled versus instrumental perspectives. *British Journal of Social Work*, 43(4), 703–719.

NICE (2015) National Institute for Health and Care Excellence Annual Conference Programme. Available at: https://www.niceconference.org.uk. Accessed 14 May 2015.

Open University (2015) People-centred designing. Open Learn Course. Available at: http://www.open.edu/openlearn/science-maths-technology/engineering-and-technology/design-and-innovation/design/people-centred-designing/content-section-0. Accessed 14 May 2015.

Poldma, T. (2015) Design thinking. In C. Edwards, H. Atkinson, S. Kettley, S. O'Brien, D. Raizman and A. M. Willis (eds), *The Bloomsbury Encyclopaedia of Design*. London: Bloomsbury, pp. 412–413.

Prouty, G. (ed.) (2008) *Emerging Developments in Pre-Therapy: A Pre-Therapy Reader*. Ross-on-Wye, UK: PCCS Books.

Rennie, D. (2006) The grounded theory method: Application of a variant of its procedure of constant comparative analysis to psychotherapy research. In C. T. Fischer (ed.), *Qualitative Research Methods for Psychologists: Introduction through Empirical Studies*. Burlington, MA: San Diego Academic Press, pp. 59–78.

Rogers, C. R. (1957) The necessary and sufficient conditions of therapeutic personality change. *Journal of Consulting Psychology*, 21, 95–103.

Rogers, C. R. (1961) *On Becoming a Person: A Therapist's View of Psychotherapy*. Boston, MA: Houghton Mifflin.

Rogers, C. R. (1974) In retrospect: Forty-six years. *American Psychologist*, 29, 115–123.

Rogers. C. (1978) *On Personal Power: Inner Strength and Its Revolutionary Impact*. London: Constable.

Rogers, C. (1980) *A Way of Being*. New York: Houghton Mifflin.

Rogers, C. and Freiberg, H. J. (1993) *Freedom to Learn* (3rd edn). New York: Merrill.

Sanders, E. (2008) On modeling: An Evolving map of design practice and design research. *ACM Interactions*. Volume XV.6, November/December 2008, 13–17.

Sanders, P. (2006) *The Person-Centred Counselling Primer*. Ross-on-Wye, UK: PCCS Books.

Slovák, P., Thieme, A., Tennent, P., Olivier, P. and Fitzpatrick, G. (2015) On becoming a counsellor: Challenges and opportunities to support interpersonal skills training. *Proc. CSCW 2015*.

Thaler, R. and Sunstein, C. (2008) *Nudge: Improving Decisions about Health, Wealth and Happiness*. New Haven, CT: Yale University Press.

Tyrer, P. and Steinberg, D. (2009) *Models for Mental Disorder: Conceptual Models in Psychiatry*. Chichester, UK: John Wiley & Sons.

Vanhove, J. (2011) Ethical framework for the implementation and use of person centred technology for persons with disabilities. ImpaCT in Europe Conference, June 2011, Cardiff.

Vines, J., Clarke, R., Wright, P., Iversen, O. S., Leong, T. W., McCarthy, J. and Olivier, P. (2012) Summary Report on CHI 2012 invited SIG: Participation and HCI: Why involve people in design? *Extended Abstracts of CHI 2012*, pp. 1217–1220.

Vines, J., Clarke, R., Wright, P., McCarthy, J. and Olivier, P. (2013) Configuring participation: On how we involve people in design. *Proceedings of CHI 2013*, pp. 429–438.

Voyer, Benjamin G. (2015) 'Nudging' behaviours in healthcare: Insights from behavioural economics. *British Journal of Healthcare Management*, 21(3), 130–135.

Wallace, J., McCarthy, J., Wright, P., Green, D., Thomas, J. and Olivier, P. (2013) A design-led inquiry into personhood in dementia. *Proc. CHI 2013*, 27 April–2 May, 2013, Paris, France.

Wallis, M. (2009) Performance, complexity and emergent objects. In J. Johnson, K. Alexiou and T. Zamenopoulos (eds), *Embracing Complexity in Design*. Abingdon, UK: Routledge, pp. 143–160.

Wilkins, P. (2010) *Person-Centred Therapy: 100 Key Points*. Hove, UK: Routledge.

Conclusion

What happens next? Themes and principles for a personalised future

Tom Fisher and Iryna Kuksa

Introduction

As a phenomenon, personalisation seems to be quite recent, facilitated in many cases by new digital technologies – genomics, 3D printing, artificial intelligence – and available in contexts formerly characterised by mass provision. But personalisation in any of these settings is not new. Being clothed, acquiring goods, learning about the past, seeing the doctor, have required personal relationships, either with the product or the person providing it, or both. Clothes have been made to measure or routinely altered, and other goods may have been the products of a crafts person who may be known personally to their owner. The early museum was a personal affair that grew out of the learned aristocrat's 'cabinet of curiosities' and this person-ality lives on in museums that carry the name of their originators, for example, Soane or Pitt-Rivers. In the developed world we are still often lucky enough to have a personal relationship with an individual doctor. However, the power and potential of digital technologies is such that the foregoing chapters point towards different relationships between consumers and all of these systems of provision of goods and services that are apparently more personal, while at the same time being part of our system of mass consumption.

As well as implying questions about persons and personhood in their articulation with systems of provision, the fact that the technologies that may enable a shift towards personalisation are recently developed means that the book as a whole points towards the future. A future orientation is built in to design, which as a profession is itself a consequence of modernisation with all its attendant progressive connotations, albeit that design has often had *subaltern* status; serving rather than leading (Dilnot 2015: 208). Different 'futures' are implied by the variety of instances of personalisation covered here, from practices with a long heritage – making clothing, shopping, seeing the doctor – to new digital technologies such as 3D printing, genomic medicine, and 'virtual' experiences. In his recent meditations on design and history, Clive Dilnot indicates that design is a 'capacity of acting' that relates both to history and to the future (2015: 133). This book reflects Dilnot's perspective – we are not prescribing a system for *doing* personalisation but rather identifying instances of design that facilitate personalisation, and considering their implications for different futures.

At the same time, as it is beyond the scope of design to bring it about, the novelty of personalisation means that simple prescriptions for it are not possible, and the diversity of examples the chapters contain suggest that they may never be. Instead of prescribing, what this concluding section hopes to do instead is to identify themes and principles that can be found in the chapters, with the intention to help the field of Design to engage productively with the phenomenon of personalisation as it appears in specific settings, identifying the opportunities it affords as well as the challenges it poses. The future relationships between people, and things and services that personalisation implies are as yet unformed, though a sense of expectation runs through the chapters that because of the power of the enabling digital technologies, personalisation will make things not only different, but also better. It is in the capacity of design practice to shape, represent and help to realise these expectations. And it is in the capacity of design discourse to challenge them.

Making things better? The positive and negative consequences of personalisation

'Better' is a loaded term and our expectations of what technologies will enable have a habit of being confounded, to the extent that we may *expect* technologies to provide less than we desire. This is the sense we have that the past has not delivered a present that resembles the future that it promised, summed up in the title of Daniel H. Wilson's 2007 book *Where's My Jetpack?* and named in the 'hype cycle' invented by the Gartner technology consultancy as the 'trough of disillusionment'.[1] The novelty of personalisation means that we are watching it take shape before us and it is in an open state, for now. This openness gives it the 'interpretive flexibility' that the sociology of technology identified in the 1980s as characteristic of the early stage of the 'social construction' of new technologies in Pinch and Bijker's scheme for the Social Construction of Technology (SCOT) (Pinch and Bijker 1984; Bijker 1995).[2]

While we might wish for 'better' as a consequence of personalisation, it is important to be alert to its potential to have both positive and negative consequences. Given that as a phenomenon personalisation is currently in a state of interpretive flexibility, we are in a moment when design can influence how it plays out. There are signs of the ethical implications of personalisation in the chapters above related to healthcare provision (Chapter 8, Golubnitchaya et al.; Chapter 7, Checkland) and to the relative lack of control that can be applied to applications of 3D printing (Sinclair). Farrington identifies both utopian and dystopian possibilities in personalisation including capacities for empowerment, and greater self-knowledge, as well as surveillance and intrusion of privacy, digital addiction, and corporate misuse of data.

Whereas with some specific technologies both common sense and the hype surrounding them can make it seem as if their internal properties determine how they play out (Fenn and Raskino 2008), given that personalisation is necessarily about humans, persons, as well as technologies, it is perhaps easier to see the social, political and psychological dimensions that affect specific instances of it. Sociological perspectives that have built on the early ideas that put social construction in the foreground, known as 'Science and Technology Studies' or STS,[3] stress the interplay of the material and social dimensions of the development of technologies (Bijker 1995; Suchman 2002; Latour 2005). Drawing from the SCOT approach, they show that stabilisation is not determined either by the technologies themselves or by social forces that 'shape' them, but comes about from a complex, historically and culturally specific interplay between material and social agents.

What this book does then, is to help us to see some of the outlines of this complex interplay of the technological, social and human forces that are currently in circulation and through which personalisation is coalescing. This is a process to which design is ideally suited to contribute, through its power to propose, prototype and refine relationships between the human and material elements in play in personalisation. The imaginative, projective, potential of design is particularly salient here, increasingly informed by critical insights that are wise to the interests that are at work in processes of technological development, and the ethical territory that in consequence they necessarily imply.[4] The imaginative element of design connects this discussion to work in the study of science and technology that focuses specifically on our expectations of technology, and the imaginative visions for it that are central to what design is taken to be (Tonkinwise 2015).

Design in personalisation: imagination and expectations

To understand the potential of design in personalisation, we can consider ways of thinking about how the future might unfold through the intertwined development of society with technologies. Both design and such imagined futures seem to fall within what Sheila Jasanoff calls 'sociotechnical imaginaries', which she defines as 'collectively held, institutionally stabilized, and publicly performed visions of desirable futures, animated by shared understandings of forms of social life and social order attainable through, and supportive of, advances in science and technology' (2015: 322).

Jasanoff's work is orientated particularly towards the political dimensions of such imaginaries, paying more attention to their features at the level of states than the activities of individuals – designers, makers and practitioners. She contrasts the relative lack of power of individual vision to bring about such imagined futures with collective efforts to embed them in social practices. It is this collective effort that is required to bring them about that characterises the sets of ideas about the future that she names imaginaries,[5] citing work that shows the importance of 'social, cultural, economic and normative structures' in achieving the effects of science on the world (ibid.: 327). There are parallels here with the relationship between the alleged role of individual designers in proposing and bringing about future visions, and the various forces that introduce what Jasanoff names as 'frictions' in that process. From a point of view on design that privileges the designer, the work of consumers in 'completing' artefacts in the open design scenario that Matt Sinclair discusses in his chapter could seem to be such a resistive force, though this personalisation seems more like an instance of how 'scientific and technological ideas [. . .] are produced together with ideas about science and technology' (Jasanoff 2015: 333). Technologies that facilitate personalisation, like additive manufacturing, have consequences for our ideas about what it is to design.

Real futures do not turn out the way we imagine them because they are also subject to political contestation, and because 'sociotechnical imaginaries are embedded in the political cultures of nations' (ibid.: 335). The ethical dimensions of political cultures are especially relevant in respect of clearly value-laden technologies, such as the biotechnology that Jasanoff discusses, referring to the study of biotechnology 'monsters' (ibid.: 325). While this book has not covered topics with quite such emotive power, there is an equivalent relationship perhaps between the use of 3D printing to produce a firearm, and concerns about limits on individuals' freedom of action. As Sinclair points out, these concerns are somewhat over-blown, given that it is easier to lash up a firearm using conventional engineering techniques than it is using 3D printing. However, the potential for new 'interpretively flexible' additive manufacturing technology to 'capture the imagination' as Guy Bingham puts it in his chapter, and to cause such concern suggests that both its material potentials and their significance in terms of political culture may be understood through the concept of the sociotechnical imaginary.

Jasanoff characterises this concept as a 'hybrid zone between the mental and the material' (ibid.: 329) and such hybridity is strongly in evidence in the cases of personalisation covered in the chapters. In many of the examples, the mental component of imagined, personalised futures appears in the form of *expectations* of what the technologies that underlie personalisation will bring about, and such expectations are also an object of sociological study. Mads Borup and colleagues (2006) provide a useful review of approaches to the subject, noting that expectations of technology may be positive or negative; we expect our lives to be improved by them, and at the same time we may fear them. As Jasanoff does with the more diffuse concept of the 'imaginary', Borup relates our collective expectations of technologies, and the ways they play out in actuality, to the political and social interests that are relevant to them.

These ways of thinking about modern industrial innovation, in terms of imagination and expectation, are useful to help understand what design brings to the process, and points to its role in shaping the potential of digital technologies in specific instances of personalisation. The key point here is that expectations of technology can be shown to be *performative*. As Borup et al. put it 'expectations are both the cause and consequence of material, scientific and technological activity' (ibid.: 286). To the extent that design is part of the 'hype cycle', it is bound up in the broad field of technology foresight (van Lente 2012), and has consequent effects on actions by investors, manufacturers, potential consumers, legislators. It is helpful to note in relation to a discussion of design's role in shaping personalisation that van Lente briefly touches on the constructivist and realist perspectives that can be applied in understanding expectations of technology, and by extension, design's role in shaping them (ibid.: 775). Whereas a realist view would distinguish between expectations, and the 'real' situation, the latter would distinguish between expectations that are plausible – or 'meaningful' in van Lente's terms – and ones that are not. Design does make expectations concrete; it has a role in the 'hype cycle'. Its power is to give meaningful form to expectations of technology, as well as to contribute to bringing them about.

This connection between design and the imaginary dimension of technology shades into science fiction, and may seem too far from van Lente's realist position to be useful, but it is nonetheless prevalent. It has been a feature of media related to technology and its development since the early twentieth century, gaining particular resonance in the social/political milieu after the Second World War (Booker 2001). The covers of *Popular Science* magazine often showed design imagination at work in relation to a particular transport technology, against a backdrop of twentieth-century urban future fantasies that stretch from those of the Italian Futurists Sant'Elia and Marinetti of 1914, through the dystopian fantasy architecture of Superstudio in the 1970s (1972), to contemporary 'concepts'. Examples of the latter include a proposal for Urban Skyfarm in Seoul, by Aprilli Design Studio[6] and the Ring Garden project in Santa Monica, by Alexandru Predonu – a finalist of the 2016 Land Art Generator Initiative competition.[7] The bio-inspired, high-rise Urban Skyfarm idea has been reported widely since 2014. It builds on concerns about the degradation of urban environments and promises to ameliorate ecological worries through the medium of vertical agriculture. The Ring Garden offers a solution to drinking water shortages in California by using solar energy to sustain a rotating desalination plant, which is also a farm producing various food crops.

The interpretive flexibility of personalisation constitutes an opening for design's future orientation, an opportunity, albeit one hedged round by its 'subaltern' status and the fact that it co-exists with the other elements in what has been referred to as an 'innovation ecosystem' (BIS 2011: 4). Recent work by Chisholm et al. (2013) identifies ways of conceptualising design's relationship to other elements in such a system – a network of commercial actors, academic research and government. These 'interacting organisations and individuals . . . suppliers, producers, competitors and other stakeholders' (ibid.: 5) include design, but as Jung et al. (2013) note, there is not as yet a 'shared understanding' of the value design can bring to such a network. While there may not be shared understanding, the cases covered in this book suggest that there are at least two aspects of the construction of personalisation to which design might make a distinct contribution. One exists in its power to encapsulate, materialise and visualise critique seen in the emerging tradition of 'speculative and critical design' (Dunne and Raby 2014, and see Malpass 2017 for an overview), the second is its ability to engage with people.

Carl DiSalvo (2012) develops this from the starting point that the normative character of design, its capacity to identify 'how things could or ought to be' (ibid.: 16), mean(s) it can be part of an 'agonistic approach to democracy' (ibid.: 4). DiSalvo works these ideas through in relation to specific design interventions, using political theorist Chantal Mouffe's formulation of contemporary political hegemony to point to design's potential to reveal power: 'Revealing hegemony is a tactic of exposing and documenting the forces of influence in society' (ibid.: 35). While such concerns are implied by some of the case studies of personalisation in the chapters above, for instance in relation to personalised medicine, further work is needed to fully elucidate and explore how design can engage with them, agonistically or otherwise.

We are, perhaps, on surer territory in relation to design's second distinctive contribution to personalisation, its potential to engage with the human, personal, dimension of our engagement with technologies. As the discussion of the construction of technologies above has shown, personalisation is more than its enabling technologies. It is people, as well as things, human as well as technological, and the intimacy with which the two are compounded in some instances of it implies a strong relationship to the human-centred, participative co-creation tradition in design (Sanders and Stappers 2008; Binder et al. 2011). It is appropriate to think a little about the concept of the person that is in play in the discussions of personalisation that the chapters cover, leading to what may be operative principles to guide the design of personalisation.

We encounter a number of conceptions of personhood in the chapters, of both wide and narrow scope. For Golubnitschaja et al. it seems to reduce to a genome, whereas for Kettley et al. personhood is centred on the intrinsically valuable human psyche. Somewhere in the middle perhaps are Checkland's social/political subjects, negotiating healthcare policy directed at them as individuals, but as part of national provision. Then in the context of material culture, there is Twigger Holroyd's skilled person re-making their embodied, personal relationship to clothing through craft skill, alongside Farrington's persons empowered or oppressed by wearable technologies. The concepts of personhood implied in these examples don't cover all the variation implied by the chapters, and they may be different enough to raise the question whether it is possible to compare them – personalisation in healthcare has such different characteristics as to appear to be a different phenomenon to personalisation in, say, fashion retail. But although they clearly have characteristics defined by the context in which they arise, they may appear more different than they are in principle. And it is principles that can be seen across examples that are useful if we are to relate the potentials of personalisation to the potentials of design.

Person-alising personalisation

Among the meanings of 'person' is a strong sense that it indicates how we project ourselves into the world, as well as denoting our actual, physical, self. Person can be contrasted with 'wight', an older word for a human being, deriving from Old English and denoting any 'creature, being or thing', living, but without the sense of character, or 'personality'.[8] This sense of personality is suggested by the derivation from the Latin *persona*, which is connected to the masks used in Roman theatre through which the characters were projected, and remains in the convention of calling the characters in a play the *dramatis personae*. The sense of physical being is found in phrases such as something being 'about my person' or someone being present 'in person'. This sense of the person as a body, has strong relationships to some of the examples in the chapters where bodies are at issue, particularly those related to medical care. The medical literature engages with the nature of personhood in direct relation to questions about the appropriate ethical treatment of actual persons – patients.

The ethical dimension of medical treatments throws into sharp relief the link between personhood, autonomy and the relationship of the person in question to other agents, human or technological (Walker and Lovat 2015). This is relevant to this discussion because some instances of personalisation seem to reduce individual autonomy rather than increasing it, particularly those that involve *personalisation for* the individual, through the autonomous operation of technology. Discussing the ethics of care at the end of life, particularly appropriate medical conduct in the Intensive Care Unit (ICU), Walker and Lovat emphasise that the essential component of personhood is *relationship*, and that it is the quality of that relationship that is the central issue at end of life. They arrive at this conclusion through a critique of an approach to personhood that takes a Cartesian view that it exists in disembodied rationality, instead offering 'an understanding of our personhood, our essence, as situated-in-the-world with others' (ibid.: 311). Quoting Eric Mathews, they note that this situatedness means that our intellect is not separable from our emotions or our relations to other people (Mathews 2012: 68–71). The 'with others' aspect of Walker and Lovat's criteria for personhood is particularly salient to designed personalisation, which might be dealing with either human or technological 'others'. Given that we need criteria on which to assess the validity of personalisation, inspired by Walker and Lovat's qualitative criteria for personhood, the *quality of the relationships with others* that a particular instance of personalisation affords seems like a productive place to start to develop such criteria.

One attractive feature of this approach to appraising the validity of designed personalisation is that it is not reductive, honouring and valuing relationships beyond the personalised experience of individual human beings in particular instances of personalisation. A tendency to be reductive seems to be inherent in systematic approaches to personalisation, which often appear to proceed by reducing the persons in question only to those features that are relevant to the personalisation process. At risk of mis-representing the complexity in particular instances of personalisation that the chapters present, 'persons' (in some of the cases described) appear to be reduced in this way, conceived of as 'a consumer', 'a genome', 'a set of skills', 'a source of data' or even 'a projected identity'. Such reduction risks downplaying, or ignoring, the relevant sets of social and political relationships that not only make the person who they are, but also have the potential to make the personalisation relevant and valuable to them. The benefit of Walker and Lovat's emphasis on relationship is that it prompts us to understand specific instances of personalisation by focusing on the quality of relationships beyond the person, whether they are doing personalisation for themselves, or having it done to/for them.

Even though it has a quite specific setting – end of life care in ICU – some aspects of Walker and Lovat's persuasive argument that the autonomy necessary to personhood inheres in relationships, resonates strongly with some instances of personalisation. Their argument against a conception of personhood as inhering solely in the ability to reason – from Kant and Descartes – is a case in point. They suggest that in the context of the ICU, the absence of an obvious ability to reason does not negate the patient's personhood, which they argue then exists in their 'socio-cultural habitus' as embodied human subjects (ibid.: 311). In practical terms this means that clinicians must operate with a concept of personhood that extends to all of those with whom the patient is in relationship. There may be a corollary here with Jon Oberlander's discussion of automated and personalised communication by an adaptive computer system, which acts in response to a user, but over which the user has no clear control (see Chapter 4).

This example goes beyond what seems a simple distinction between personalisation 'by' and personalisation 'for' a user, because here a user cannot exercise their powers of reason over the system and they would not be capable of doing so if they were given the chance, because of the level of technical understanding it would require. As Oberlander puts it, 'A system may be so complex and subtle that giving those it affects access to it, or even just awareness of it, does not de-fuse its ethical implications' (this volume, p. 83). In other words, it is not possible for non-technical people to 'live with' this technology and influence its development. The most that can be done is to give the user the chance to 'de-personalise' their interaction with an adaptive system, to turn off its personalised features so that it is more apparent what these are doing. This at least demonstrates that the relationship exists, even if it does not give the user reasoned control over it. In Walker and Lovat's formulation this respects their personhood, enhancing the user's autonomy by making the relationship more evident, if not much richer. A further step in this direction would be to make it possible for users to 're-personalise' their interaction with an adaptive system, allowing them to deploy a variety of self-made 'personas' in the interaction, which would each elicit their own 'personalised' response from the system. This, among other ways of customising interactions is the remedy to restore control, simultaneously making the user's *relationship* with the adaptive system more complex, and exposing its artificiality.

Relational personalisation and personalised relationship

The principle of relationship is central to examples of personalisation that relate to more conventional settings such as the everyday consumption of goods. In the cases that Sinclair, Kent, Twigger Holroyd and Bingham discuss, the relationship between people and various aspects of material culture – shopping for fashion, craft, additive manufacturing – is affected because of, and beyond, personalisation as tightly defined. There is a curious parallel between the need to 'de-personalise' adaptive systems to preserve the user's autonomy described in Oberlander's chapter (Chapter 4), which also features in Twigger Holroyd's craft personalisation. In this case the barrier to autonomy, and therefore to personalisation, that truly honours the *person* is again a lack of *capacity* to personalise. One of Twigger Holroyd's participants expresses this in terms of limits to her imagination about what she might do to alter clothes that she owns but is not satisfied with: 'I can't see it, I can't visualise, I can't imagine what you would do'. The more deeply inflected personal and therefore personalised relationship to objects of material culture that high-level craft skills can facilitate enhances more than just their owner's physical relationship with them, it helps them to imagine beyond the perfect surfaces of conventionally acquired goods.

There are echoes in this example of Colin Campbell's (1987) 'imaginary hedonism', his observation that modern consumption is driven more by imagined consumption experiences than by direct physical experience with actual goods. By implication, Campbell restricts daydreams about consumption to new products bought, not ones that someone might make or personalise. Even his 'craft consumption' (2005) is crafting by assemblage of new items, not by making or re-making. Clearly, the values that accrue to personalised products might be negative as well as positive. The long-standing association of home-made or repaired clothes with poverty stands against the attraction of the brand new; shop-bought is better, more modern, more desirable, possible to fantasise about. In contrast, Twigger Holroyd's success in helping individuals re-claim a 'craft commons' opens up the possibility of an imaginative consumption based in personalised material engagement that includes imagining positive new experiences for objects that do not yet, quite, exist.

The technologies of additive manufacturing that Sinclair and Bingham discuss have a clear relationship to craft practices, apparently superseding them but, in fact, supplementing them and pointing towards 'future crafts' (Bonanni et al. 2008). Bespoke and therefore personalised prosthetic devices, from teeth to limbs to eyes, have a long history, and as Bingham sets out, these technologies have made the production of bespoke medical products much easier and cheaper and made possible new forms of implants and limb prostheses. Bingham makes the point that in the latter case, the patient/wearer/user of the limb is able to specify its 'look and feel' so that it is aesthetically, as well as functionally, personalised. However, despite the fact that additive manufacturing and a simple online interface makes possible perhaps the most personal example of personalisation in personalised sex toys, which are rich with potential for both imaginary and actual hedonism, this mass consumer personalisation faces an equivalent problem to that thrown up in Oberlander's example – the complexity of the technology gets in the way of the potential to maximise the personalised relationship. Sophisticated knitting techniques are no less difficult to master than 3D CAD, but their relative technical simplicity, in respect of the materials required and the social hinterland they point to and can build on, means they and other such craft techniques may be a more immediate route to richly relational personalisation.

Although they have a clear focus on personalisation in the provision of healthcare services, the pair of chapters by Golubnitschaja et al. and Checkland seem further from the field of design than the others, although, as we have just seen, there is plenty of personalisation going on in relation to the design of healthcare products. Here, the way that relationships are implicated in the design of the personalisation is perhaps both more obvious and more potent. In some of the other chapters, where personalisation is close to everyday consumption, it is perhaps easier to restrict evaluations of the relationships in play to matters that are close to the technology that enables personalisation. Even in the case of the topics of these chapters, however, such 'crude empiricism' is possible and commentators such as Klein and Kleinman (2002) warn against this. However, it is more difficult to ignore the political and moral dimensions of personalisation in Checkland's and Golubnitschaja's chapters. The ideological gloss that is put on the state provision of health services through the principle of personalisation that Checkland discusses is not easily overlooked.

In a similar way, it does not require a great deal of searching through the literature to uncover robust and credible critiques of personalised medicine based on genomics, which point to its scientific shortcomings, the ideological overtones of its convenience for commercial interests and its consequences for individuals' conception of what it is to be a healthy person. To take the last, Jacqueline Savard identifies that among other effects, personalised healthcare reduces individual autonomy by challenging what it means to be healthy, turning every person into a patient and shifting the ontology of health, illness and disease (2013: 197–198). As she puts it: 'Illness [. . .] becomes not so much a matter of experience, but the possibility of developing disease according to one's genetics' (ibid.: 199). She notes that this approach to health and illness may have conflicting consequences for individuals' sense of responsibility for their health – they may act more responsibly, or less. While the personalised medicine programmes that Golubnitschaja et al. describe require individuals to follow lifestyle regimes that minimise the risks associated with their genetic make-up, a sense that health is 'all in the genes' may mean individuals conclude their actions are irrelevant. Personalised medicine therefore has a propensity to 'both empower and absolve individuals of responsibility for their health' (ibid.: 199) and design could engage with both responses to facilitate conformity with a life regimen, through communication design. In the case of the latter choice, the medical profession is placed in a similar position as to a patient who chooses unhealthy practice. Drinking, over-eating or smoking are instances of such behaviours that feature in current public discourse (Daily Mail 2015).

Whether responses to such habits, or to not conforming to a regimen dictated by personalised genomic diagnosis, are framed in terms of public health or personal choice is a political matter, which has direct consequences for the design of healthcare provision. Savard is careful to avoid technological determinism by pointing out that there is nothing inherent in medicine based in genetic information that promotes discrimination, but she notes that it does 'enable it [discrimination] to be done more scientifically' (ibid.: 200) – this may make it easier to design prejudice into healthcare systems. She goes further in suggesting that the ease with which non-expert patients get access to their genetic information has potentially negative consequences that do seem to be a function of technology, as do some of the consequences of personalised additive manufacturing. Here, however, this ease of access promotes 'a reductionist, "anti-social" view of health, illness, and disease' (ibid.: 200) with illness as a personal failure, rather than a product of an unhealthy environment.

This emphasis on the individual in personalised medicine points strongly to its political implications, specifically the sense that it is a consequence of neoliberalism, played out in health provision. Savard gives a convincing definition of neoliberalism that connects it to the features of personalised healthcare, and to some extent to other instances of personalisation covered in this book. As the '(re)privileging of liberal principles, including the notion that individuals are atomistic, rational agents whose existence and interests are prior to society' (p. 201), neoliberalism aligns with the 'anti-social' implications of some personalisation. In the context of health provision, a personalised approach runs counter to inclusive community-wide approaches to health problems. As Checkland's chapter sets out, the promise of individual choice and apparently increased autonomy ensures that there will be losers as well as winners, the latter being those members of society who for reasons of wealth, education and culture are likely to benefit from healthcare available on a consumption model.

Personalised medicine seems to be an instance where personalisation provides a vision of the future in which the 'hype' has taken hold, driven by particular, commercial, interests. Joyner and Paneth (2015) are scathing in their critique of the likelihood of actual benefits deriving from such an approach making a clearly evidenced argument that 'the promise of improved risk prediction, behaviour change, lower costs and gains in public health for common diseases seem unrealistic'. Although they do not use the word hype, they suggest that proponents of personalised medicine should temper 'their narrative of transformative change and [. . .] communicate a more realistic set of expectations to the public' (2015: 1000). Personalised medicine then, seems to be an example of personalisation where the promise of increased autonomy actually equates to atomisation rather than empowerment for individuals. The consequent effects on the relationship of the patient to the system of health provision are clearly a matter of dispute, and arguably negative.

Conclusion

It is not a simple matter to draw together the threads in a collection of essays as diverse as these, even though they all engage with the same topic. Personalisation offers us a set of paradoxes, but that we may be able to judge it by working out whether a particular manifestation increases the vitality and richness of relationships of persons to others, or impoverishes them. It is paradoxical, in that while in principle it promises to increase the individual autonomy necessary to personhood, it cannot do that if it impoverishes relationships. It is paradoxical in that it can emerge 'bottom up', through individuals' actions or 'top down' through the design of systems.

The degree to which a specific instance of personalisation might affect relationships, and the ways in which it might do so, is grounds for critical contestation to which design can contribute. Design's focus on human persons – whether identified as 'users', 'customers', 'carriers of social practice' or otherwise – and their (our) relationship to the made world gives it purchase on this critical contestation that may not be available from other perspectives. Accounts of technology development may take a 'realist' or 'constructivist' view – the former privileging the technology, the latter its social construction. Given that personalisation seems frequently to be driven by developments in technology, or at least enabled by them and that design is frequently the practical bridge between the human, social and the technological, design clearly can have a significant role to play in how personalisation plays out.

So, *Design for Personalisation* is necessarily a collective effort of engaging with the future, in full understanding of the critical contestation this implies and of the power of the interests that underlie it. As Clive Dilnot puts it, design is a 'capacity for acting' in relation to both history and the future (2015: 133), which must be alert to the degree to which its practices have built into them preferences for what sort of future there should be. In the case of a more personalised future, the imaginaries to which design contributes indicate how personalised products should be, the types of experiences they should generate, the collective purposes they should serve. These collective purposes have values attached, so one of the functions of design in the sphere of personalisation is to question those purposes, to offer alternative future worlds. Ideas about the future may be positive or negative and this is evident in the sociological literature on expectations of technology (Borup et al. 2006) and as we have seen, personalisation generates both hopes and fears. However, it is important to recognise that our expectations of technologies may condition their reality – we should be careful what we wish for and design can help us take that care.

Notes

1 See http://www.gartner.com/technology/research/methodologies/hype-cycle.jsp
2 SCOT has four components: (1) interpretive flexibility (i.e. the technology can be interpreted in a number of ways by ...), (2) relevant social groups that influence the technology's development, which implies (3) closure and stabilisation of the form of the technology in (4) a wider social and political milieu. See Klein and Kleinman (2002) for a more recent summary and critique. Bijker later (1995) added a further concept of the 'technological frame' to the above four, which Klein and Kleinman relate to a Kuhnian (1970) paradigm as a 'shared cognitive frame that defines a relevant social group and constitutes members' common interpretation of an artifact' (2002: 31).

3 See Fallan (2010) for an overview and introduction to the relationship of SCOT and STS to Design and Design History.
4 See, for instance, Mahmoud Keshavarz's work on the practices of power that are embedded in systems of passport control (2016).
5 Jasanoff quotes Arjun Appadurai for the phrase 'an organised field of social practices' (2015: 327).
6 http://www.worldarchitecturenews.com/project/2014/24426/aprilli-design-studio/urban-skyfarm-in-jung-gu-seoul.html.
7 http://inhabitat.com/solar-powered-ring-garden-marries-desalination-and-agriculture-for-drought-stricken-california.
8 See the Oxford English Dictionary: www.oed.com.

References

Binder, T., Ehn, P., De Michelis, G., Jacucci, G. and Linde, G. (2011) *Design Things*. Cambridge, MA: MIT Press.
BIS (2011) *Innovation and Research Strategy for Growth*. Cm 8239, London: HM Stationery Office.
Bijker, W. B. (1995) *Of Bicycles, Bakelites and Bulbs*. London: MIT Press.
Bonanni, L. A., Parkes, A. J. and Ishii, H. (2008) Future craft: How digital media is transforming product design, in *Proceedings of the 2008 Conference on Human Factors in Computing Systems*, CHI 2008, April 5–10, Florence, Italy.
Booker, M. Keith (2001) *Monsters, Mushroom Clouds and the Cold War: American Science Fiction and the Roots of Postmodernism, 1946–1964*. Westport, CT: Greenwood Press.
Borup, M., Brown, N., Konrade, K. and Van Lente, H. (2006) The sociology of expectations in science and technology. *Technology Analysis & Strategic Management*, 18(3–4), 285–298.
Campbell, Colin (1987) *The Romantic Ethic and the Spirit of Modern Consumerism*. Oxford: Blackwell.
Campbell, Colin (2005) The craft consumer: Culture, craft and consumption in a post-modern society. *Journal of Consumer Culture*, 5, 23–42.
Chisholm, J., Evans, M., Cruikshank, L. and Cooper, R. (2013) Towards a taxonomy: Classifying design innovation policies in Europe, *CADMC 2nd Academic Design Management Conference*, Cambridge, 4–5 September 2013.
Daily Mail (2015) How obese patients have cost the NHS £7 million: Hospitals forced to spend cash buying specialist equipment such a huge mortuary slabs and reinforced beds. Daily Mail online, Published 24 October, updated 26 October, available at: http://www.dailymail.co.uk/health/article-3287288/NHS-spends-millions-larger-equipment-obese.html. Accessed 24 August 2016.
Dilnot, Clive (2015) History, design, futures: Contenting with what we have made, in Tony Fry, Clive Dilnot and Susan Stewart (eds), *Design and the Question of History*, London: Bloomsbury, pp. 133–243.
DiSalvo, Carl (2012) *Adversarial Design*, Cambridge MA: MIT Press.
Dunne, A. and Raby, F. (2014) *Speculative Everything: Design, Fiction, and Social Dreaming*. Cambridge, MA: MIT Press.
Fallan, K. (2010) *Design History: Understanding Theory and Method*. London: Berg.
Fenn, J. and Raskino, M. (2008) *Mastering the Hype Cycle: How to Choose the Right Innovation at the Right Time*. Cambridge, MA: Harvard Business Press.

Jasanoff, Sheila (2015) Imagined and invented worlds, in Sheila Jasanoff and Sang-Hyun Kim (eds), *Dreamscapes of Modernity: Sociotechnical Imaginaries and the Fabrication of Power*, Chicago, IL: University of Chicago Press, pp. 321–341.

Joyner, Michael and Paneth, Nigel (2015) Seven questions for personalized medicine. *Journal of the American Medical Association*, 314(10), 999–1000.

Jung, J. Y., Evans, M. and Cruickshank, L. (2013) Identifying core knowledge: Towards a shared understanding of design management through comparing different stakeholders' perspectives. *Proceedings of the 2nd Cambridge Academic Design Management Conference*, 3–5 September.

Keshavarz, Mahmoud (2016) Material practices of power – Part 1: Passports and passporting. *Design Philosophy Papers*, 13(2), 97–113.

Klein, Hans, K. and Kleinman, Daniel Lee (2002) The social construction of technology: Structural considerations. *Science, Technology, & Human Values*, 27(1), Winter 2002, 28–52.

Kuhn, Thomas (1970) *The Structure of Scientific Revolutions*, Chicago, IL: University of Chicago Press.

Latour, B. (2005) *Reassembling the social. An introduction to actor-network-theory*. Oxford: Oxford University Press.

Malpass, M. (2017) *Critical Design in Context: History, Theory and Practices*. London: Bloomsbury Academic

Mathews, Eric (2012) Old age and dependency, in Christopher Cowley (ed.), *Reconceiving Medical Ethics: Bloomsbury Studies in Philosophy*, London: Bloomsbury Academic, pp. 59–71.

Pinch, Trevor and Bijker, Wiebe (1984) The social construction of facts and artefacts: Or how the sociology of science and the sociology of technology might benefit each other. *Social Studies of Science*, 14, 339–341.

Sanders, E. B.-N. and Stappers, P. J. (2008) Co-creation and the new landscapes of design. *CoDesign*, 4(1), 5–18.

Sant'Elia, Antonio and Marinetti, Filippo Tommaso (1970 [1914]) Manifesto of Futurist Architecture, in Ulrich Conrads (ed.), *Programs and Manifestoes on 20th-Century Architecture*, London: Lund Humphriesm, pp. 34–38.

Savard, Jacqueline (2013) Personalised medicine: A critique on the future of healthcare. *Bioethical Enquiry*, 10, 197–203.

Suchman, Lucy (2002) Located accountabilities in technology production. *Scandinavian Journal of Information Systems*, 14(2), Article 7. Available at: http://aisel.aisnet.org/sjis/vol14/iss2/7.

Superstudio (1972) *Microevent/Microenvironment*, in W. Braham and J. A. Hale (eds), *Rethinking Technology*, London: Routledge, London, 2007, p. 196.

Tonkinwise, Cameron (2015) Just design: Being dogmatic about defining speculative critical design future fiction. *Medium*. Available at: https://medium.com/@camerontw/just-design-b1f97cb3996f#.i9jowd6lz. Accessed: 20 January 2016.

van Lente, Harro (2012) Navigating foresight in a sea of expectations: Lessons from the sociology of expectations. *Technology Analysis & Strategic Management*, 24(8), 769–782.

Walker, Paul and Lovat, Terence (2015) Concepts of personhood and autonomy as they apply to end of life decisions in intensive care. *Medicine, Health Care, and Philosophy*, 18(3), 309–315.

Index

activity maps 156
actor maps 156
Actor Network Theory 175
additive manufacturing (AM) 8, 91, 113–130, 195, 199–200, 202; *see also* 3D printing
Adidas 2, 7, 24, 35, 44
adolescence 162–163
Adorno, Theodor 6, 53, 55–58, 60–61, 62, 64, 67, 68
advertising, targeted 3, 4, 82; *see also* marketing
aesthetics: Benjamin 63–64; Habermas 61; relational 178; slow fashion 30; wearable technologies 68; *see also* art
Affective AutoTutor 87
Agee, J. 55
agency 1, 3, 10; choice and self-efficacy 137; culture 56; human and machine 85–86; moral 108; Person-Centred Approach 172; protection of 2; slow fashion 29
Akama, Y. 172, 178–179
Aldersey-Williams, H. 96, 107
algorithms 83, 100, 171
Alton Lane 35
AM *see* additive manufacturing
amateur fashion making 6, 34–50, 200
Amazon 82, 142–143
Anderson, C. 107
Anderson, D. M. 22
animal tracking devices 10–11
Anya Hindmarsh 25
Appadurai, Arjun 204n5
Apple Watch 51, 74, 161
apps 2, 7, 9, 65, 125
Arduino 91
Arnould, E. J. 22, 26
Arnstein, S. R. 183

art 5, 53, 56–57, 61, 62–64, 67, 68; *see also* aesthetics
'aura' 53, 62–64, 65, 68, 69
authenticity 63, 64, 69
autonomy 8, 73, 87; art 61, 63; culture 56; de-personalisation 200; Person-Centred Approach 10, 172, 182, 183; personalised medicine 202; personhood 198, 199, 203; user models 83, 84

Bates, M. 183
Benjamin, Walter 6, 53, 62–64, 65, 67, 68
Bespoke Innovations 121–122
bespoke products 3, 200; additive manufacturing 115, 116; consumer involvement in new product development 98, 99; fashion 25, 30, 35; medical implants 119
Bezaitis, M. 172
big data 2, 26
Bijker, W. B. 193, 203n2
Bingham, Guy 8, 113–130, 195, 199–200
bioinformatics 155, 168n2
biology 10–11
biometric data 5, 51, 74, 150
birth 162
Blair, Tony 134, 140
blogs 4, 20, 26, 37
Bluetooth 2
BMW 2
body scanning technologies 7, 27–28, 35, 122, 126
Borup, Mads 195
Bourriaud, N. 178
Bozdag, E. 83, 84
brands: crowdsourcing 109; digital technology 26; fashion 4, 17, 18, 21, 24–25, 27; service-dominant logic 22
Bratich, J. Z. 37

Breward, C. 36
Broussard, Diana 66
Brush, H. M. 37
Bryson, J. J. 85
Burberry 25, 27

CAD *see* computer-aided design
Cahn, J. E. 80
Cameron, David 137
Campbell, Colin 200
Campbell, R. I. 97–99, 105
capitalism 53, 55–56, 57, 58, 61, 63
Caplan, Ralph 93
Carroll, M. 183
Casemore, R. 178
Cell Cycle 100–101, 125–126
Chamberlain, P. 180, 185
Checkland, Kath 9, 133–149, 185, 197, 201, 202
children and families 135
Chisholm, J. 196
Chloé 18
choice, in public services 134–140, 144, 145, 202
Chopard 25
co-creation 1, 7, 197; additive manufacturing 123–124, 127; fashion 4, 6, 17, 18, 20, 24–28, 30; service-dominant logic 21
co-design 1, 91; additive manufacturing 123–124; consumer involvement in new product development 97, 98, 99; crowdsourcing comparison 101–102; fashion 6, 28, 29, 30; human-centred design 155, 185; industrial design 96; ladder of participation 183; mass-personalisation 115; Person-Centred Approach 178
co-production 1, 186; fashion 17, 18, 26; human-centred design 185; service-dominant logic 22
co-research 1, 172, 184, 185
coaching systems 74
collaboration: amateur fashion making 45; collaborative consumption 27; crowdsourcing 109; PPPM 151; professional and amateur 107
communication 54, 153–155, 163, 167, 180
communicative action 59, 60, 61, 68
communities of practice 3
computer-aided design (CAD) 200; additive manufacturing 114, 116–117, 119, 125; Kadushin's work 105, 106; Liberator gun 104, 108, 109
constructivist perspective 195–196, 203
consumerism 55, 60, 67, 142
consumers 2, 91–92, 192, 194–195; additive manufacturing 122–128, 129; constraints on 108; crowdsourcing 101–103; fashion 17–18, 19–21, 23–24, 26, 30–31; involvement in industrial design 8, 92–95, 96–99; mass customisation 99–101; service-dominant logic 21; user-centred design 96
consumption 17, 19, 27, 30, 192
Converse 24
Cooper, Z. 137
costs: healthcare 150; mass customisation 23; mass production 94, 113
counselling services 166–167, 181, 182
craft 6, 28–29, 37, 48, 199–201
CrAg project 80, 88n1
Crane, D. 17
Creative Commons 106
criminal justice 135
Critical Agent Dialogue 80, 88n1
critical design 5–6, 173
critical theory 6, 52–53, 55–64, 69
crowdsourcing 8, 92, 101–103, 109; consumer involvement in new product development 98, 99; fashion design 27; professional expertise 107
culture industry 55–57, 60, 64
customerisation 22
customisation 2, 7, 19–20, 22–23, 85, 88; animal tracking devices 11; consumer and designer involvement 97, 98; fashion 4, 17, 23–24, 25, 30; personalisation distinction 3, 75, 115; service-dominant logic 22; user-initiated 83, 84, 87; *see also* mass customisation; personalisation
Cute Circuit 51, 65–66
Cutler, T. 134, 144

Dant, T. 46
Darzi Report (2008) 133–134, 142, 145
data 2–3, 9, 171; big data 2, 26; biometric 5, 51, 74, 150; health and privacy 161–162; PPPM 158–159; user models 82–83; wearable technologies 65, 67, 68
databases 150, 153–154, 162, 165
Davis, Stan 99
dbCHRONICLE bag 66

208   Index

De Mul, J. 44
de-personalisation 8, 84–85, 86, 87–88, 199, 200
decoration 24
Defense Distributed 103–104
deficit model 171, 174, 186
Del Nord, R. 160
Democratising Technology project 178–179
design 194–197, 203; consumer involvement in industrial design 8, 92–95, 96–99; critical 5–6, 173; fashion 18, 23, 28–30; generative 100–101; human-centred 22, 151, 155–156, 160, 163, 166, 178, 185; imaginative element of 194; metadesign 44–45, 48; Person-Centred Approach 170, 173, 181–186; PPPM 152–153, 160, 163, 167; service-dominant logic 21; *see also* open design; participatory design; user-centred design
Design for Manufacture (DfM) 115
design research 173–175, 178–186
design thinking 156, 163, 167, 174, 187n3
designers 8, 91–92, 106–109, 194–195; amateur versus professional 92, 95–96; consumers as 92, 93, 95, 99, 109; fashion design 18, 20, 23, 27–30, 54; industrial design process 93–94, 96–97; learning 157; metadesign 44; new product development 97–99; wearable technologies 57
'desirability lens' 156
devolution 146n1
DfM *see* Design for Manufacture
diagnosis 152, 162, 174
dialogue 21, 80, 183
Dickens, Philip 115
differentiation 47
digital fabrication technologies 8, 94–95, 96, 100, 106–107, 109, 113–114; *see also* 3D printing
Digital Forming 127–128
Dildo Generator 124–125
Dilnot, Clive 192, 203
Direct Metal Laser Sintering (DMLS) 119
direct payments in healthcare 136
disability 2, 9, 186
DiSalvo, Carl 196–197
disease prevention 150–151, 161
Dixon, A. 138
D'Mello, S. 87
doctor–patient relationships 159–161
dress 54
Duffy, S. 144
dystopia 6, 51–52, 193

e-commerce 23, 27, 80, 82
e-textiles 172
ECS *see* ethical counselling services
education 135, 153, 157–158, 167
emancipation 52, 58–59, 69
Embleton-Tudor, L. 177
empathy 176, 179–180, 181, 186
employment 135
empowerment: capacity for 193; healthcare 24, 138–139, 141, 143, 144, 161; Person-Centred Approach 177; personalised fashion choice 6, 54, 58, 64; public service users 9, 138, 140; wearable technologies 52, 53, 62, 65, 68
Enlightenment 58, 60
EOS 119
EPMA *see* European Association for Predictive, Preventive and Personalised Medicine
equity 137, 138, 143
error 82–83
ethical counselling services (ECS) 166–167
ethical self-expression 61, 66–67, 68
ethics: Habermas 60–61; healthcare 198; open design 108; participatory design 179; Person-Centred Approach 170, 181; personalisation 82; political cultures 195; responsibilisation 139
European Association for Predictive, Preventive and Personalised Medicine (EPMA) 151, 157, 164
Evans, W. 55
expectations 193, 195–196, 203
experimentation 45
expertise 92, 95–96, 107, 108–109; CAD 114; Person-Centred Approach 172, 175; power relations 184

false consciousness 53, 56
Farrington, Conor 6, 51–70, 193, 197
fashion 4–5, 6, 17–33, 192, 197, 199–200; additive manufacturing 122–124, 125–126; amateur fashion making 6, 34–50, 200; choice and individuality 52, 53–55, 57–58, 61–62, 64; critical theory 69; definition of 54; fast fashion 20–21, 31; Internet 26–28; longevity 29, 47–48; mass customisation 3, 23–24; personal identity 19–20; service-dominant logic 21–22; slow fashion 28–30; smart technologies 7; wearable technologies 51–54, 57, 62, 65–69
fast fashion 20–21, 31

feedback 158, 159
Ferguson, I. 139, 144–145
fetishisation 9
Fiell, C. 93
Fiell, P. 93
Fila Adatto 7
Finlayson, J. G. 58, 60
Fischer, G. 92
Fisher, Tom 1–13, 192–205
Fotaki, M. 137
Franke, N. 46
Frankfurt School 52–53
Fraunhofer Institute ILT 119
Freeth, R. 185
Friedlander, E. 62
Fuad-Luke, A. 172
Fused Deposition Modelling 113
Futurists 196

Geczy, A. 54
gender 17, 18; *see also* women
general practitioners (GPs) 136–137; *see also* doctor–patient relationships
generative design 100–101, 173
geometries 114
Geuss, R. 53
Gheorghe, C. 5
Givenchy 18, 27
Glendinning, C. 145
Golubnitschaja, Olga 9–10, 150–169, 197, 201
Google 84
governmentality 6, 68
GPs *see* general practitioners
Graesser, A. 87
Grant, B. 178, 186n1
Greener, I. 136
Grounded Theory 182
Gucci 25
guns *see* Liberator gun

H&M 20
Habermas, Jürgen 6, 53, 58–62, 68
Hack Chair 105
Hackney, F. 36–37
Haenlein, M. 100
Hallnäs, L. 175
Hansen, M. B. 65
Harrods 25
HCD *see* human-centred design
health 2, 3, 9–10, 193, 197, 201–202; biometric data 5; deficit model 174; ImPaCT project 186; medical AM personalisation 116–122, 128–129;

'nudge' psychology 171; Person-Centred Approach 10, 170, 171, 173, 185; personalisation in the NHS 133–149; personhood 198, 199; predictive, preventive and personalised medicine 10, 150–169; wearable technologies 24, 51
health literacy 137
hearing aids 116–117, 128
Hermès 25
Holbrook, M. B. 23
Hollander, A. 64
Holroyd, Amy Twigger 6, 34–50, 197, 199–200
homemade clothes 6, 34–50, 200
Hong Kong 23
Hopkinson, Neil 115
Horkheimer, Max 52–53, 55, 60
housing 135
Hull, C. W. 113
human-centred design (HCD) 22, 151, 155–156, 160, 163, 166, 178, 185
'hype cycle' 193, 195–196

Iacobelli, F. 79
Icon pendant 122–123
identification 47
identity: amateur fashion making 36, 42, 46; ethical self-realisation 61; fashion choice 52, 54, 55, 58; fashion design 17, 18, 19–20, 21; user models 83
IDEO 155–156
ideology 53, 55–56
ILEX (Intelligent Labelling Explorer) 73, 74–78, 86
'imaginary hedonism' 200
ImPaCT project 186
implants 119–121
inclusive design 2
individualisation: fashion 21, 30, 31; healthcare 167; pseudo-individualisation 56; public services 145
individuality: fashion 17, 30, 54–55, 56, 57–58; homemade clothes 39; Person-Centred Approach 182; PPPM 163; uniqueness 47; wearable technologies 66, 68, 69
industrial design 8, 92–95, 96–99
Industry 4.0 2, 4
inequalities 137, 139, 141
informed consent 182
Ingram, D. 61
innovation: bottom up 3; disruptive 23; innovation communities 27; open 1; social 6

integrative modelling 155
intellectual property (IP) 103, 105, 106
intelligent tutoring systems 74, 82, 87
interactome design 153–155, 156
Internet: amateur fashion making 37; data 2–3; fashion 26–28; medical information 161; open design 104; searches 82; web-based portals 123–124, 125–128; *see also* e-commerce; online retail; social media
Internet of Things (IoT) 2, 4, 170, 172, 178
Interpersonal Process Recall 182
Invisalign 118
invisibility 82, 83
IoT *see* Internet of Things
IP *see* intellectual property
iPad 25
iPhone 7, 65
Ive, Jonathan 91

Jacq, Bernard 153
Jaeger-LeCoultre 25
Jasanoff, Sheila 194–195, 204n5
Jawbone Up 74
jewellery 100–101, 122–124, 125–126
Jiao, J. 3
Jones, I. 180, 182
Joyner, Michael 202
Jung, J. Y. 196

Kadushin, Ronen 105–106
Kapalla, Marko 9–10, 150–169
Kaplan, A. 100
Karaminas, V. 54
Katz, A. 103, 104–105, 106
Kay, Judith 82–83
Keen, Andrew 91–92
Kent, Tony 6, 9–10, 17–33, 150–169, 199–200
Kettley, Richard 10, 170–191
Kettley, Sarah 10, 170–191, 197
Kim, Sangho 102
Kinematics Cloth 126
Kleeman, F. 101
Klein, Hans K. 201, 203n2
Kleinman, Daniel Lee 201, 203n2
knitting 35, 36, 37–45, 46, 48, 200–201
Koskinen, T. 152–153
Kuksa, Iryna 1–13, 192–205
Kummerfeld, B. 82–83

Lacoste 19
ladder of participation 183
Lamb, Norman 141

language: Habermas 59, 62; personalisation systems 82; personality and language use 79–80, 81, 86, 88; style 78; *see also* natural language processing
Lanvin 27
laser sintering 113, 119
Latour, B. 175
LayerWise 120–121
Le Grand, J. 138
Leadbeater, Charles 138, 139, 144
learning 157
Leckey, Mark 5
Lemke, Heinz 9–10, 150–169
Levi's 28
Levitt, B. E. 177
Liberator gun 103–104, 106, 108–109
Liebenberg, L. 138
Liedtka, J. 167
lifestyles 5, 153, 154, 158, 163, 201
lifeworlds 58–61, 68, 175, 179
Light, A. 172, 178–179
Lin, G. I. 80
linguistic style 78
Local Motors 102–103
longevity 29, 47–48
Louis Vuitton 25
Lovat, Terence 198–199
Lownsbrough, H. 138, 139
Lucas, Rachel 10, 170–191
Luckman, S. 37, 46
Lusch, R. F. 21–22
luxury brands 24–25, 30

M-PIRO *see* Multilingual Personalised Information Object
Maker Movement 8, 91, 92, 96
Makerbot 91
manufacturing 3, 91; customerisation 22; digital fabrication 94–95, 96, 100, 106–107, 109, 113–114; industrial design process 94; mass customisation 22–23; *see also* additive manufacturing
Marathe, S. S. 84
marketing 3, 163; differential segmentation 19; micromarketing 30; PPPM 167; service-dominant logic 21; *see also* advertising
Martin, R. L. 156
Marxian perspective 53
mass customisation 1–2, 8, 91, 92, 99–101; consumer involvement in new product development 98, 99; definition of 3, 22; fashion 3, 4, 23–24, 30; mass-personalisation distinction

122; professional expertise 107; *see also* customisation
mass media 63, 68
mass-personalisation 115, 122, 123–124, 127, 128–129
mass production 106, 133; costs 94, 113; fashion 21, 22, 35, 52, 68; re-evaluation of 37; techniques 113, 115; uniformity 23; users 96; wearable technologies 66, 67
'masstige' 20
material culture 17, 199–200
materials 39–40, 101, 106, 119
Mathews, Eric 198
McCartney, Stella 18, 27
McDonald, R. 138–139
McDowell, C. 36
McGuirk, Justin 91
McLean, M. 39
Mearns, D. 183–184
media 63, 68, 161
medical implants 119–121, 128
Medical Information and Model Management System (MIMMS) 164–166
mental health services 10, 170, 172, 173–174, 184, 185; *see also* therapy
Merchant, Nilofer 95
Meroni, A. 22
metadesign 44 45, 48
MGM *see* model-guided medicine
Mi Adidas 2, 7
micromarketing 30
Miliband, David 133, 142
MIMMS *see* Medical Information and Model Management System
mobile technologies 7, 9, 28
model-guided medicine (MGM) 158, 163–166
money 59–60
Moovel 2
moral agency 108
Mouffe, Chantal 197
Mugge, R. 47
Müller, M. 23
multidisciplinary communication 153–155
Multilingual Personalised Information Object (M-PIRO) 77–78
multiple reproduction 93
Murphy, D. 185
Mymuesli 2

National Health Service (NHS) 9, 133–149, 161
natural language processing (NLP) 8, 73–81, 86, 87

Needham, C. 134–136, 141, 144
neoliberalism 2, 55, 139, 144, 145, 202
Nervous System 100–101, 125–126
Net-a-Porter 27
networks 156
new product development (NPD) 97–99, 101–103, 104, 107; *see also* product development
NHS *see* National Health Service
Nielsen, T. H. 60
Nike: Fuelband 74; NIKEiD 24, 95, 100
non-directivity 177–178
Non-Intentional Design 178
Norman, D. A. 85, 91
NPD *see* new product development
'nudge' psychology 171

Oberlander, Jon 8, 73–90, 199, 200
OBL 119–120
online retail 17, 24, 26–28; *see also* e-commerce; Internet
open design 8, 103–104, 105, 107–108, 194–195; consumer involvement in new product development 97, 98, 99; Digital Forming 127; Person-Centred Approach 178
open innovation 1
opened design 98, 99, 104–106
oppression 52, 53, 57, 62, 65, 68
originality 47
orthodontic aligners 118, 128
Oudshoorn, N. 97

Pacif-i 2
Paneth, Nigel 202
parenting 2
Pariser, E. 82, 88
participation, levels of 172–173, 183
participatory design 91; fashion 28, 29; human-centred design 155; Person-Centred Approach 10, 172, 173, 179, 181, 184, 186
participatory medicine 160
patient–doctor relationships 159–161
patient profiling 152, 153, 154, 158–159
PCA *see* Person-Centred Approach
Peacock, M. 139
Peckham, S. 139–140, 145
Pennebaker, J. W. 79
perinatal morbidity 162
Perry, Katy 51, 69
Person-Centred Approach (PCA) 10, 170–191
personal anecdote, policy by 140–142, 145

personal health budgets 135, 136–137, 141–142, 145
personal identity *see* identity
personal responsibility 163; *see also* responsibilisation
personalisation 1–4, 10–11; additive manufacturing 115, 116–129; Adorno 55; algorithmic 171; amateur fashion making 6, 34–48; constraints on users 108; critiques of personalised medicine 201–202; cultural choice 57; customisation distinction 3, 75, 115; definitions of 3–4; ethical counselling services 166–167; fashion choice 54–55, 61–62, 64–65; fashion design 6, 17–18, 24–26, 27, 29, 30–31; future for 192–203; longevity 47–48; National Health Service 9, 133–145; natural language processing 73–78; non-directivity 178; Person-Centred Approach 170, 177, 178, 184–185; personality and 8, 73, 86, 87–88; positive and negative consequences of 193–194; predictive, preventive and personalised medicine 9–10, 150–151, 152–153, 155–156, 167; problems with 82–85, 87; public services 9, 133, 134–137, 140, 142, 144–145, 153; relational 200–201; smart technologies 7; social policy 8–9; software 7; user involvement 96, 97; wearable technologies 52, 65–67, 68, 69; *see also* customisation
personality 8, 10, 73, 87–88, 197–198; brand 18; natural language processing 78–81; Person-Centred Approach 175, 176; problems with 85–87
personhood 1, 179–180, 184–185, 192, 197–198, 199, 203
Personhood Project 179–180
Piller, Frank T. 4, 23
Pinch, Trevor 97, 193
Pine II, B. Joseph 1, 23, 99–100
Piore, Michael 133
policy 8–9, 139–142, 143, 144, 145, 146n1
politics 142–143
popular culture 55–57, 64
positivism 52–53
postmodernist perspectives 19, 30
power 59–60, 97; health data and privacy 161–162; hegemony 197; Person-Centred Approach 172–173, 175, 182, 184; user needs 185–186
Prada 25

predictive, preventive and personalised medicine (PPPM) 10, 150–169
Predonu, Alexandru 196
Pringle 35, 44
privacy 3, 7, 52, 193; customisation and 84; health data 161–162; user models 82, 83
product development 2, 93–94, 97–99; crowdsourcing 101–103, 107; fashion design 27, 28; open design 104
prosthetic fairings 121–122, 128, 200
prosumers 6, 20
prototyping 94, 114, 180
puberty 162–163
public art 5
public services 9, 133–137, 138, 140, 142, 144–145, 153
purposive-rational action 59, 60

Raasch, C. 103
Rally Fighter 102–103
Ralph Lauren 18, 19
Rapid Prototyping (RP) 114
Raspberry Pi 91
re-personalisation 8, 84–85, 86–88, 199
re-use 47–48
realist perspective 195–196, 203
Redström, J. 96, 175
reflection on practice 172–173, 183–184
Relational Design 178
relationships 21, 198–199, 203
research and development 113
responsibilisation 138–140, 145, 151
responsiveness 136, 140, 145
retail 4–5, 6, 17, 20–21, 26–28, 171; *see also* e-commerce
reworking 35, 37, 41–44, 47, 48
Ring Garden project 196
rituals 63
Robinson, R. E. 172
robots 85
Rogers, Carl 170, 171, 175–177, 186
Rushmore, J. 39

Sabel, Charles 133
Sanders, Elizabeth B.-N. 97, 124, 170, 173, 174
Sangiorgi, D. 22
Savard, Jacqueline 150, 201–202
Sawyer, J. 80
Scherzinger, Nicole 51
Schreier, M. 46
Science and Technology Studies (STS) 194
SCOT *see* Social Construction of Technology

scrutable user modelling 83, 84, 85, 87–88
search engines 88
seed objects 123–124, 125
Segall, M. 143
segmentation 19
Selective Laser Melting (SLM) 119
self-efficacy 137
self-management of health 161–162
self-reflection 184
Sennett, R. 35
service design 9, 22, 29, 157, 174
service-dominant logic (S-DL) 21–22, 29
sewing 36–37, 38, 39–40, 46, 48
sex toys 124–125, 200
sexuality 17, 18
signifiers 17
Sigurdsson, G. 63
Simmel, Georg 47, 55
Simonse, L. 156
Sinclair, Matt 8, 91–112, 194–195, 199–200
Siri 7
Skov, L. 23
Sleeswijk, V. F. 30
slow fashion 28–30
smart garments 5, 51–52, 53–54, 65, 68–69; *see also* wearable technologies
Smythson 25
social care 3, 24, 135–136, 141, 145, 185–186
social change 5, 6, 68
Social Construction of Technology (SCOT) 193, 194, 203n2
social media 20, 37, 161, 163
social model 174
social norms 47
social shopping 27
social status 17–18
'sociotechnical imaginaries' 194, 195
software 7, 106; *see also* computer-aided design; natural language processing
spaces 4–5
standardisation 39, 106
Stappers, P. J. 97, 124
Steen, M. 155
Stegall, M. 157
Stereolithography (SL) 113, 118
STS *see* Science and Technology Studies
Sundar, S. S. 84
suppliers 21
surveillance 52, 161–162, 193
'the system' 59–60, 68
Szeless, M. 40

TAC-TILE Sounds project 180–181
targeted advertising 3, 4, 82
technology 3, 10, 26, 106, 192, 203; animal tracking devices 10–11; Bluetooth 2; body scanning technologies 7, 27–28, 35, 122, 126; *Democratising Technology* project 178–179; design 92; digital fabrication 8, 94–95, 96, 100, 106–107, 109, 113–114; expectations of 193, 195–196, 203; health 9, 10, 24; mass customisation 23, 24; model-guided medicine 164–166; PPPM 158–159; prosumers 20; retail 4; smart 7; Social Construction of 193, 194, 203n2; sociology of 52; wearable technologies 5, 6, 24, 51–54, 57, 62, 65–69, 74, 161; *see also* additive manufacturing; computer-aided design; Internet
therapy 171, 173, 175–177, 181–182, 184, 186
Thomson, M. 152–153
Thorne, B. 183–184
3D printing 7, 8, 107, 113–130, 192; ethical issues 195; fashion design 23, 26; lack of control 193; Liberator gun 103–104, 108–109; Maker Movement 91; mass customisation 100
3D Systems 114, 121
timescale 172–173, 181–182
Timmermans, J. 83, 84
tone of voice 78
Tonkinwise, C. 95
Tooze, J. 104
TopShop 20, 25–26
tracking devices 74
Traid 35
translational bioinformatics 155, 168n2
transparency 83
Tseng, M. M. 3
Turney, J. 46
Twitchell, J. B. 17–18, 19

Ultimaker 91
unconditional positive regard (UPR) 176, 179, 180
uniqueness 47, 48, 64
Urban Skyform 196
urban spaces 5
user-centred design 96, 172, 173, 178, 185; consumer involvement in new product development 97, 98, 99; public services 153

user-designers 91
user experience 160
user-generated content 27
user models 82–85, 87
user needs 30, 185–186
utopia 6, 51, 52, 193

value creation 21
Van Lente, Harro 195–196
Vargo, S. L. 21–22
Verbeek, P-P. 9, 108
Vines, J. 181
virtual worlds 4–5, 17, 24

Walker, M. A. 80
Walker, Paul 198–199
Wallace, Jayne 179–180, 181
Wallis, M. 180, 182
waste 83
watches 25

wearable technologies 5, 6, 24, 51–54, 57, 62, 65–69, 74, 161
Web 4.0 7
web-based portals 123–124, 125–128
Whistles 25–26
White Papers 140, 143
White, S. K. 62
Whittaker, S. J. 80
Wilkins, P. 182
Wilson, Cody 104, 106, 108
Wilson, Daniel H. 193
Witkin, R. W. 56, 57–58, 63
women 29, 36, 37–38

Xilloc 120

Yamamoto 18
Yr digital printing service 26

Zara 20
Zebracki, M. 5